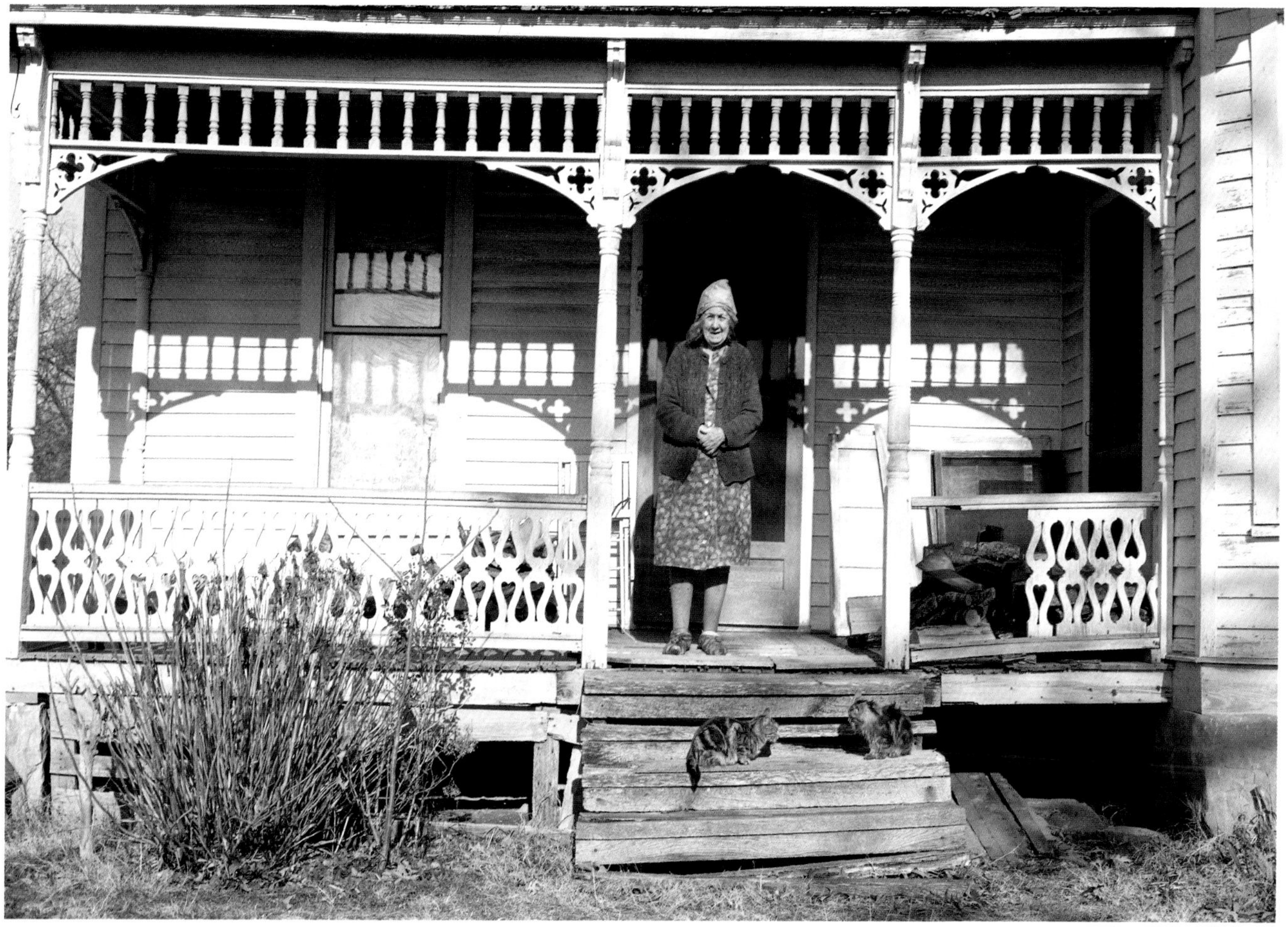

IF THAT'S THE HOUSE I'M THINKING, it stood outside of old Bigelow, down there in what we call the Fourche Bottoms. That lady lived in that house all by herself. Just her and about a hundred cats. I can tell you where that house stood, if it's the one I'm thinking of, but I don't know if it's still there or if they tore it down. You can go out and see for yourself. I tell you how to get there.

Get on Prince Street, over there at the stoplight, and follow that street right out of town. That's gonna take you past the graveyard and up on the bridge over the river, take you right into Perry County. Now you're on Highway 60. You pass through Toad Suck and see the Toad Suck Park off on the left. 60's gonna twist around out there, it's gonna take a hard curve to the right, then it's gonna straighten out. *You just stay with it* on that straightaway.

When you come up on the crossroads at Highway 113, hang it to the left and come on into old Bigelow. Not much left of Bigelow, but you'll know it when you hit it. You gonna see the foundation of the old hotel out there.

Keep a lookout for Old Dixie Road. That's what you looking for, *Old Dixie Road*. That road's gonna take you over to the Fourche Bottoms where that old lady's house stood.

A spinster lady she was, real friendly, talked to everybody that come by. Then she died. After she was gone the kids wouldn't go near that house. They said it was a haunted house after she died. They said they heard noises, and they were sure it was her ghost spooking around that house. But I'm thinking it was just all those cats, prowling around, looking for her.

Travis White
Conway, Arkansas

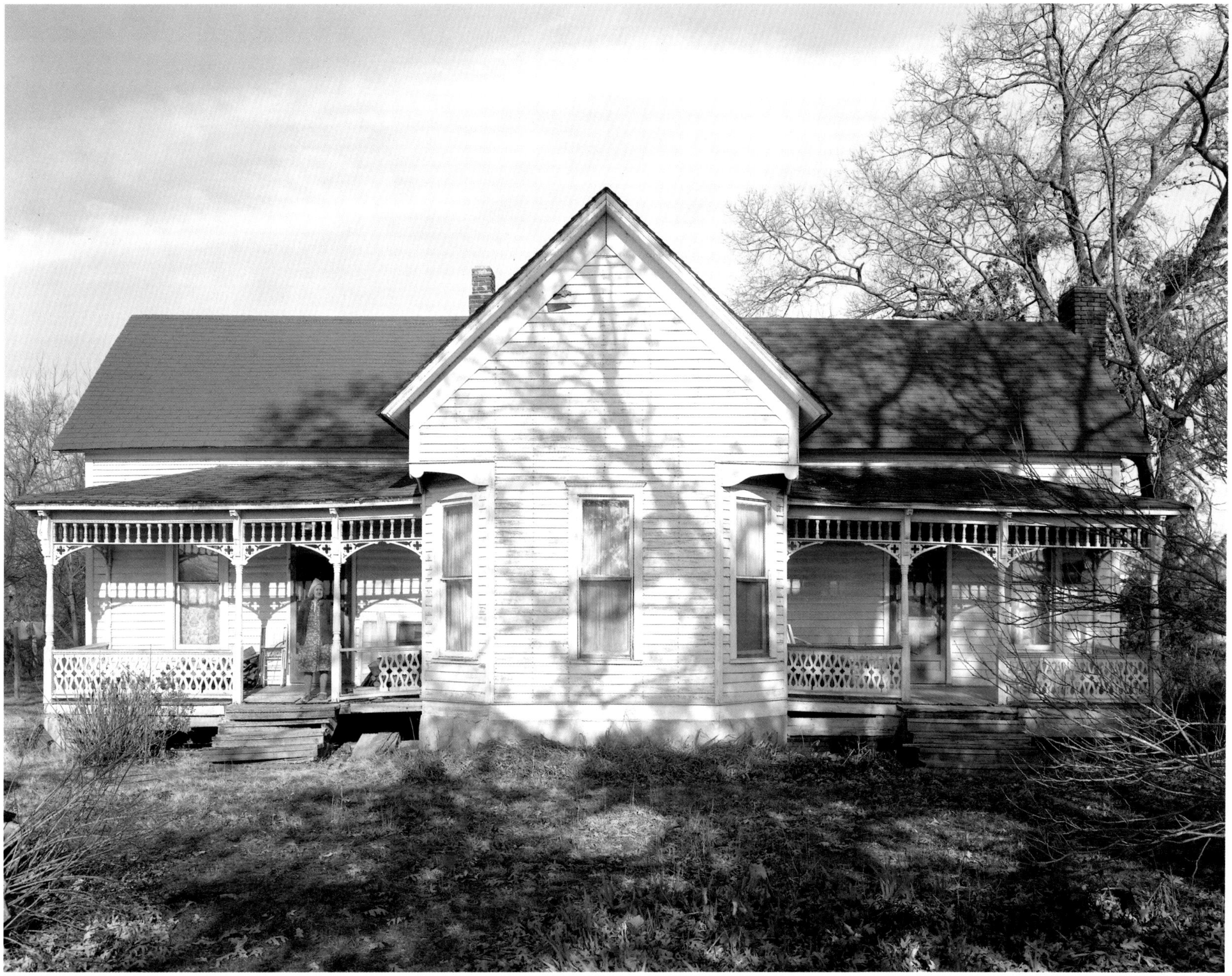

Wood frame Queen Anne double house
Bigelow (Perry County), Arkansas
(no longer standing)

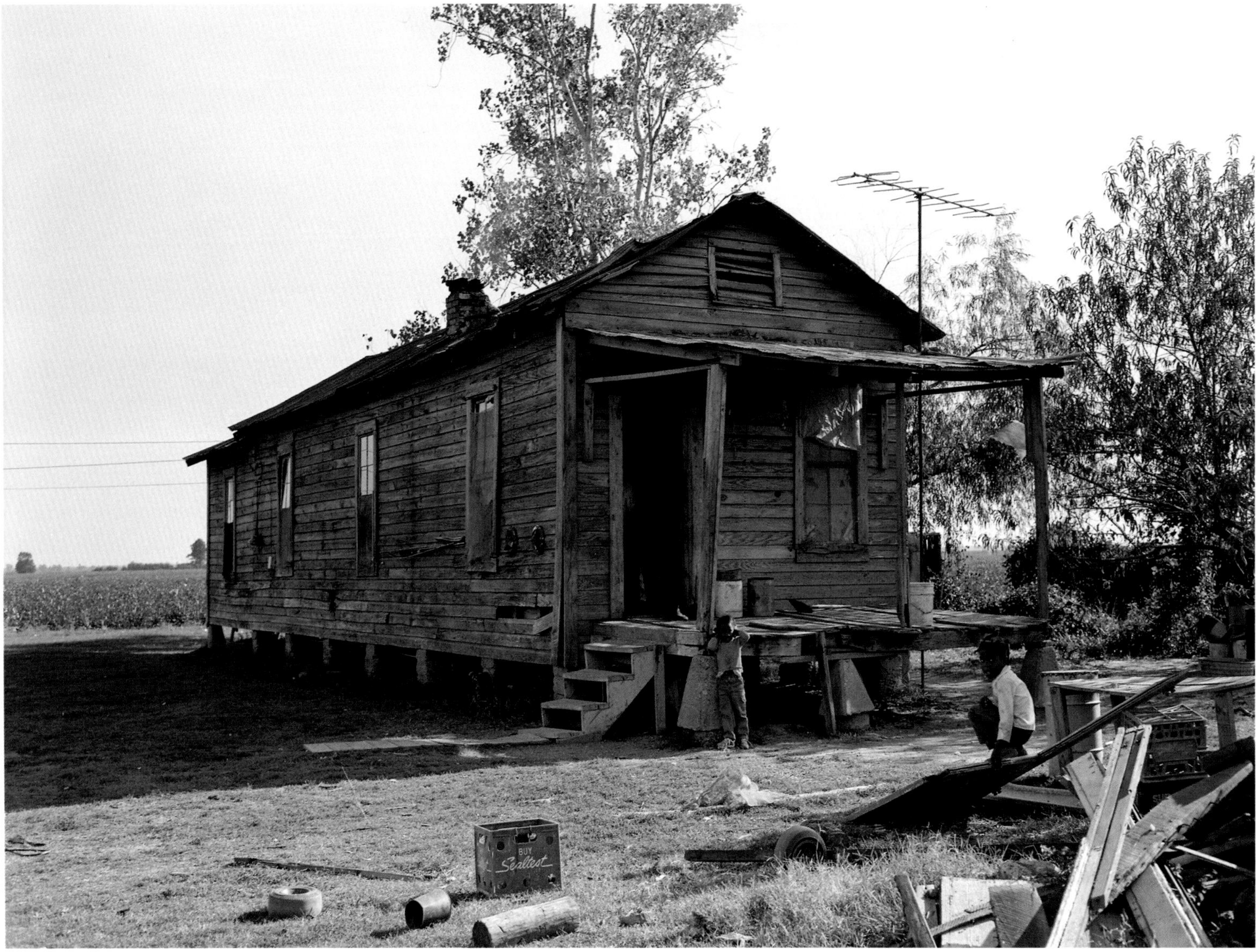

Wood frame shotgun house with three rooms plus addition
Francis County, Arkansas
(no longer standing)

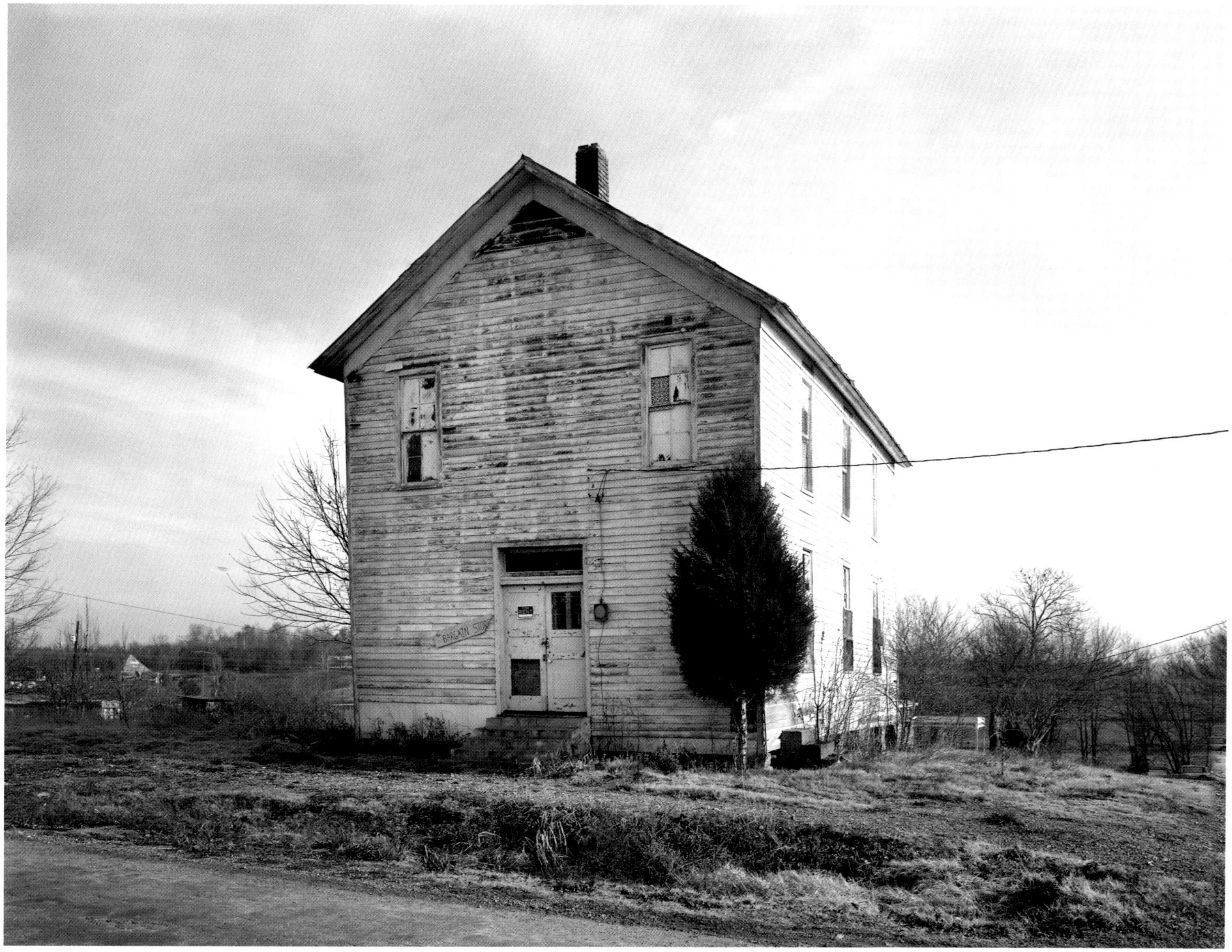

Abandoned wood frame, two-story meeting house
Desha (Independence County), Arkansas
(no longer standing)

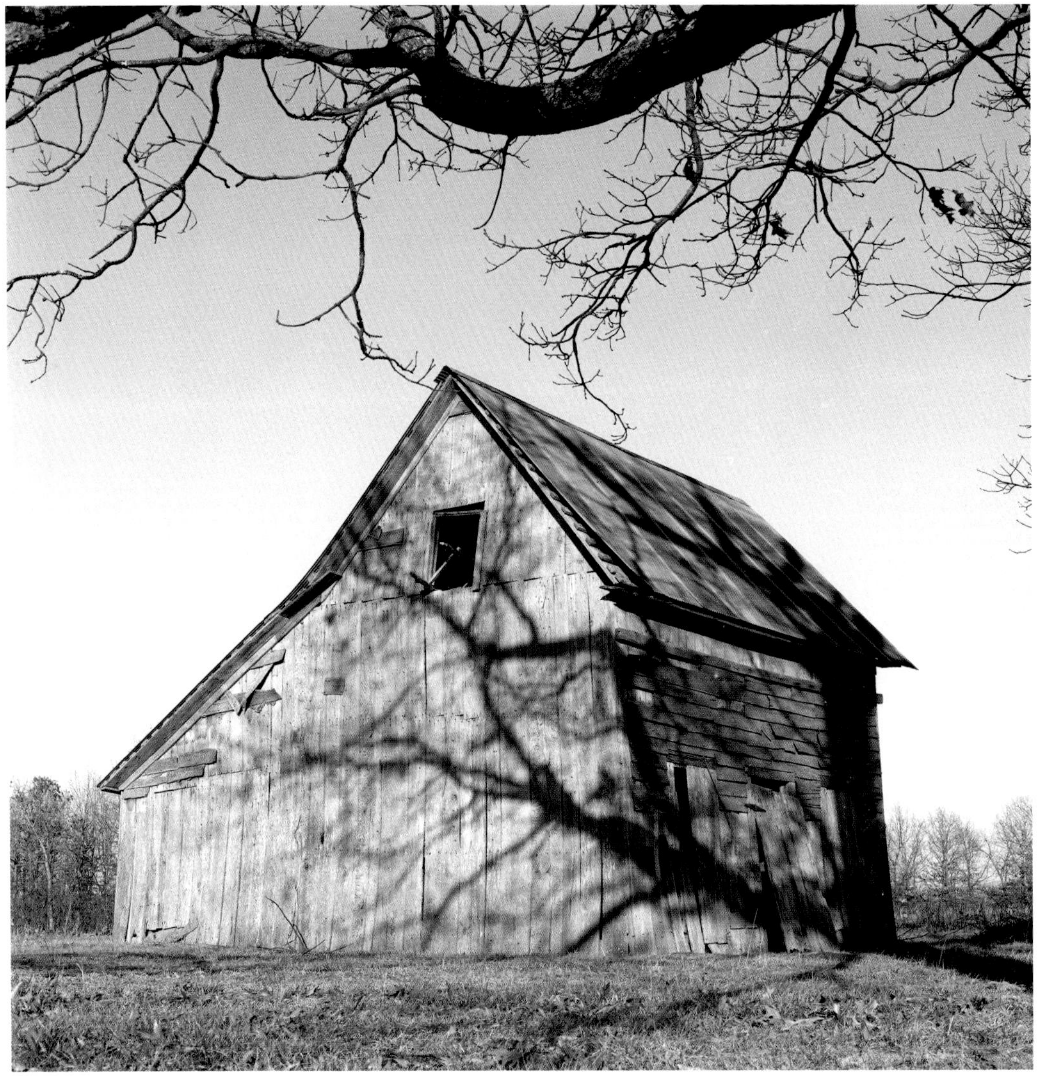

Wood frame barn
Boone County, Arkansas

THE TRUE BASIS FOR ANY SERIOUS STUDY of the art of Architecture still lies in those indigenous, more humble buildings everywhere that are to architecture what folklore is to literature or folk song to music and with which academic architects were seldom concerned.

These many folk structures are *of the soil,* natural. Though often slight, their virtue is intimately related to the environment and to the heartlife of the people. Functions are usually truthfully conceived and rendered invariably with natural feeling. Results are often beautiful and always instructive.

Frank Lloyd Wright
from *The Sovereignty of the Individual*

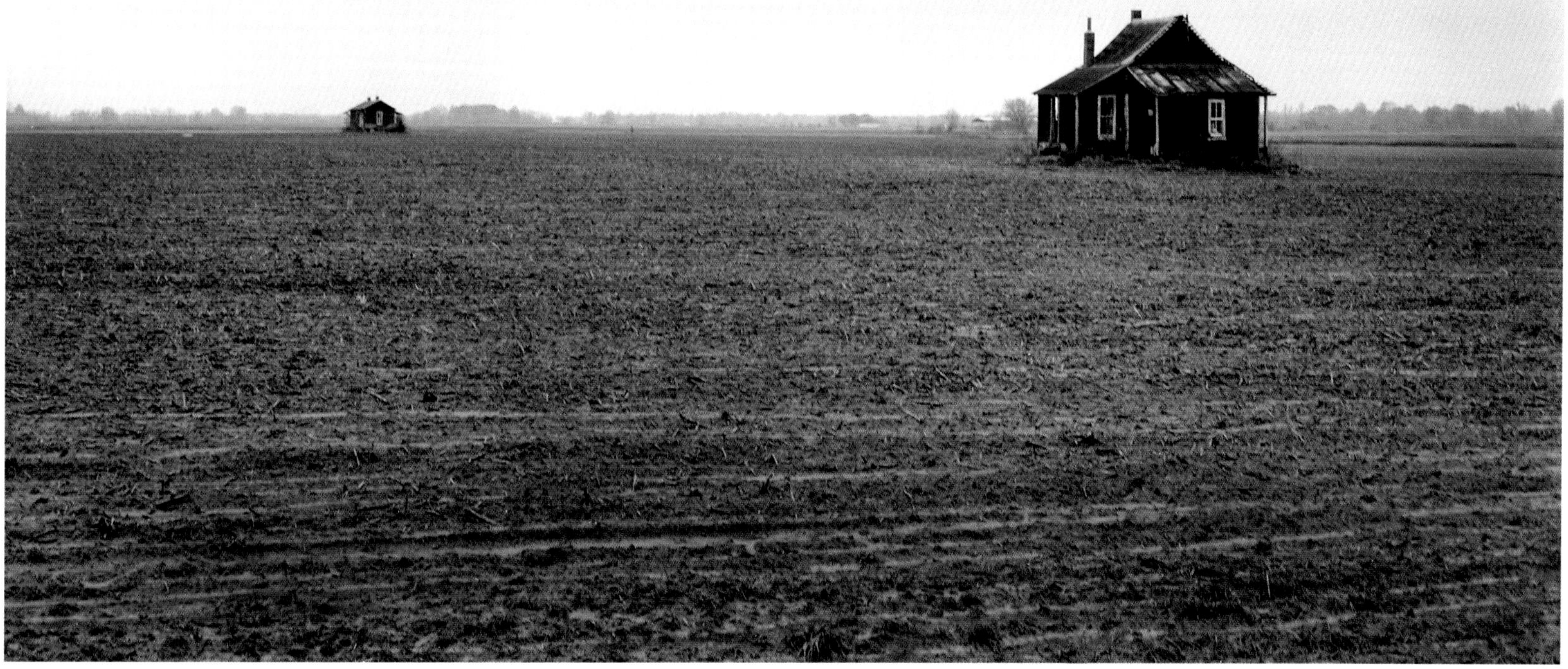

Sharecropper houses in cotton field
Monroe County, Arkansas
(no longer standing)

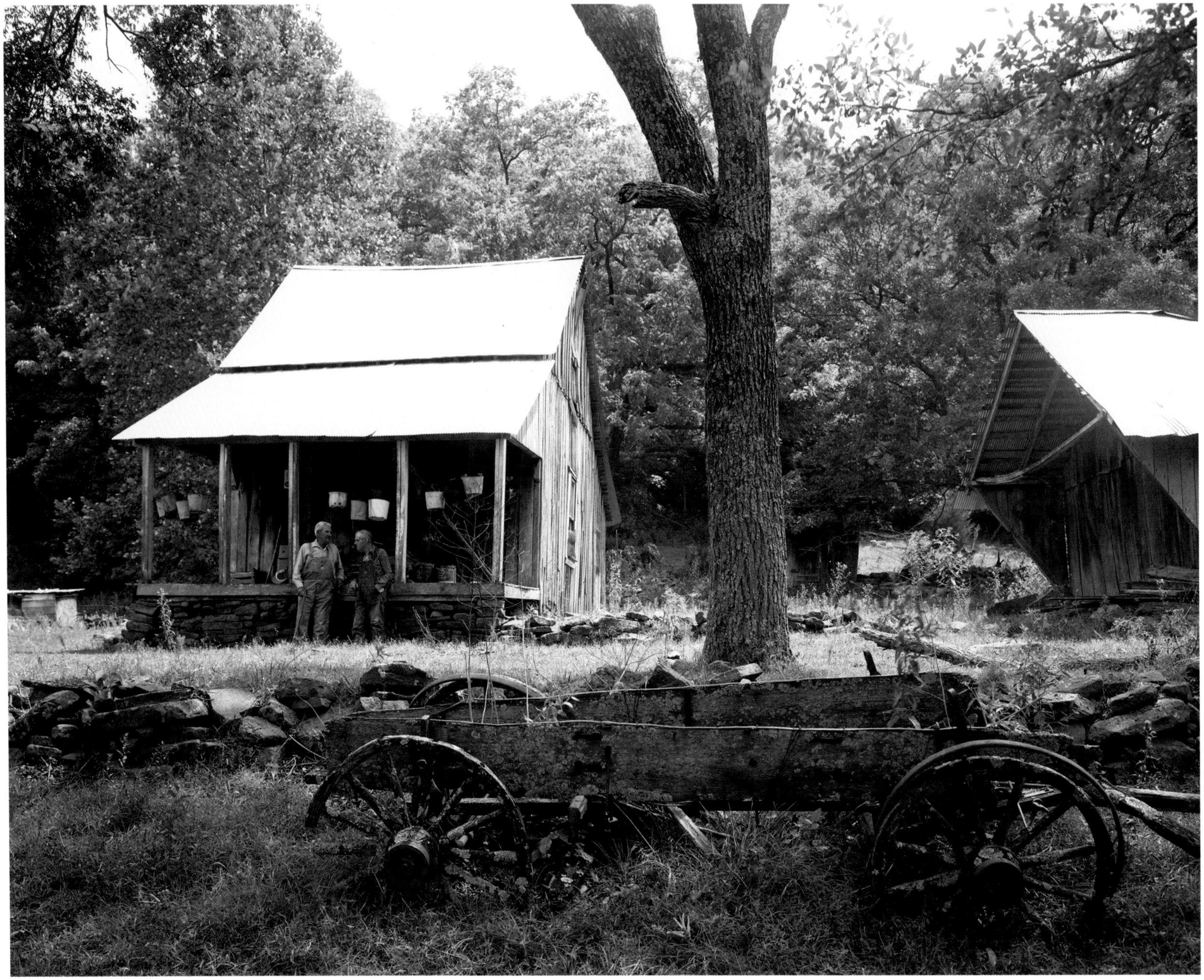

Board and batten Ozark house
Madison County, Arkansas

PHOTOGRAPHS OF VERNACULAR ARCHITECTURE

OF THE SOIL

AND STORIES OF CHANGING TIMES IN ARKANSAS

GEOFF WINNINGHAM

The Fay Jones School of Architecture
The University of Arkansas Press
Fayetteville
2014

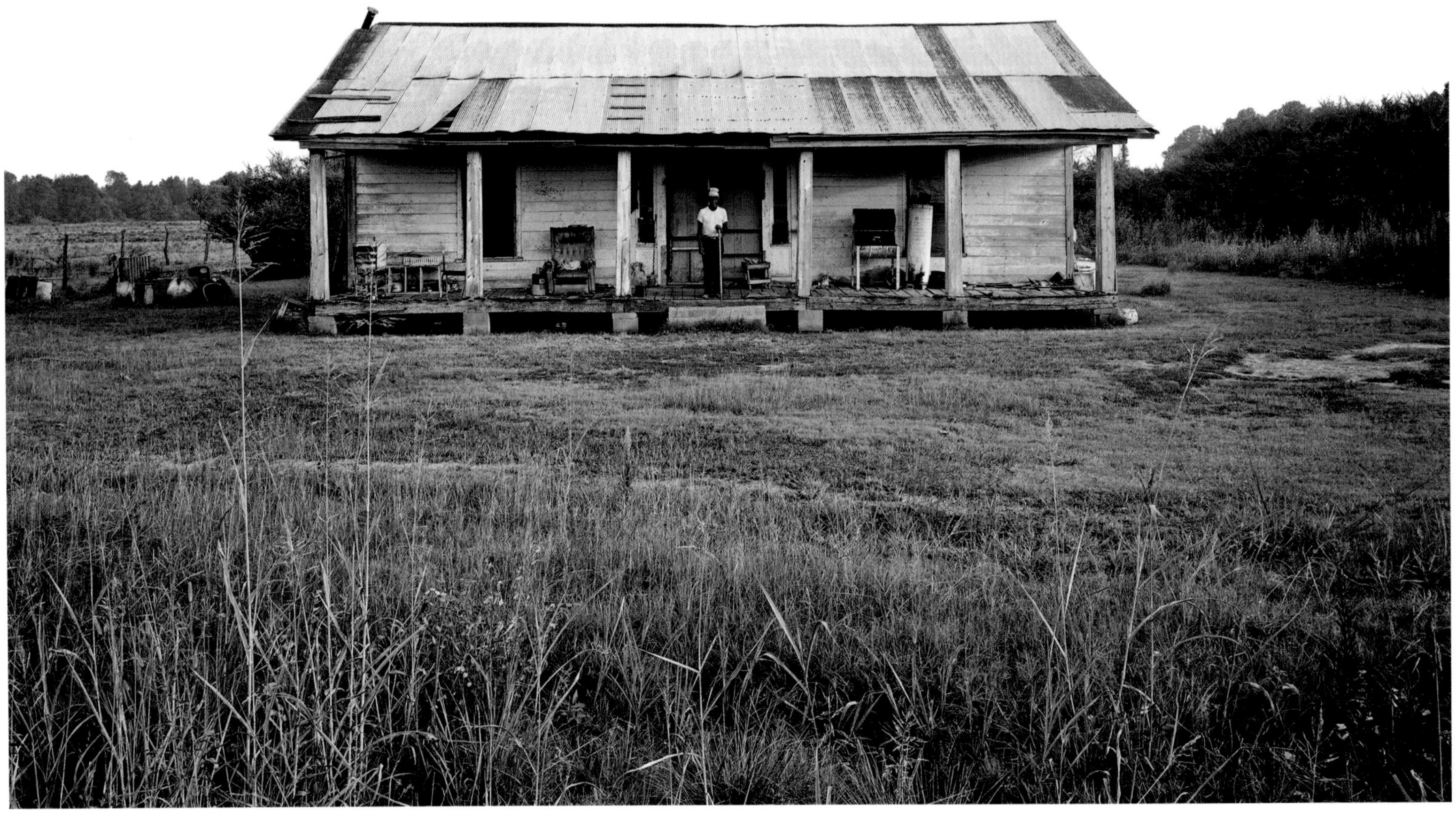

Greek Revival cottage with battered columns
Mineral Springs (Howard County), Arkansas
(no longer standing)

Preface

In August of 1980, I made the first in a series of trips across the state of Arkansas, driving along back roads and highways, through small towns and rural areas of the state. My traveling companion for most of these trips was Cyrus Sutherland, professor in the Fay Jones School of Architecture at the University of Arkansas. Our project was to identify and photograph the best examples of the vernacular architecture of the state.

Cy was an inspiring colleague to work with. Each day that we traveled and worked together, I experienced his passion for both classical and vernacular architecture. Born and reared in Arkansas, Cy earned a degree in architecture from Harvard, then returned home to practice architecture and to teach at the state university in Fayetteville. I often recall a story that Cy told me about the sabbatical year that he had spent touring the Roman Empire with his wife and three children in a Volkswagen van. He was convinced that his oldest son had chosen archaeology as his life's work due to the childhood experience of exploring classical ruins on that trip. Looking back, I regard my travels with Cy as a cumulative architectural tour of another sort, in which he introduced me to the best dogtrot houses, wood frame churches, octagonal barns, and one-of-a-kind hog houses in the state.

Nothing seemed to delight Cy more than the discovery of classical architectural elements in humble structures. I recall one afternoon, driving west of Nashville, Arkansas. As we approached the town of Mineral Springs, Cy moved forward onto the edge of his seat, surveyed the landscape to the north of the highway, and began to prepare me for what I would see just ahead. "When we round this curve, take a look out into the field to the right," he said, "and you will behold the most beautiful Greek Revival cottage in all of Arkansas." Around the curve, I looked off the road to the right, but all I saw was a dilapidated little shack with a patched roof of corrugated metal and a porch littered with junk. Noting my confusion, Cy pointed out the perfect symmetry of the little house, its elegant battered columns, and the precise classical details of its window framing. How on earth, I asked, would elements of Greek Revival style, turn up in a sharecropper's house in rural Arkansas? Cy explained that classical architectural styles had spread across America in the late 19th and early 20th centuries, largely through widely distributed carpenter's guides and pattern books. The Greek Revival style, in particular, held vast popular appeal because so many Americans looked to Greece for the roots of democracy and regarded Greek temples as the ultimate statement in architectural perfection. Most likely, the tiny house in the field outside Mineral Springs would have been painted white, he explained, to suggest the look of marble.

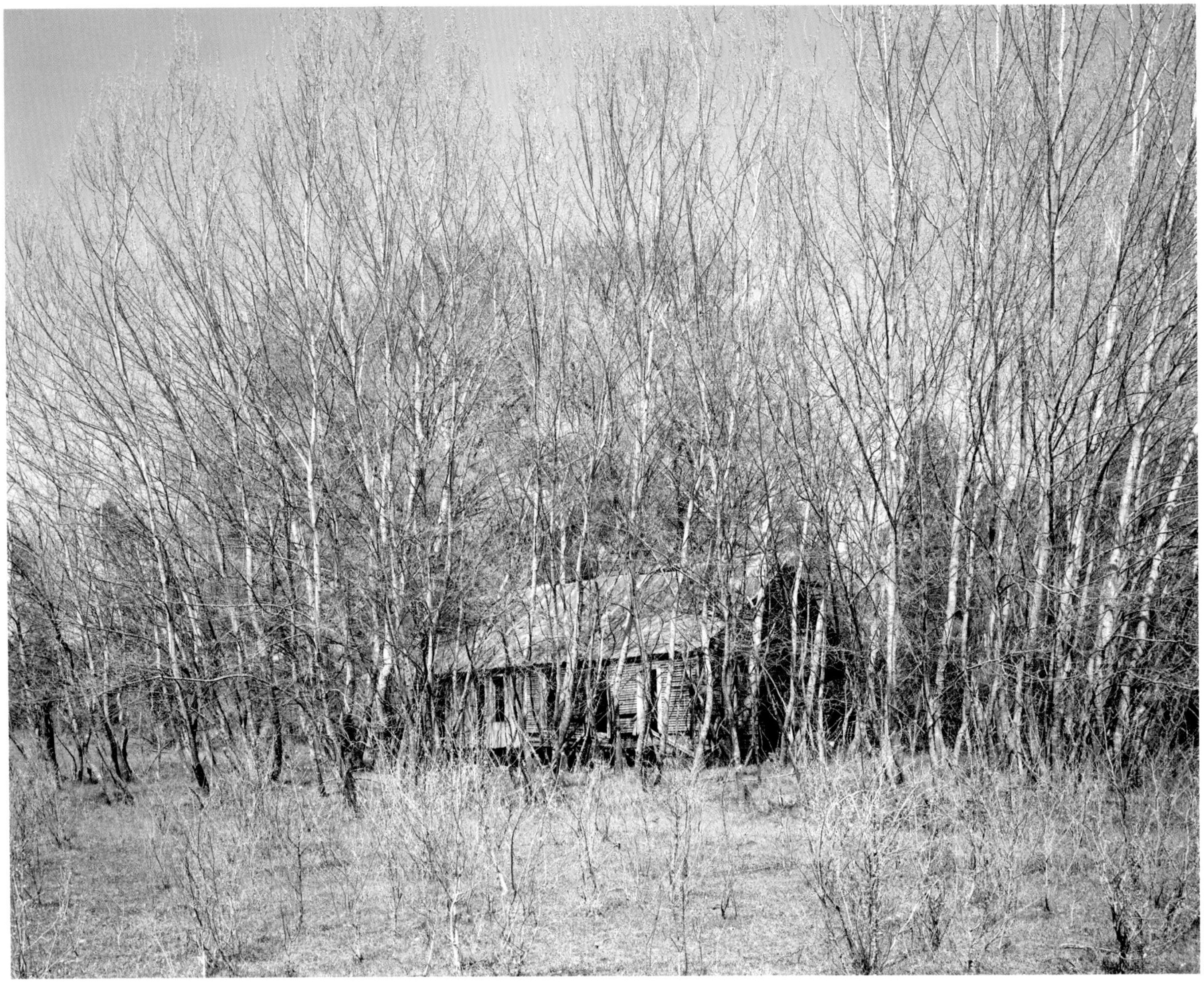

Abandoned dogtrot log house
Howard County, Arkansas
(no longer standing)

The first year of our work on the project was commissioned by First Federal Savings and Loan Association, and in the spring of 1981 First Federal selected a hundred photographs to frame and hang in their new building in Little Rock. With our commitment to First Federal fulfilled, our project might have ended then, but Cy and I decided to keep working, in hopes of compiling a comprehensive collection of Arkansas vernacular architecture. We continued to travel and to photograph for two more years. I worked with Cy—and at times with Parker Westbrook—into the spring of 1983, by which time we had made photographs of over 1,000 structures. During those years, I would often return five or six times, often on my own, to the same store or church building, in order to photograph the structure in different light or with a surrounding landscape of a different season. By 1983, lacking any outside funding and with each of us pulled in different directions by other interests, Cy and I put our project on hold.

It wasn't until Cy died in 2008 that I looked at my Arkansas photographs again. Working with a digital film scanner, I made high resolution digital files of over 500 negatives, then I produced a set of proof prints from the scans. For the first time, I had a comprehensive overview of my photography from the project, and it was clear that I had more than enough good photographs for a book. A book, however, needs a text, and so I began to cast about for prose or poetry that would complement the pictures. In January of 2010, I returned to Arkansas, looking for a poet or a writer with whom I might collaborate. My first stop was in Bingen, Arkansas, a tiny community just north of Nashville, where I had photographed the Wolff Store half a dozen times on the '80s. I was shocked to see that the store was gone. There was not so much as a trace of the foundation left where the old store had once stood. In the months that followed, as I searched for more of the buildings that I had photographed almost thirty years earlier, I would learn that most of the buildings were gone. Many had been lost due to fires or storms, while others had been torn down or had simply crumbled into ruins. At some point it dawned on me that what I had been photographing were the vanishing architectural ruins of my own culture.

As I stood on the side of the road in Bingen, holding my 8 x 10 black and white print of the Wolff Store in the air in front of me, trying to imagine it where it had once stood, a man walked out the front door of a nearby house. As he stopped to pick up his newspaper, he noticed me and waved in my direction. I walked down the road and introduced myself to Clay Hester, who took a look at my photograph of the old store and began to talk. I sat with Clay at his breakfast table and listened for almost two hours. I knew then that I did not need a poet or a writer for the text I wanted for my book. I only needed to revisit the sites of as many of the buildings that I had photographed as possible, look around each community, find people who knew the buildings or remembered them, listen carefully, and write the stories they would tell me.

G. W.

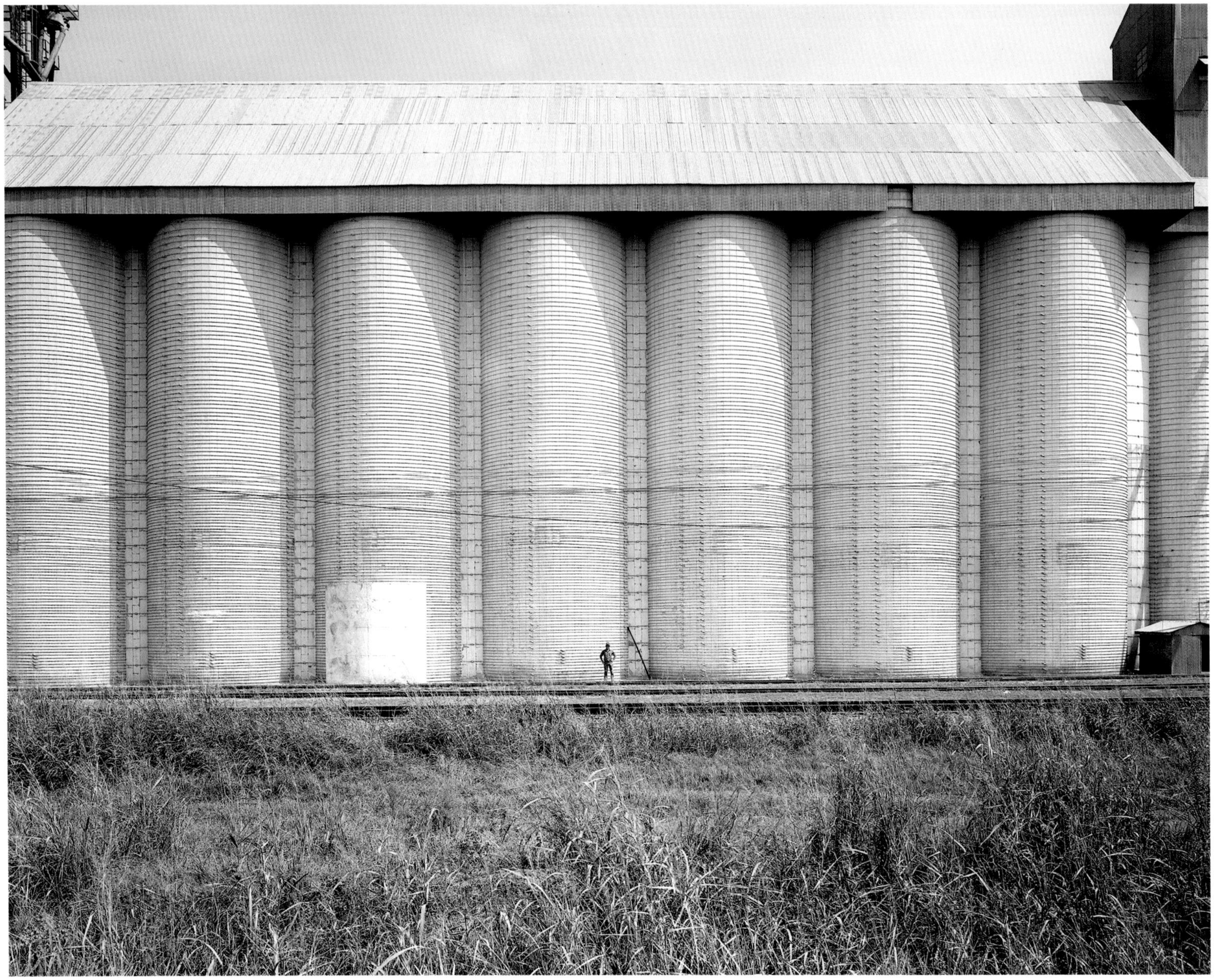

Corrugated metal on wood frame grain silo
Stuttgart (Arkansas County), Arkansas
(demolished)

This book is dedicated to the memory of the late Cyrus Sutherland, professor of architecture at the University of Arkansas, inspiring teacher, dear friend, and mentor to many, whose vast knowledge and love of vernacular architecture inspired this project.

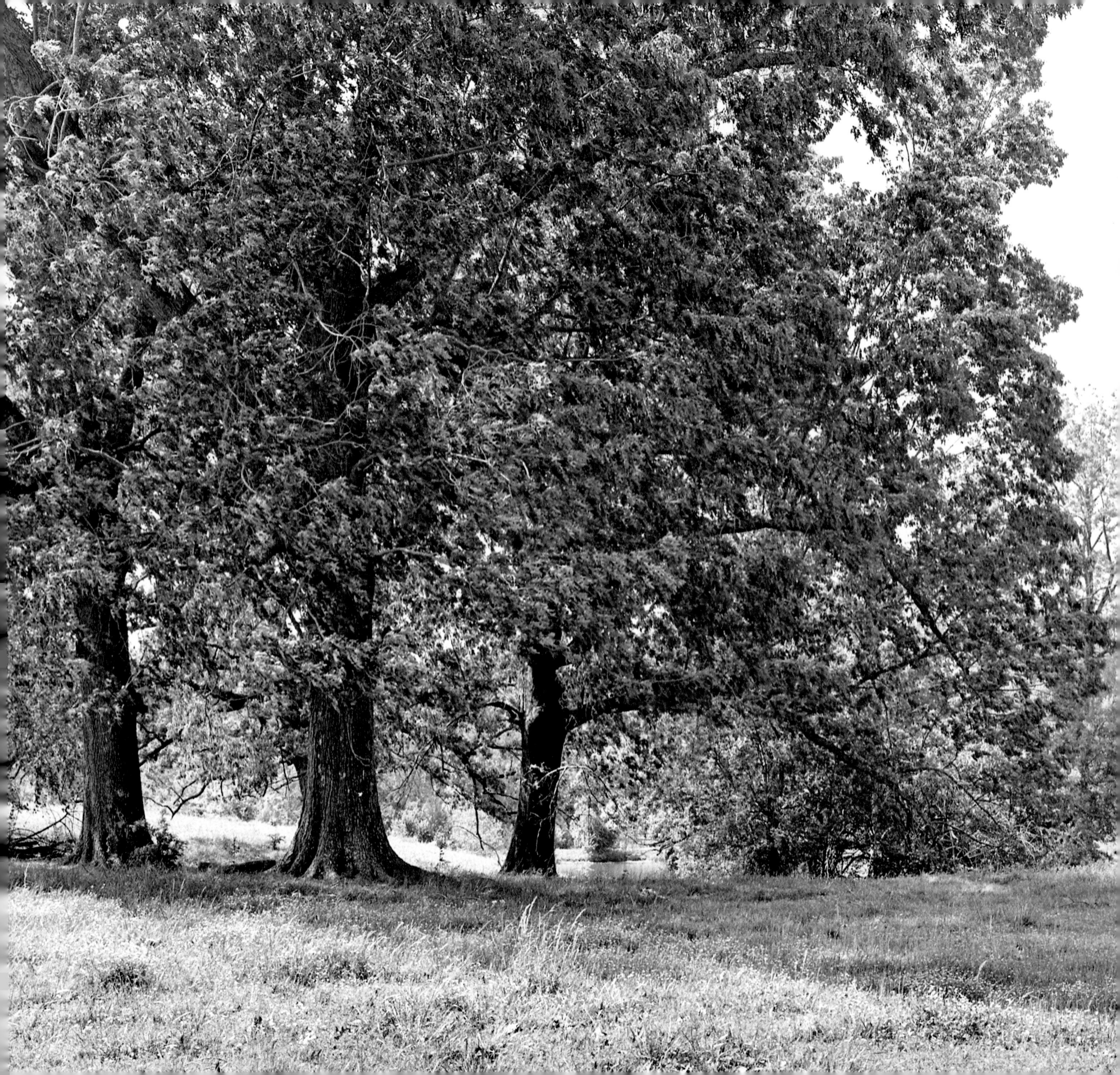

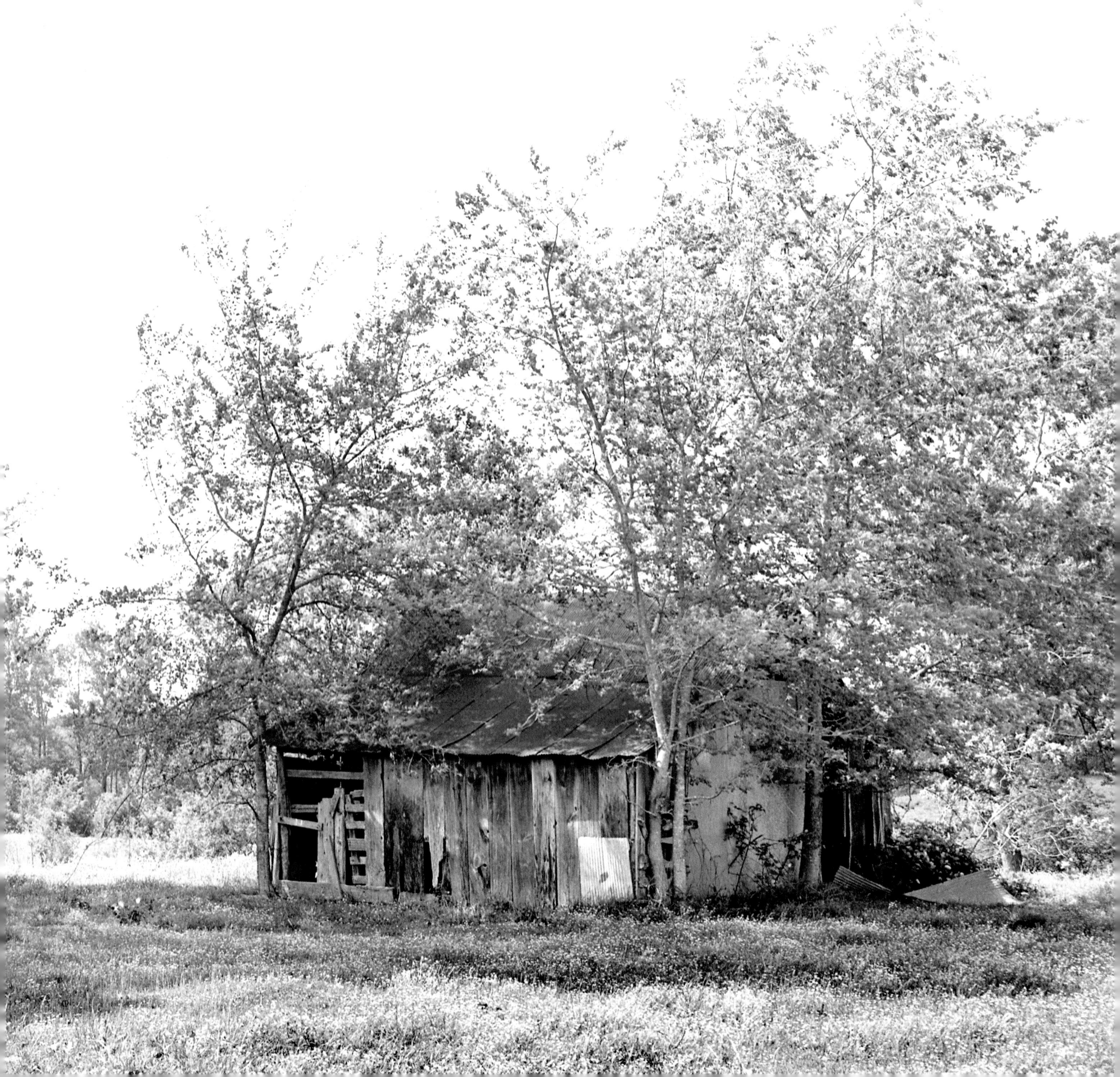

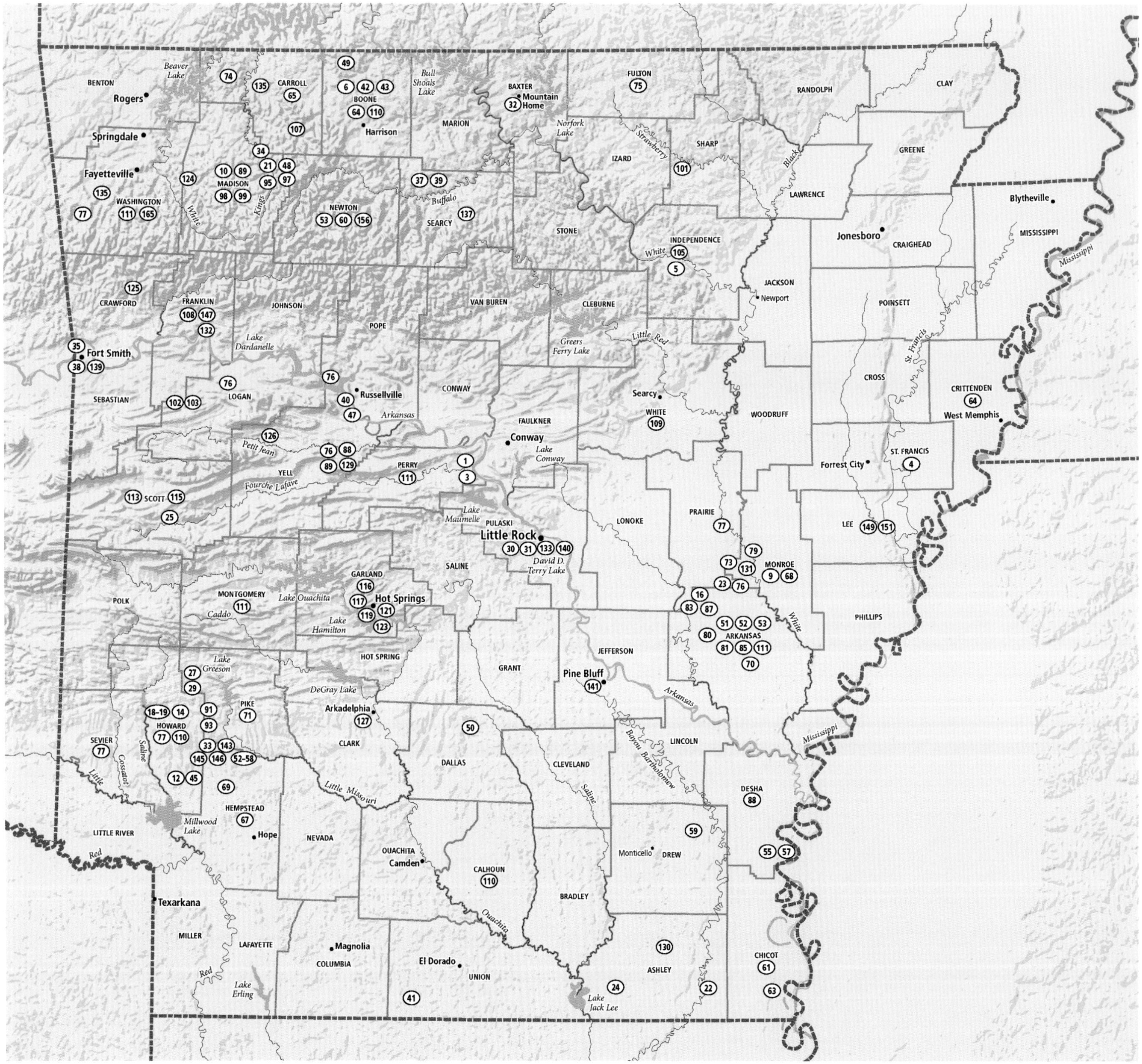

The state of Arkansas and the locations of the photographs in this book. See pages 158–159 for a full index of photo locations.

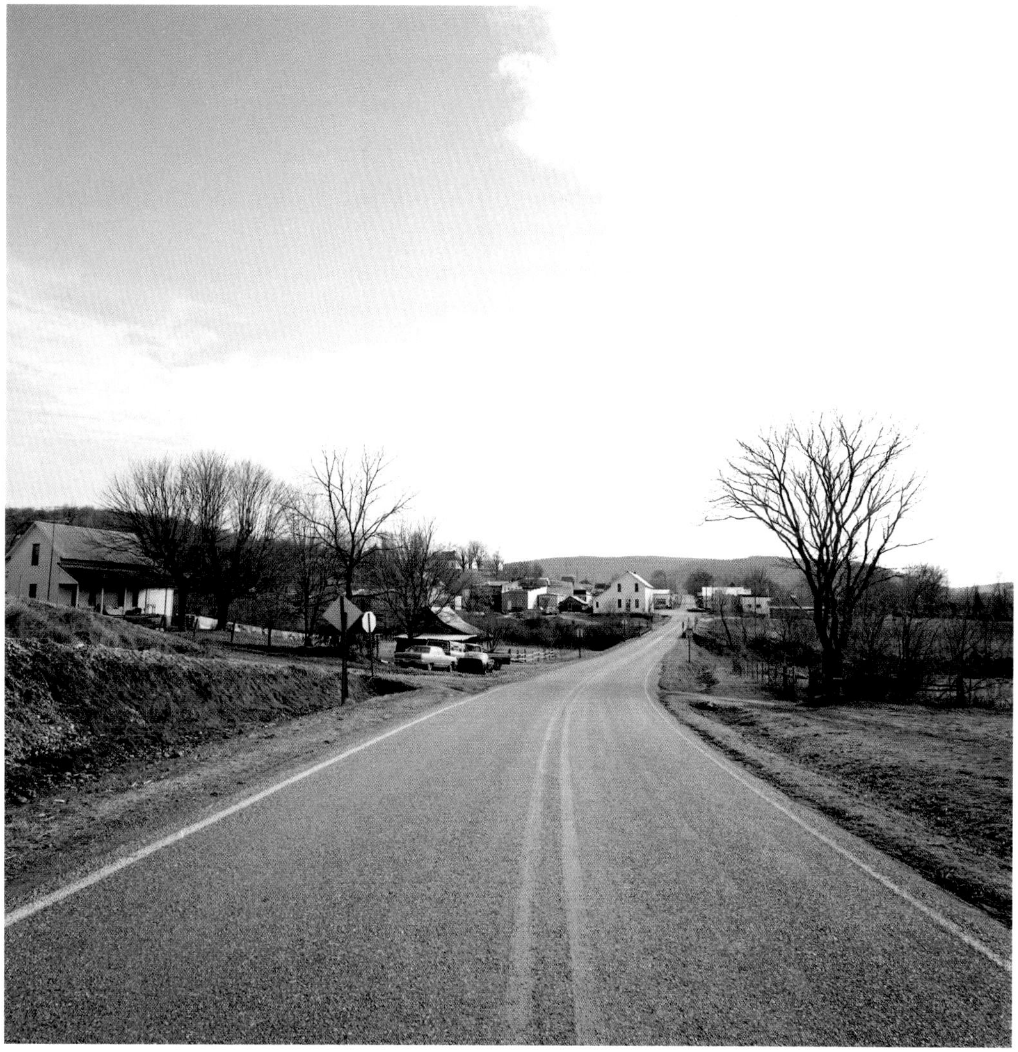

Highway 21, south into Kingston (Madison County), Arkansas

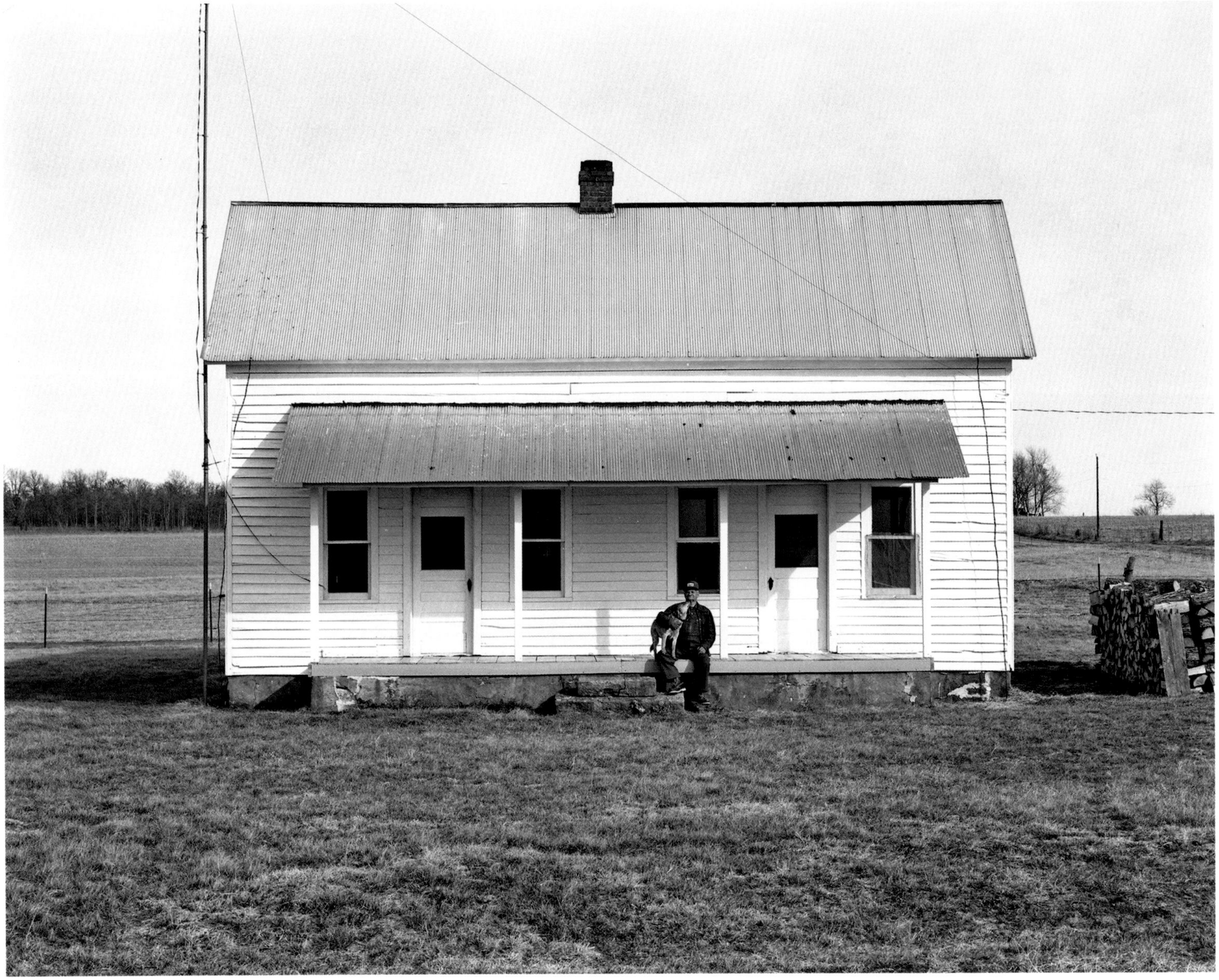

Wood frame saddlebag house
Parkdale (Ashley County), Arkansas

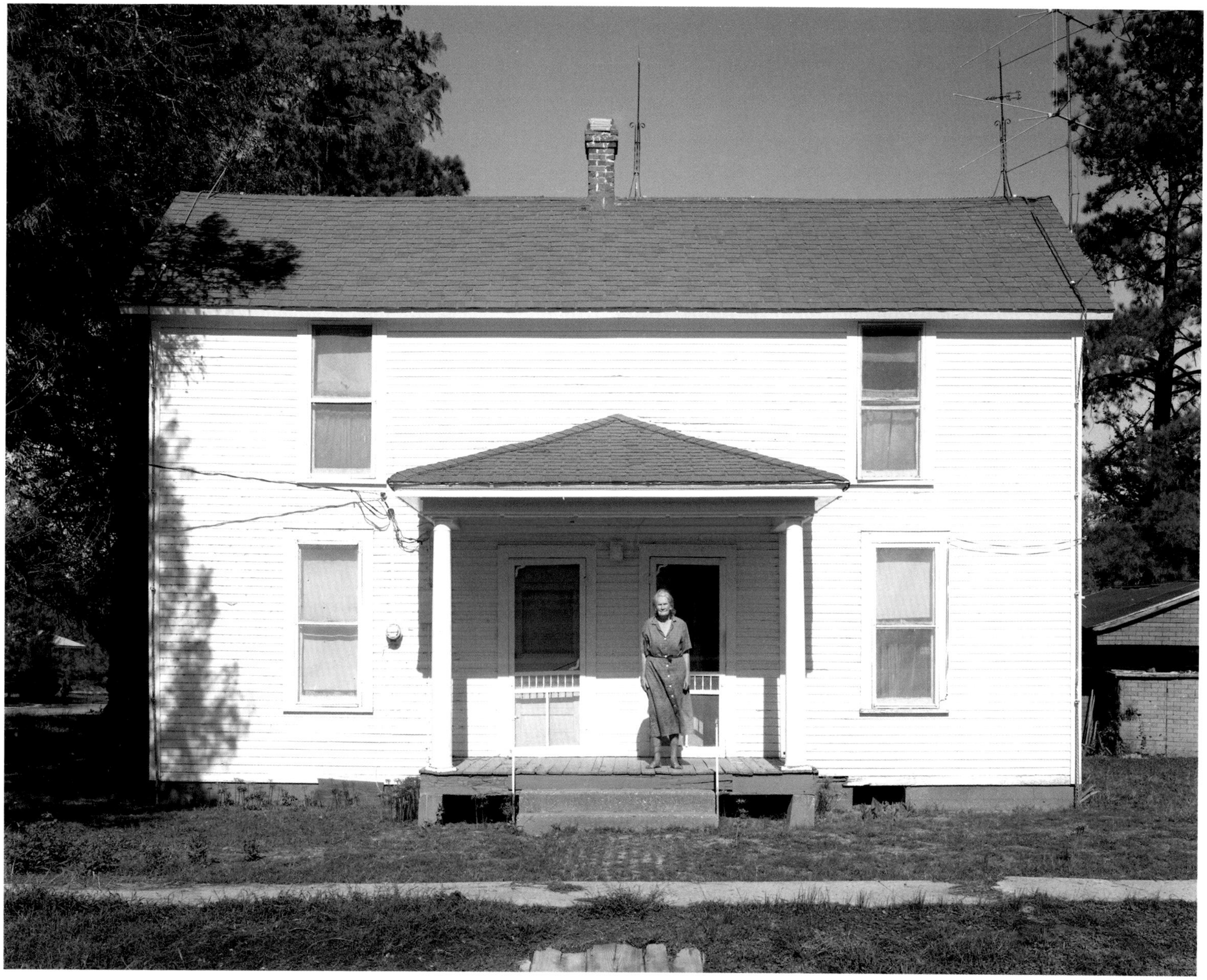

Two-story, wood frame double house
Ulm (Prairie County), Arkansas

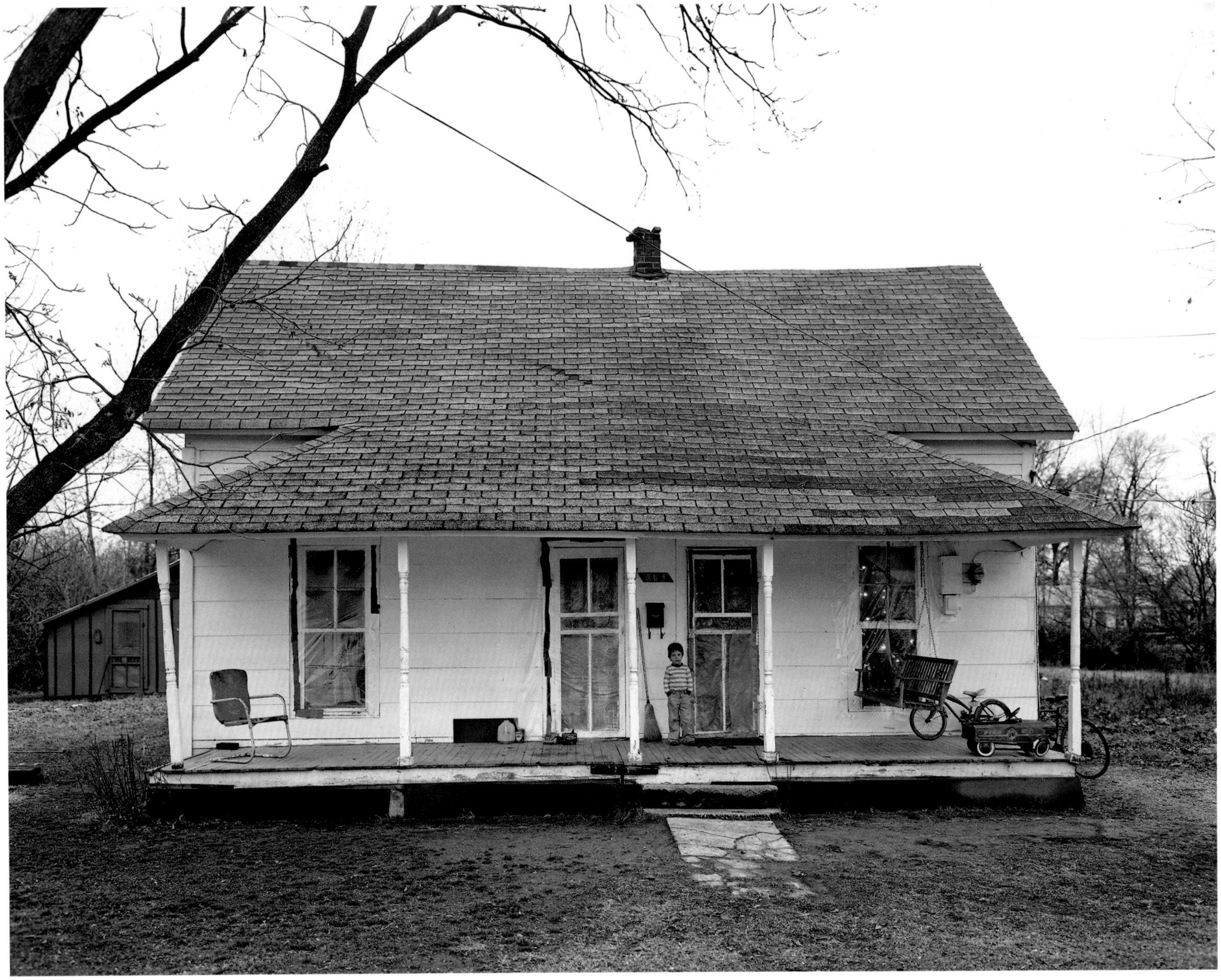

Asymmetrical wood frame double house
Crossett (Ashley County), Arkansas

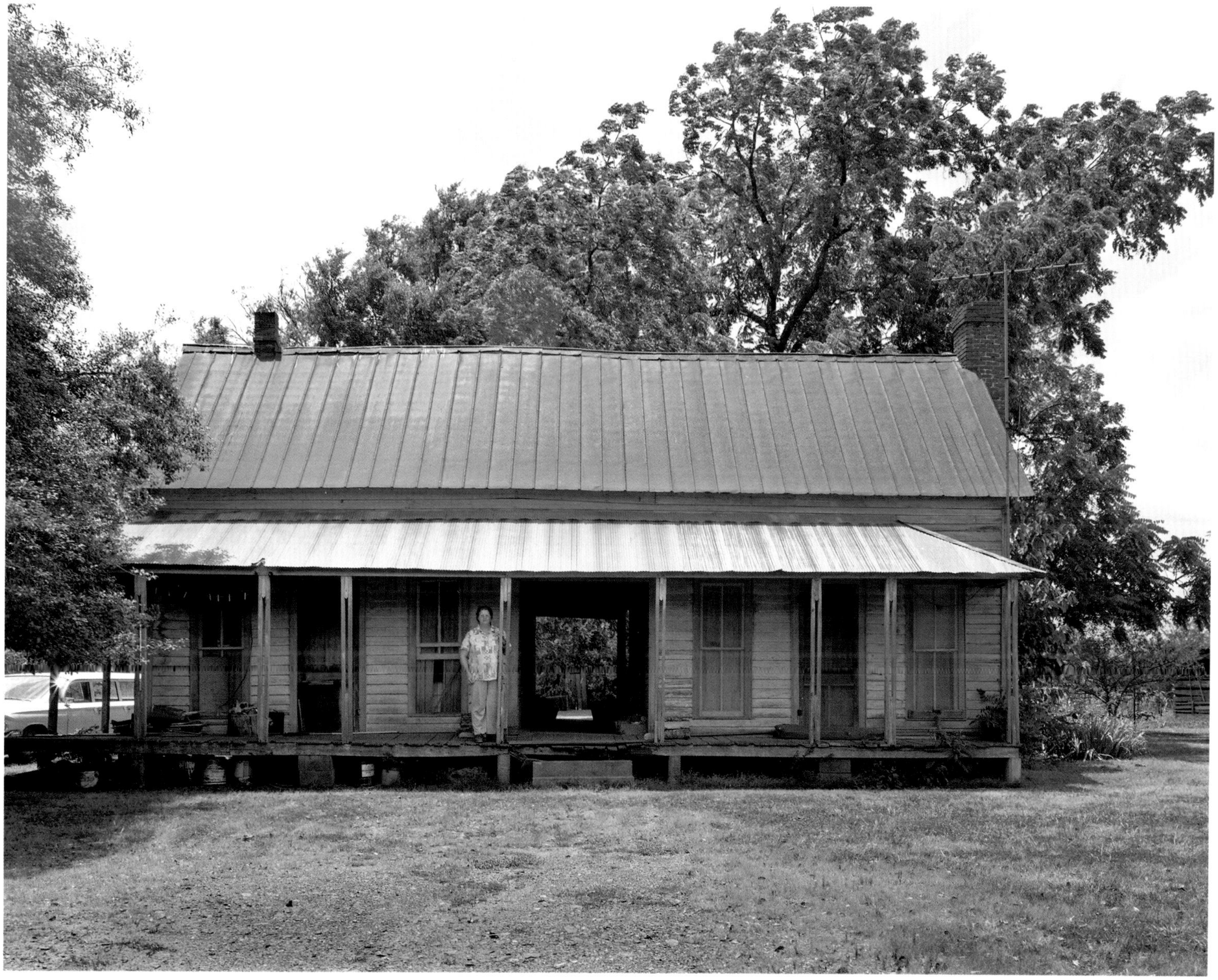

Wood frame, double pen dogtrot house
Parks (Scott County), Arkansas
(no longer standing)

THAT STORE THERE WAS BUILT BY LEONARD DAVIS. Called him Red Davis. Red Davis built that store in 1946. I don't know that for a fact, but that's what I been told many times. Leonard was his real name, but everybody called him Red. He built that store in 1946, and he worked there until he died. That's what I been told.

On the back a that store, Red built a shop where he'd work on trucks and cars and you-name-it. Tractors and whatever needed fixing. Red was a *mechanic,* and he would fix them all at the back of his store. In the front of the store was a little shop where he'd sell candy and tobacco and such. And then the gas pumps were here. It was the kind of pump where you pump it up by *hand*—maybe you never seen one of them—you pump it up, then the gas just kind of siphered down. Say you pump up ten gallons, then the gas would just unload itself into the tank. Maybe you never seen one of them old hand pumps. They long gone.

That car in the pitcher there, that's Donald *Jean's* car. Donald Jean *Young*. And that's him in the pitcher, the one with the sideburns, *crotched* over. The one leaning back against the store, looking this way, that's Leonard *Marfew.* And the third guy, that's Red Bissell. That's another Red—called him Red, too—same thing they called old man Davis. Looks like we had a lot a Reds around here. Anyway, they're all *dead* now, ever one of 'em.

I own that store now. Bought it from Doodle Lee in seventy-eight. He bought it from Marvin Kaufman. Kaufman, he bought it from Davis. So it was Red, Kaufman, Doodle, and me. That's the story of that store up to now. That was the chain of command. Now Doodle, he was one helluva mechanic, just like Davis was, but by the time I took hold of the store, it was mostly just a place where everybody would come to play *dominoes*.

On a *bad* day—you know, when nobody could get out to work—there be fifteen, twenty men there. That's where they all *go*. Sit there and play dominoes, talk, cuss, smoke, and tell stories. It got to where the women wouldn't even come around the place because all the men would be cussing and carrying on so bad. It was strictly a *man's* place. ▶

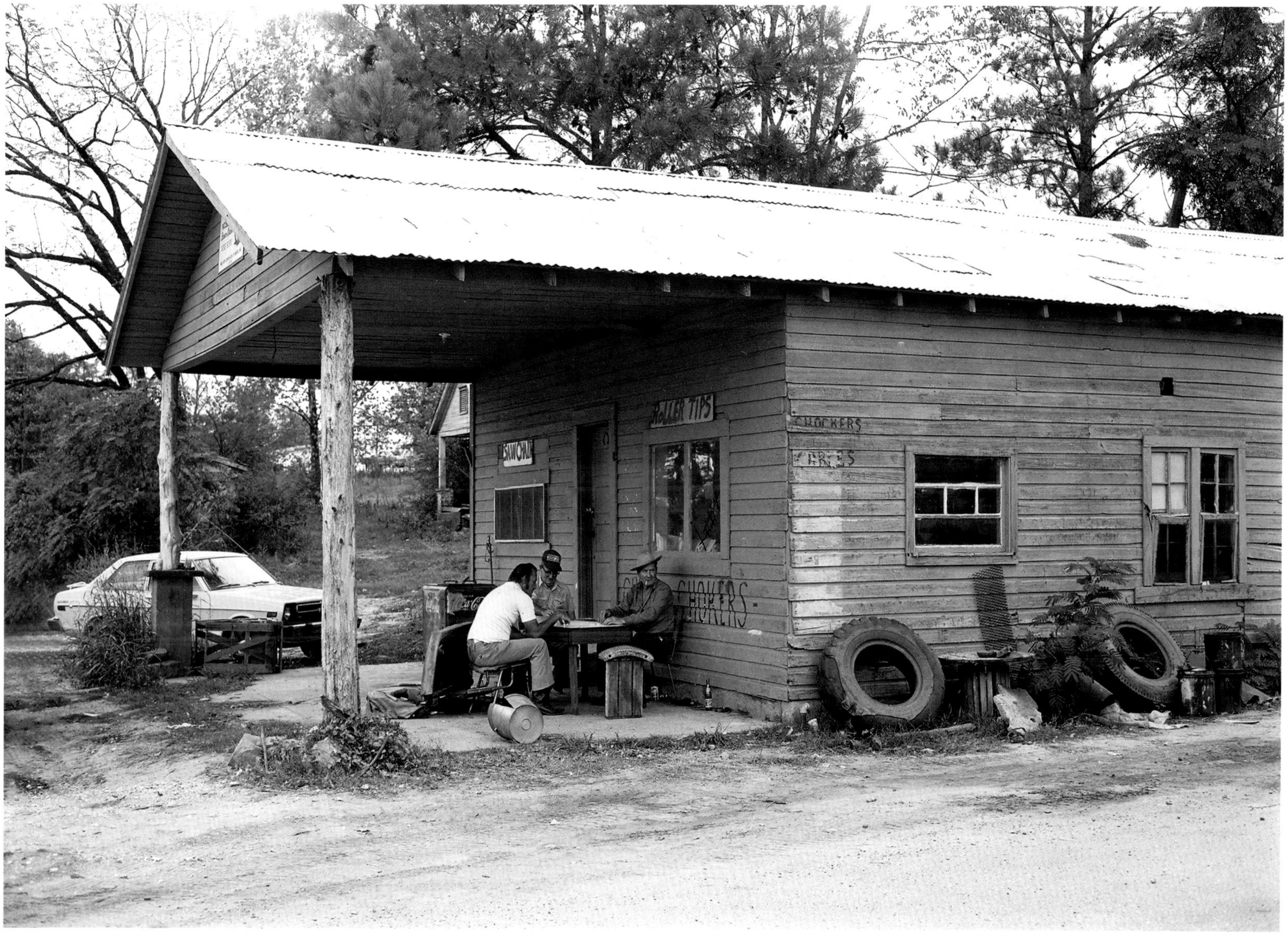

Wood frame roadside repair shop with deep overhang
Highway 70
Newhope (Pike County), Arkansas

I remember one day when James—that was *James Larry* Young, Donald Jean's little brother—he got all riled up about something and took his *chain* saw and cut his initials in that post there, one of them posts that's holding up the roof. You can see it for yourself, still there, *J-L-Y,* cut in the post where James went at it with his chain saw.

My story? I was born here in Newhope, but we left when I was five years old. We went to Amarillo, Texas. That was during the war. My old man was a carpenter, an alcoholic, and about anything else you want to call him. Then we went on from Amarillo to Oklahoma City, and my daddy got so bad my momma had to leave him. There was four of us kids, and I was the oldest, about nine years old at the time, and she left him. We bounced around for a while, stayed with kinfolks, and wound up back here when I was eleven years old. I been here ever since.

I hauled logs all my life. That's all I *ever* done. I hauled logs this morning in my sleep, in my *dreams*. I got up and told my wife this morning, them *damn logs* are gonna kill me yet. I done a lot of hard work in my life, and now it's catching up with me. When I wasn't hauling logs, I was farming. Growing soy beans down in the river bottoms. But it wasn't any money there. It wasn't nothing but a occupational *hazard*, and I got out of that one *real* fast. From time to time, I made a little *sorghum*, and I thought about brewing some *whiskey*, but then I thought better and gave up that idea.

Then, my wife and me, we grew *chickens* for years. We had thirty thousand chickens in two big houses out there in the back. Tyson give us the chickens and the feed, and we growed 'em. We growed all those chickens for all those years and I kept telling my wife to get some *pitchers* of those birds. But hell, she didn't get *one* damn pitcher. Those big old white birds sure was *pretty,* sitting up there real proud. And damn if we don't have *one* single pitcher of 'em now. But times are *changing*, no doubt about that. I remember when the road through this little town was nothing but dirt. Then we *paved* it. That was '64 and '65, and I was still in high school when I worked on that crew, paving that road going out of here toward Dierks. Next thing you know, we had a water tower and a *post office.* Time just flies, don't it? But it's real different now. A woman just moved in here from California with four kids, all between nine and` sixteen. *No daddy*. I'm told she don't know who the daddy of those kids was. They go to school over in Dierks, and they all been suspended. The town's just changing. On weekends, the corners are covered up with blacks. A few weeks ago, somebody lit fire to the school building. I heard it said that they *know* who it was, but they can't prove it. All things considered, I wouldn't know what the future is or where it's all going. I just wouldn't know.

But I tell you what I *do* know. I remember that old *tire* sitting there, that one right there in the pitcher, the one that's got no *tread* on it. And I know for sure that I was owning that store when you got that pitcher, because that was *my* old tire, sitting right there all those years.

P. T. Henry
Newhope, Arkansas

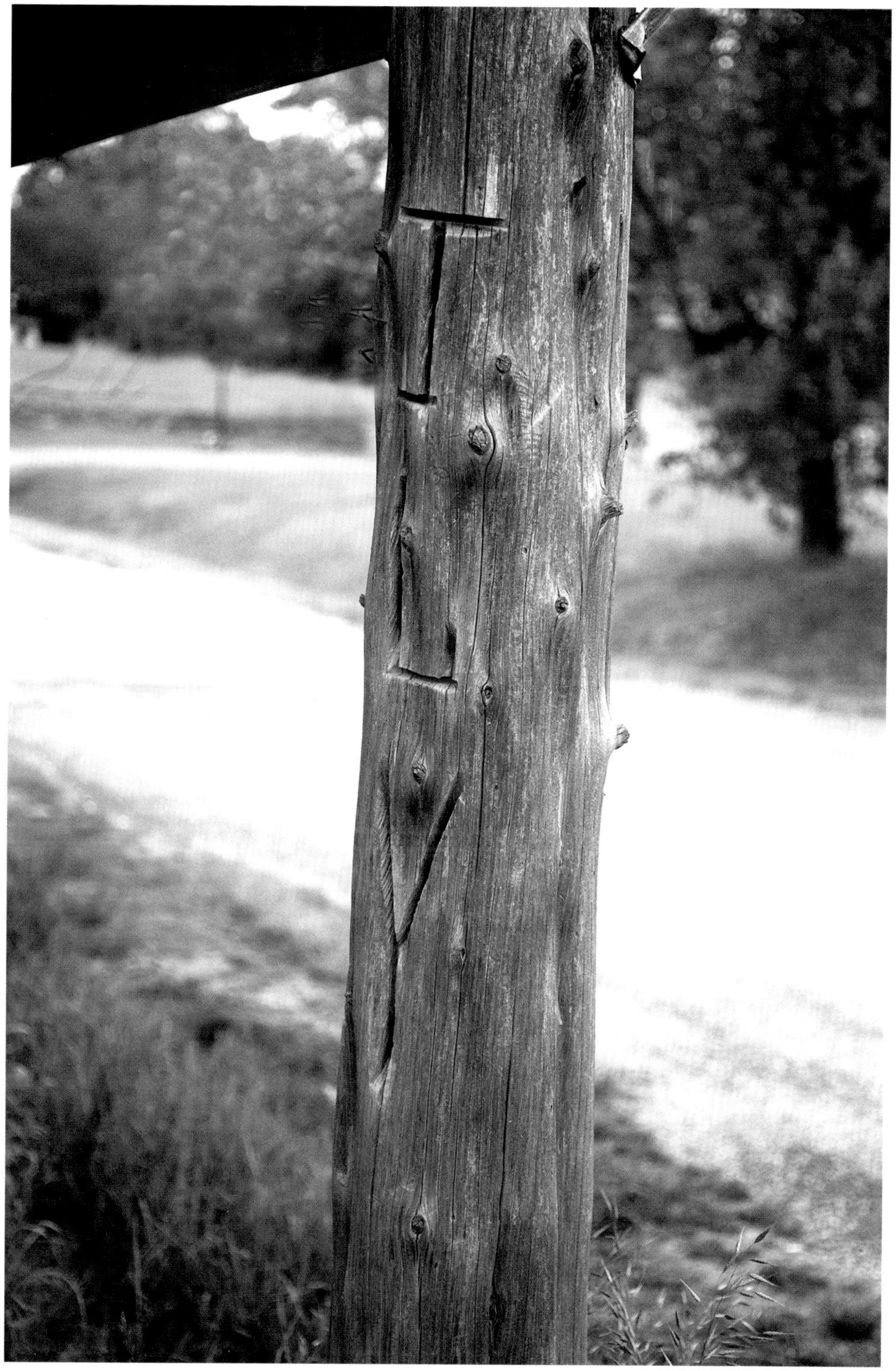

Initials carved with a chain saw in support post of
P. T. Henry's roadside repair shop
Newhope (Pike County), Arkansas

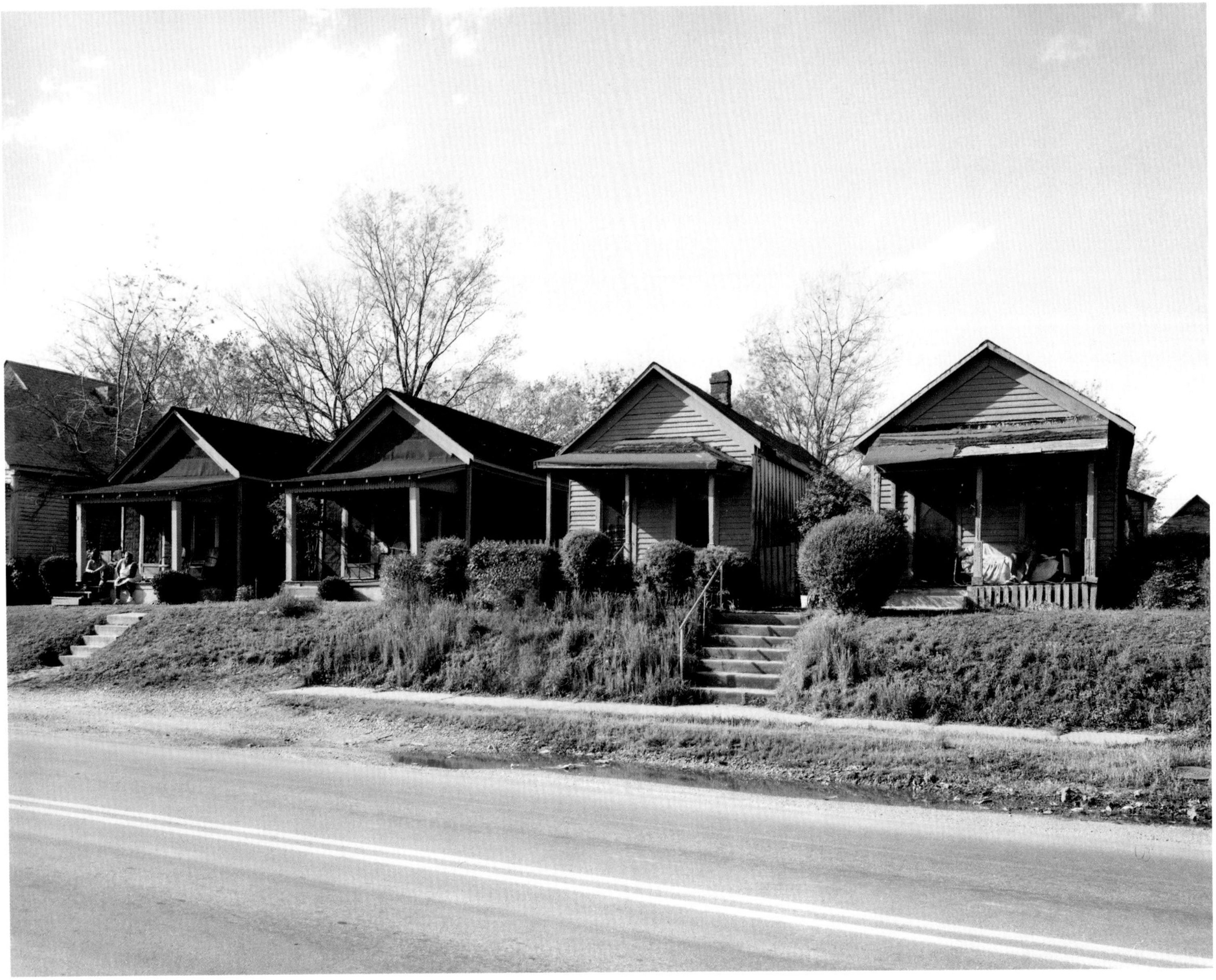

Wood frame shotgun houses
Little Rock (Pulaski County), Arkansas
(demolished)

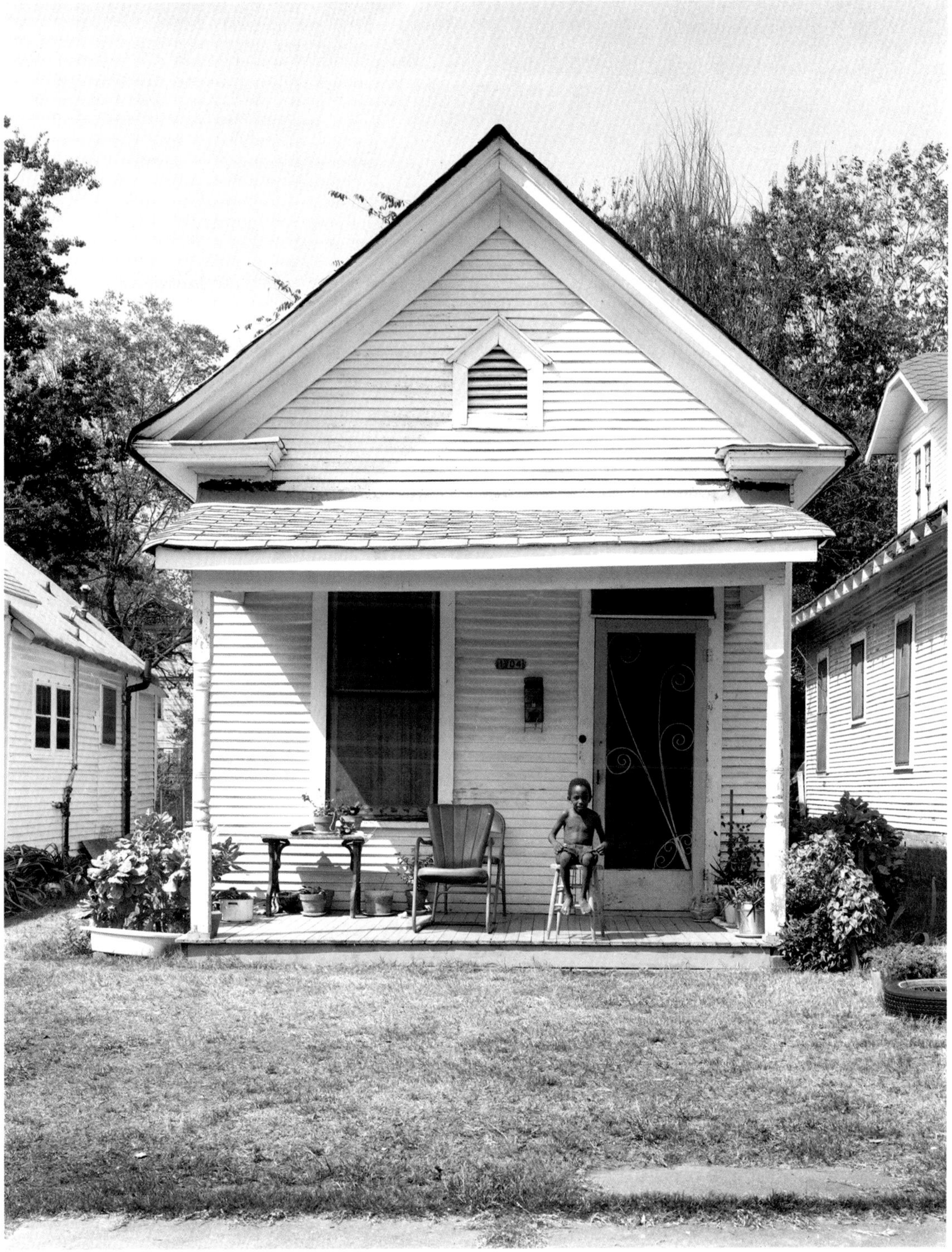

Wood frame shotgun house
Little Rock (Pulaski County), Arkansas
(demolished)

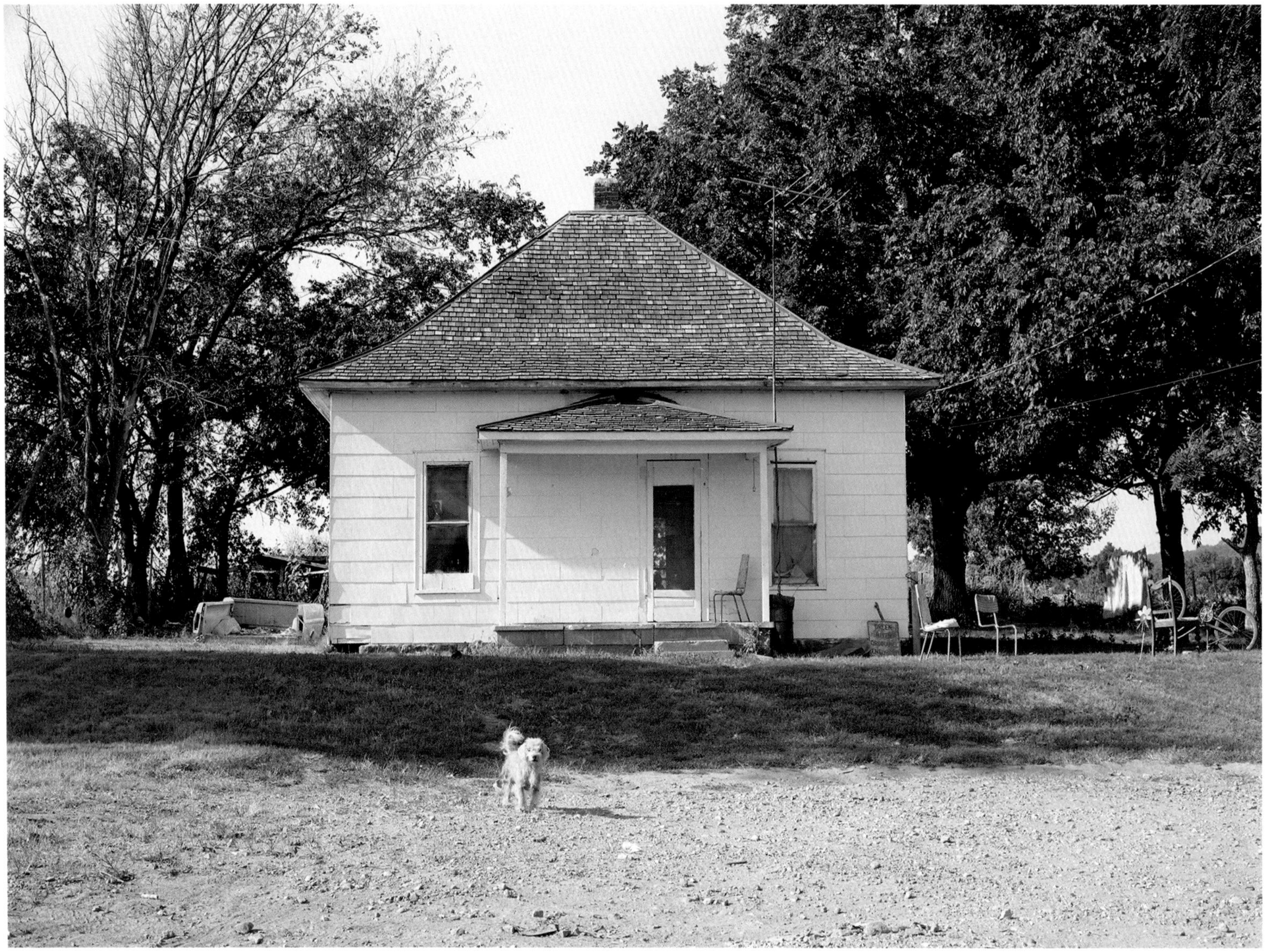

Converted double house with curved eaves
Mountain Home (Baxter County), Arkansas

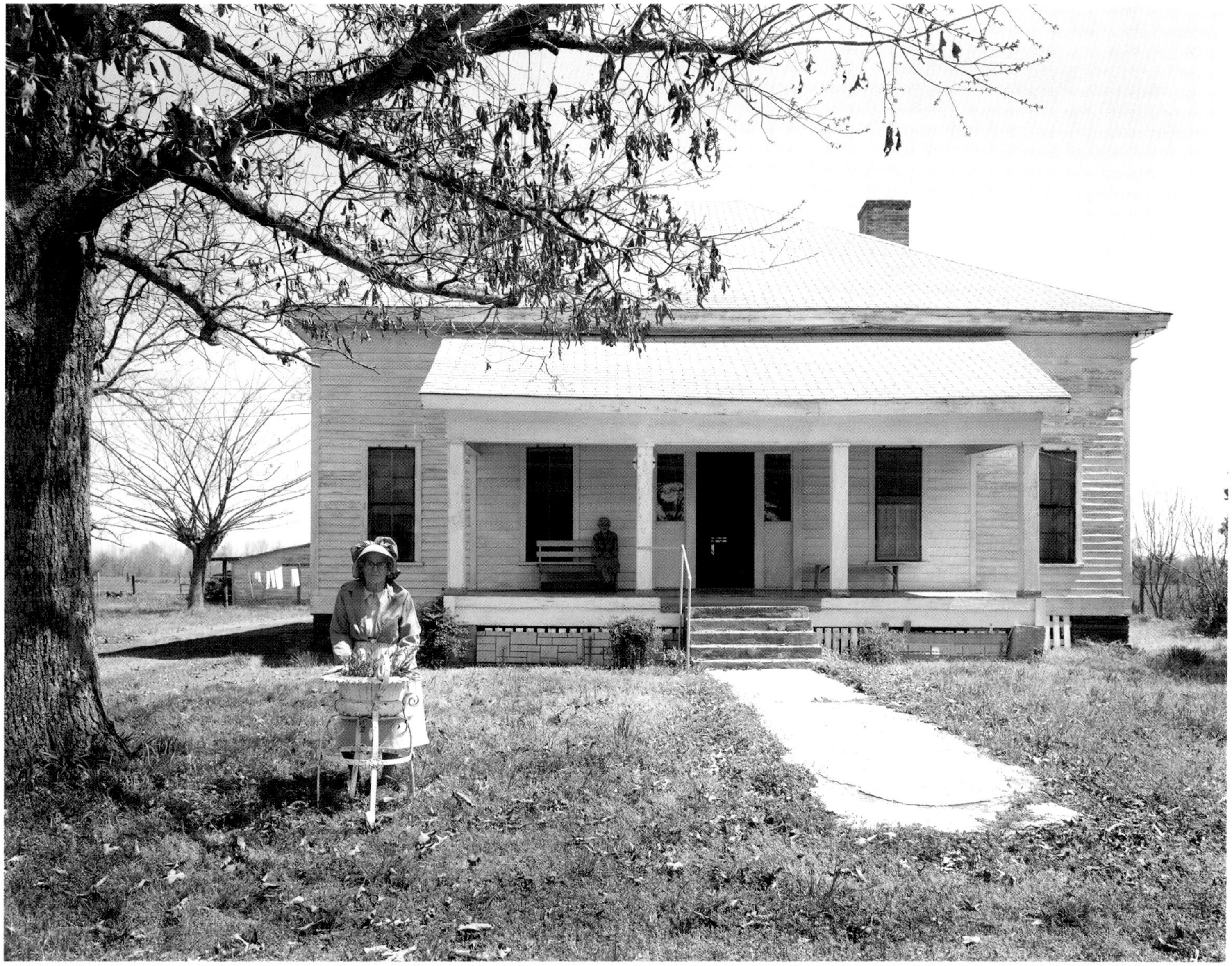

Enclosed dogtrot house with flush porch siding
Bingen (Hempstead County), Arkansas
(no longer standing)

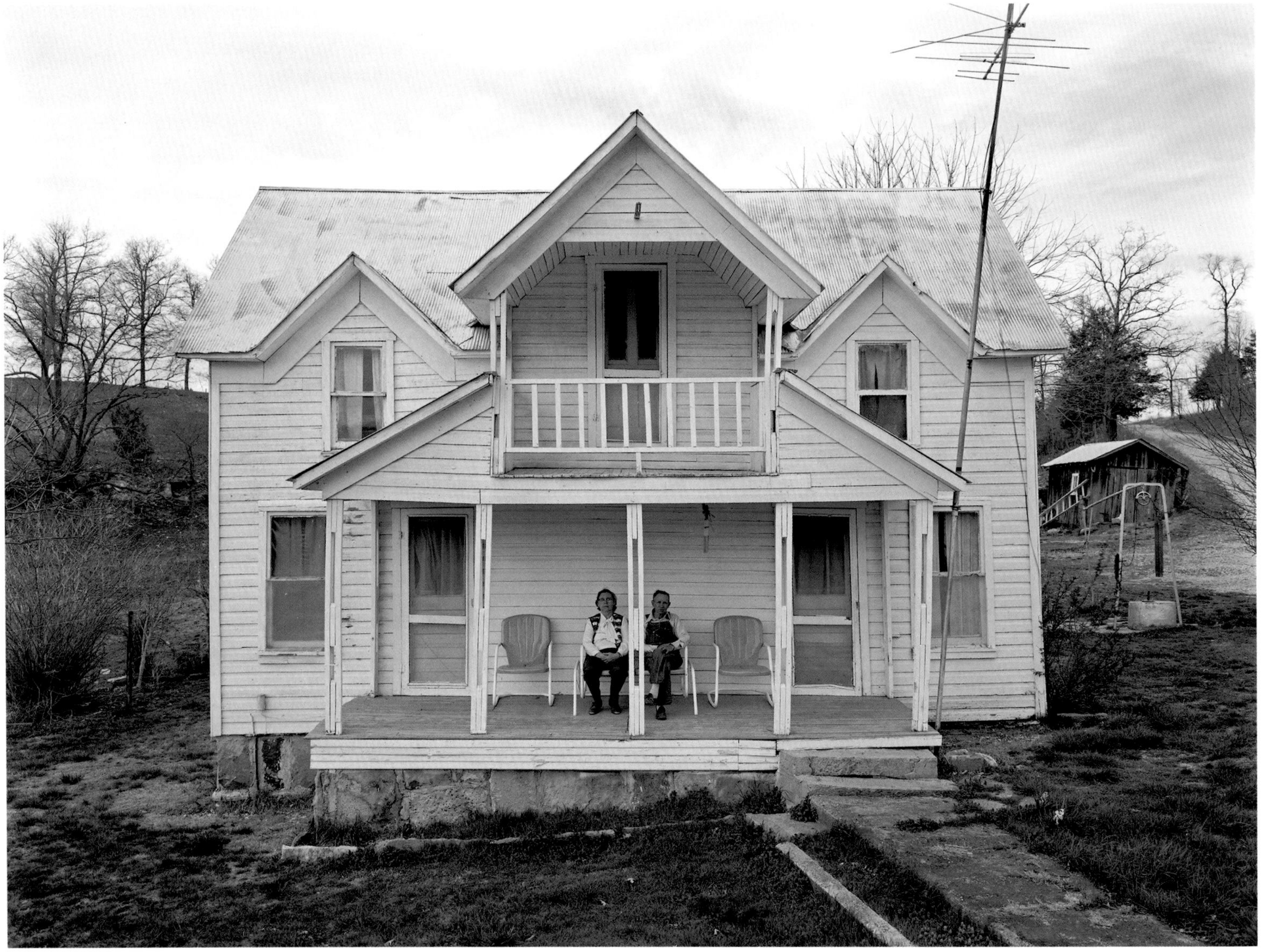

Wood frame double house with added porch
Alabam (Madison County), Arkansas
(demolished)

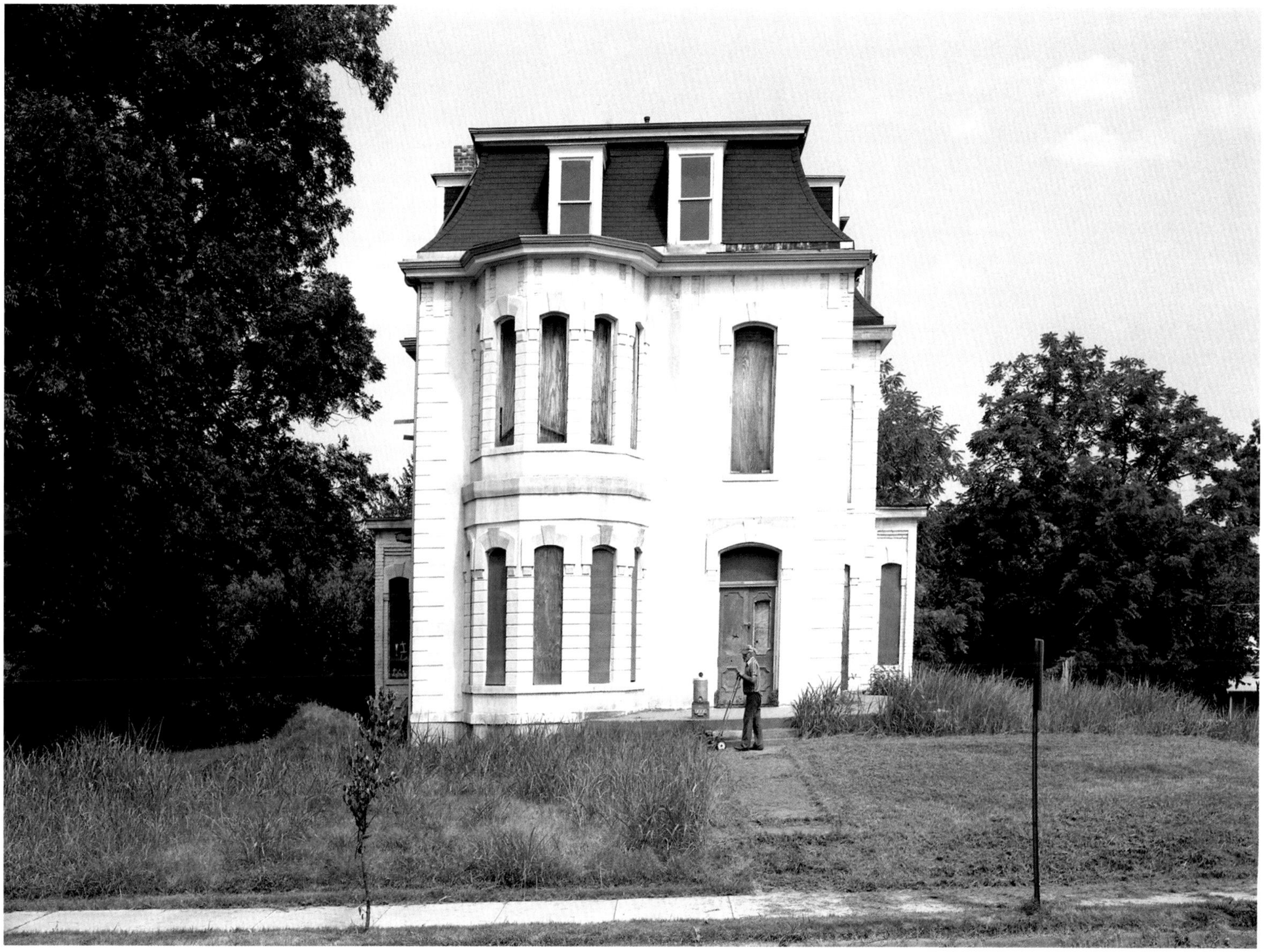

Stucco-faced Second Empire townhouse
Fort Smith (Sebastian County), Arkansas
(demolished)

I REMEMBER THAT FELLA. We were friends, actually. His name was *Bill*, Bill Long, and he was out of Los Angeles, California. He came here to St. Joe in '78. Or maybe it was '79. He came with his friend William, who stayed with him. William *Mann* was his name, and he was from back out East. William was a real *handsome* man. Very distinguished, you would say, but he had some years on him. I would say he was eighty-something years old. Bill had a few gray hairs in there himself, but I would guess he wasn't more than fifty-five at most.

They came to St. Joe and Bill bought the property there where that little rock house stood, right alongside the highway in the center of town. That little house used to be a café and a bus station. Miss Jesse Henley built it, and I heard it called the Jesse Henley Building. Jesse and her husband, they had a two-story hotel next to it, and that's where she fed their customers, in her little café there. To the side of that little house they had their hotel, but all of that just fizzled out sometime in the '60s.

After Miss Jesse left, the little place was a flea market, a junk store, this and that and the other. Then Bill showed up, like I said, about '78, and he bought the property, the little café and the hotel, too. The whole deal. Bill and William moved into the hotel, lived on the ground floor, and turned the second floor into a bird operation. Bill raised cockatiels, finches, parakeets, and you name it. The whole second floor was full of birds. The little stone house next door, the old café, it was his showroom, and he did a good business there. He put up signs on the highway coming into town, and he would stand there in front of the store, showing off this bird or that. People coming through town would stop to see what was what, and first thing you know, they were driving away with a bird or two.

The way I met Bill was right after they moved in. It was wintertime, and I heard that they needed some firewood. Of course, I was a *young* man then, and I was still living with my mother outside of town. I went and chopped a good load of firewood and took it to them. Bill seemed to like what I brought him, and he would order more firewood whenever he needed it. We got real friendly and pretty soon I had to sit down and play a couple of games of chess before he'd pay me for the firewood. One thing led to another and that's how our friendship started. ►

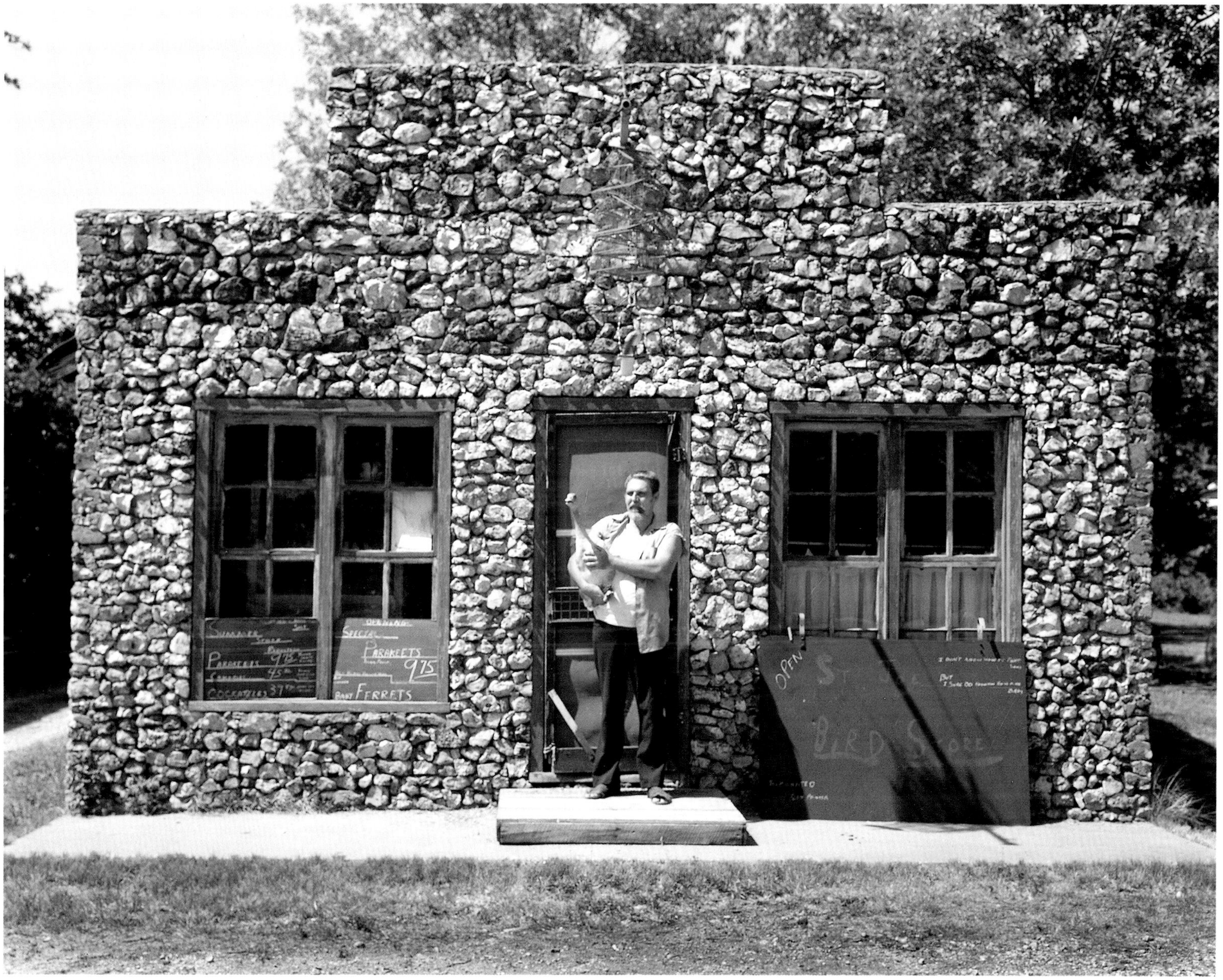

Rock-faced commercial building
St. Joe (Searcy County), Arkansas
(no longer standing)

I think the two of them came to St. Joe for the quiet. That and the fact that it was off the beaten track. They pretty much stayed to themselves, didn't mix a lot with the locals here. I was one of the only people that got to know them. When Bill learned that my mother was real good with birds, he asked us to move in and live with them in the old hotel, which we did. My mother would feed those baby cockatiels by hand and raise them for Bill. The only thing that people in St. Joe ever talked about as far as Bill was concerned was about the big *snake* that got away from him.

There was this woman that lived here, and she was sort of a strange one. She liked to keep snakes. Lots of 'em. *Big* snakes. And the way the story goes is that Bill was keeping one of her big snakes for her, a big *python* snake, and he let it get away from him. That's what people said, anyway. They were saying, if that woman had one big snake, she might of had more, and if there was more than one snake loose, then they were out there multiplying. People in St. Joe still talk about it. They still talk about the big snakes that got away from Bill and god knows how many are out there now.

Anyway, some time in the '80s, Bill got all involved in Scientology. He took a trip to Florida and stayed in L. Ron Hubbard's compound down there. When he came back to St. Joe, he had a totally different outlook on life. He was like a different man. He sold the property, the old café and the hotel, and he left to go back to California. He left William here with my mother and me, and William was quite a handful by then because he was just getting older and older. We took care of him as long as we could, then we located a sister of his that was still living back out East. So we put together some money and we bought a bus ticket for William. We sent him back out East to live with his sister.

That was all a long time ago now, and that's the last I heard of either one of them.

Duane Ingram
St. Joe (Searcy County), Arkansas

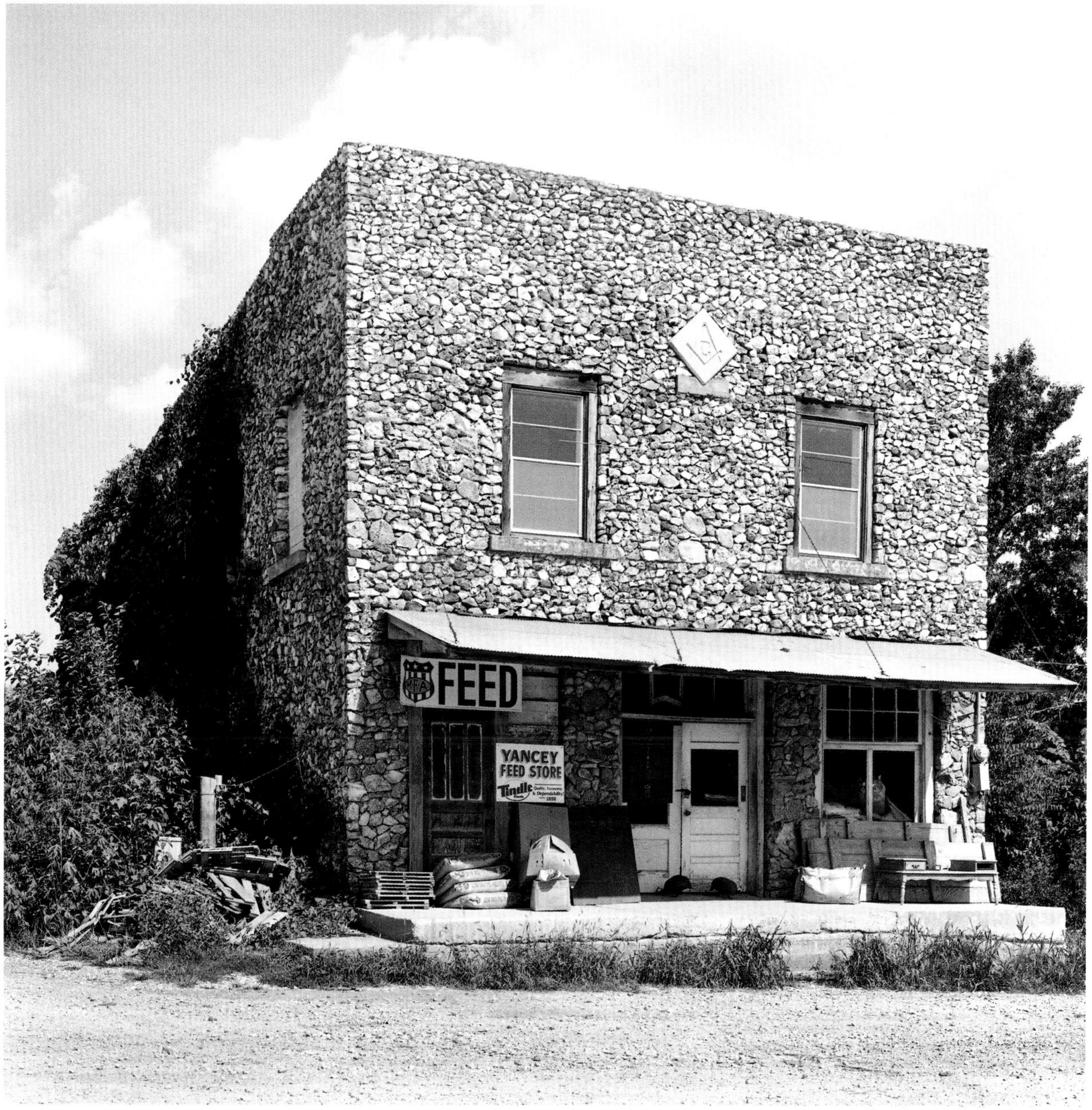

Rock-faced commercial building
St. Joe (Searcy County), Arkansas
(no longer standing)

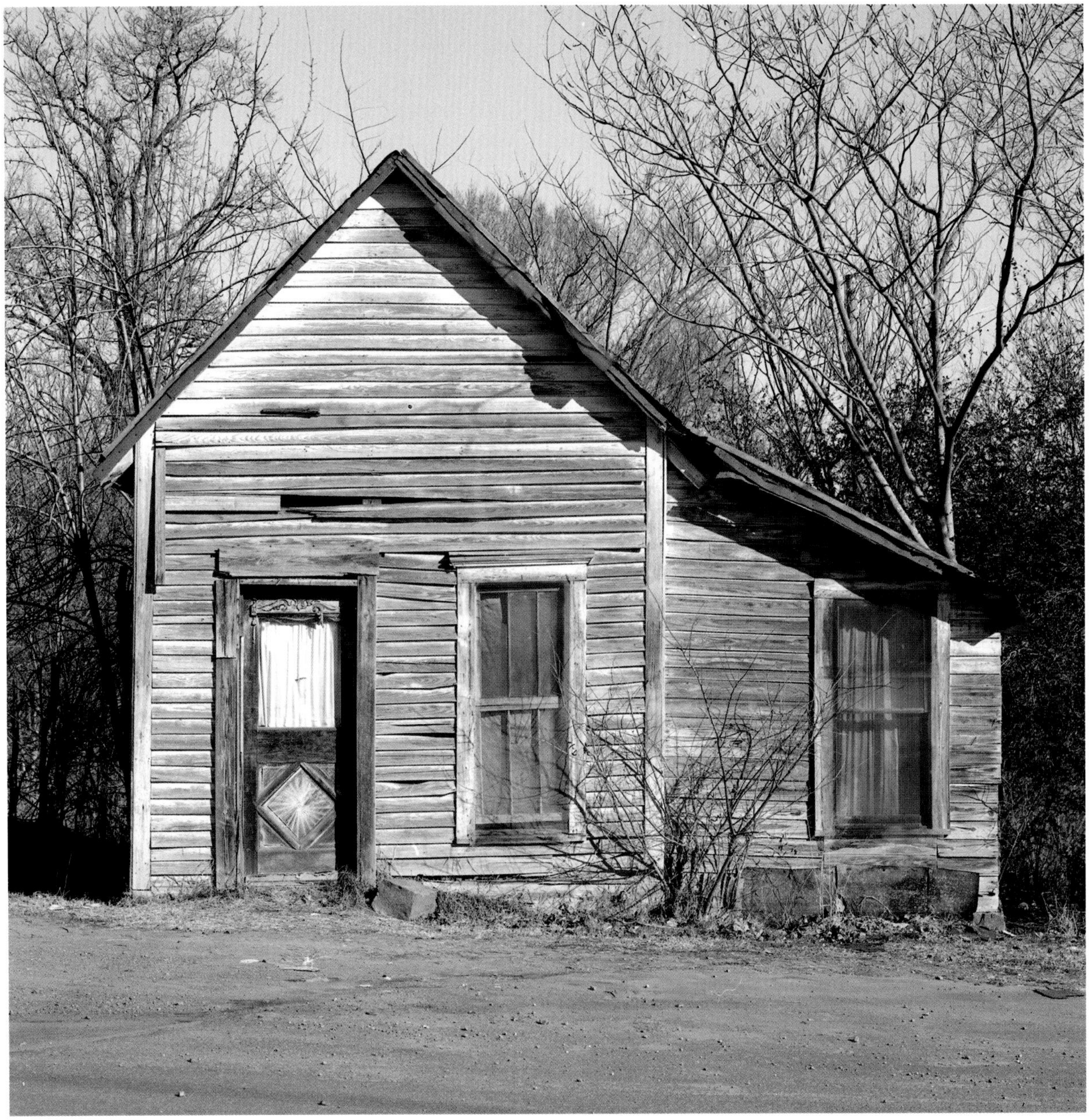

Gable-ended house with added lean-to rooms
Dardanelle (Yell County), Arkansas
(no longer standing)

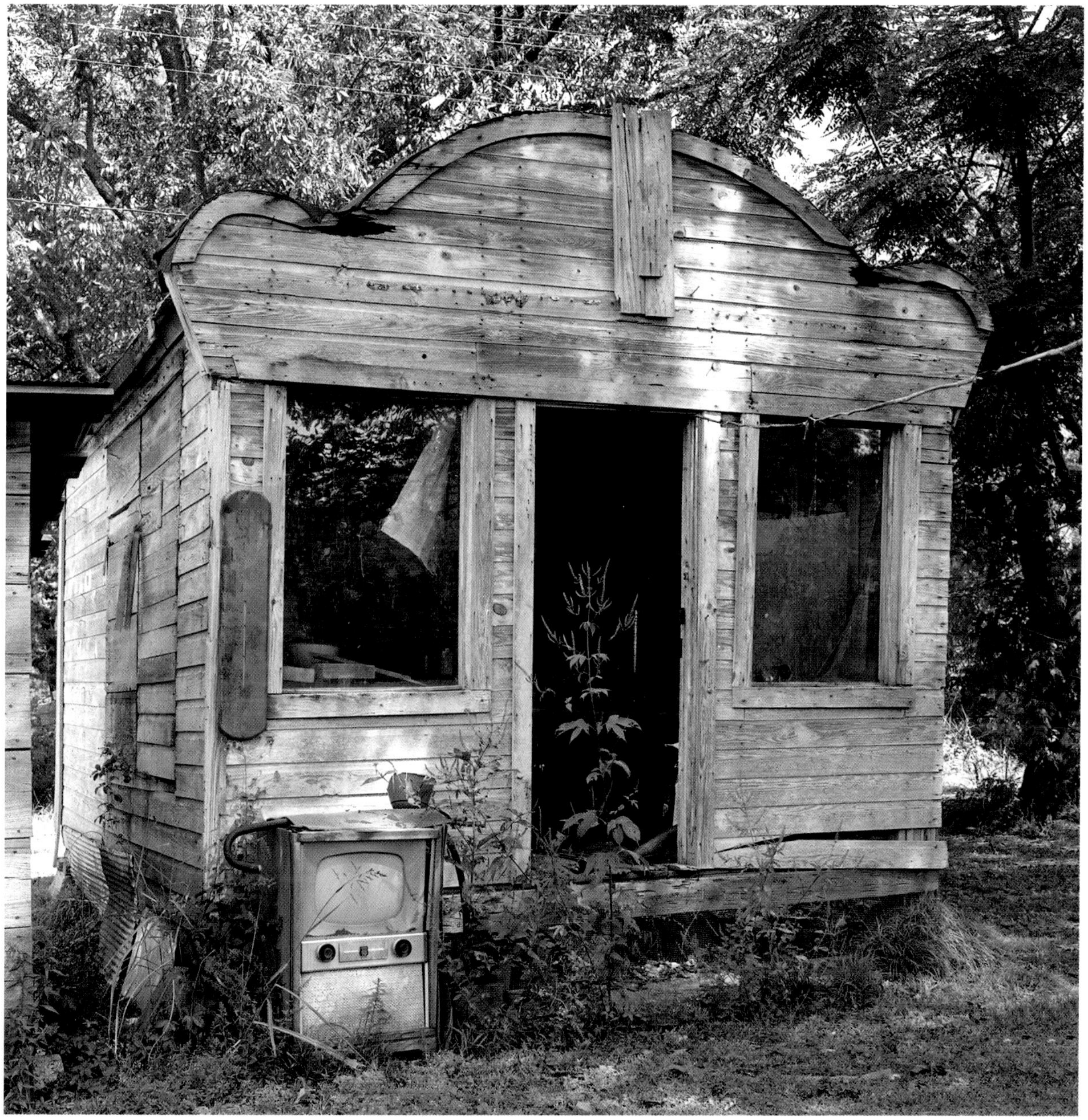

Whimsical commercial structure with "German" siding
Three Creeks (Union County), Arkansas
(no longer standing)

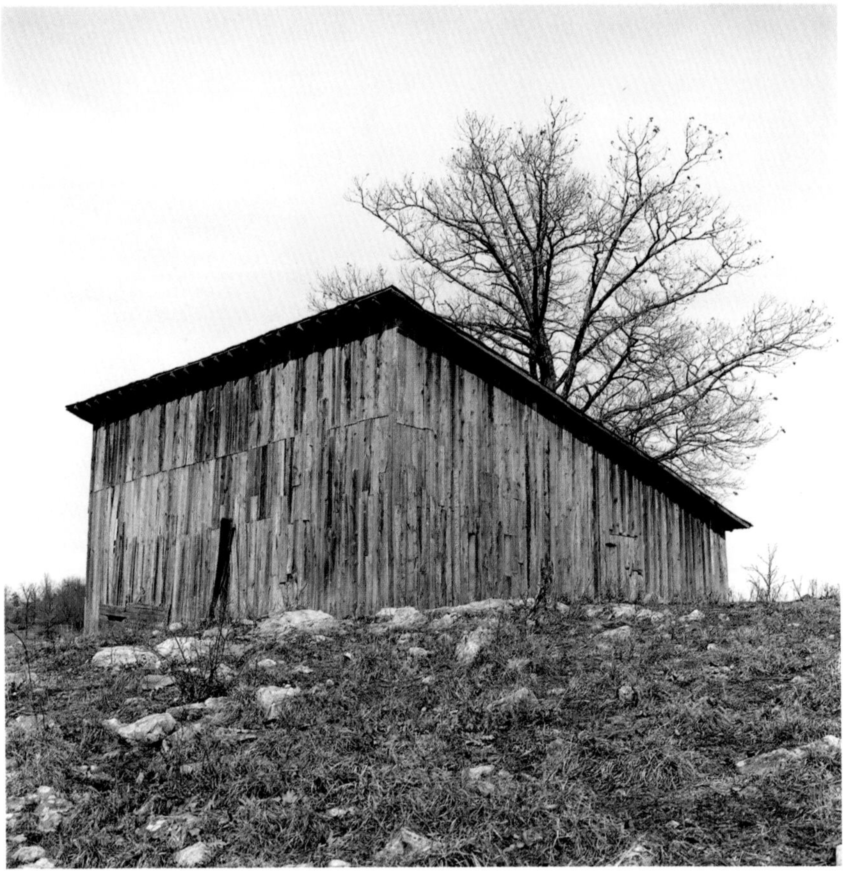

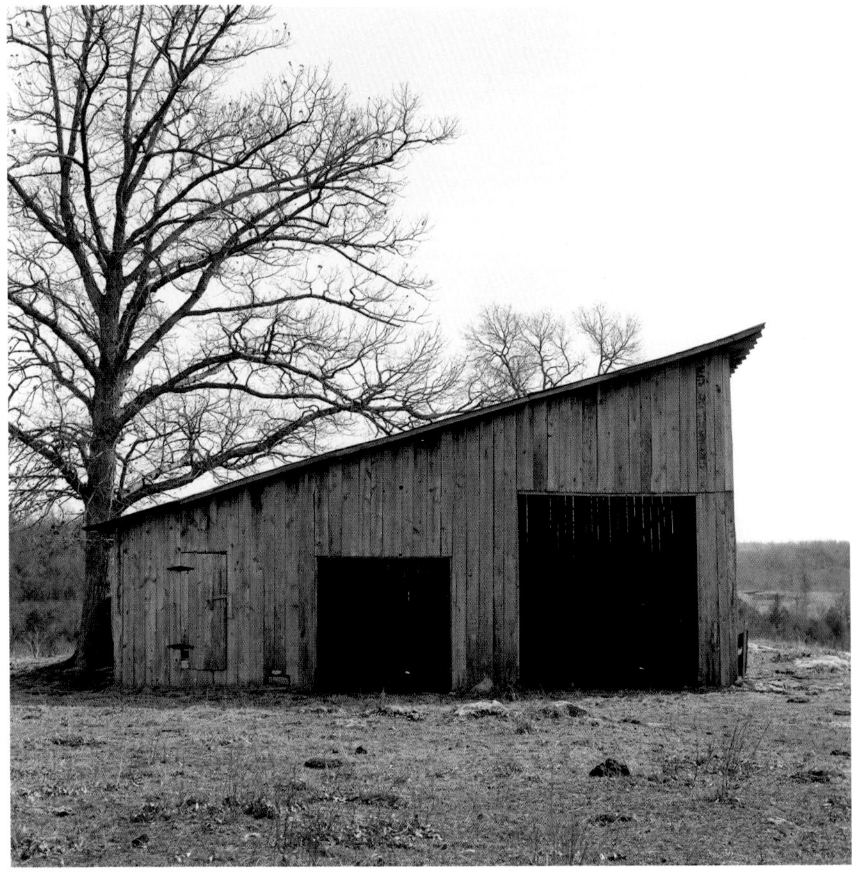

Storage barn of plain vertical board construction
Boone County, Arkansas

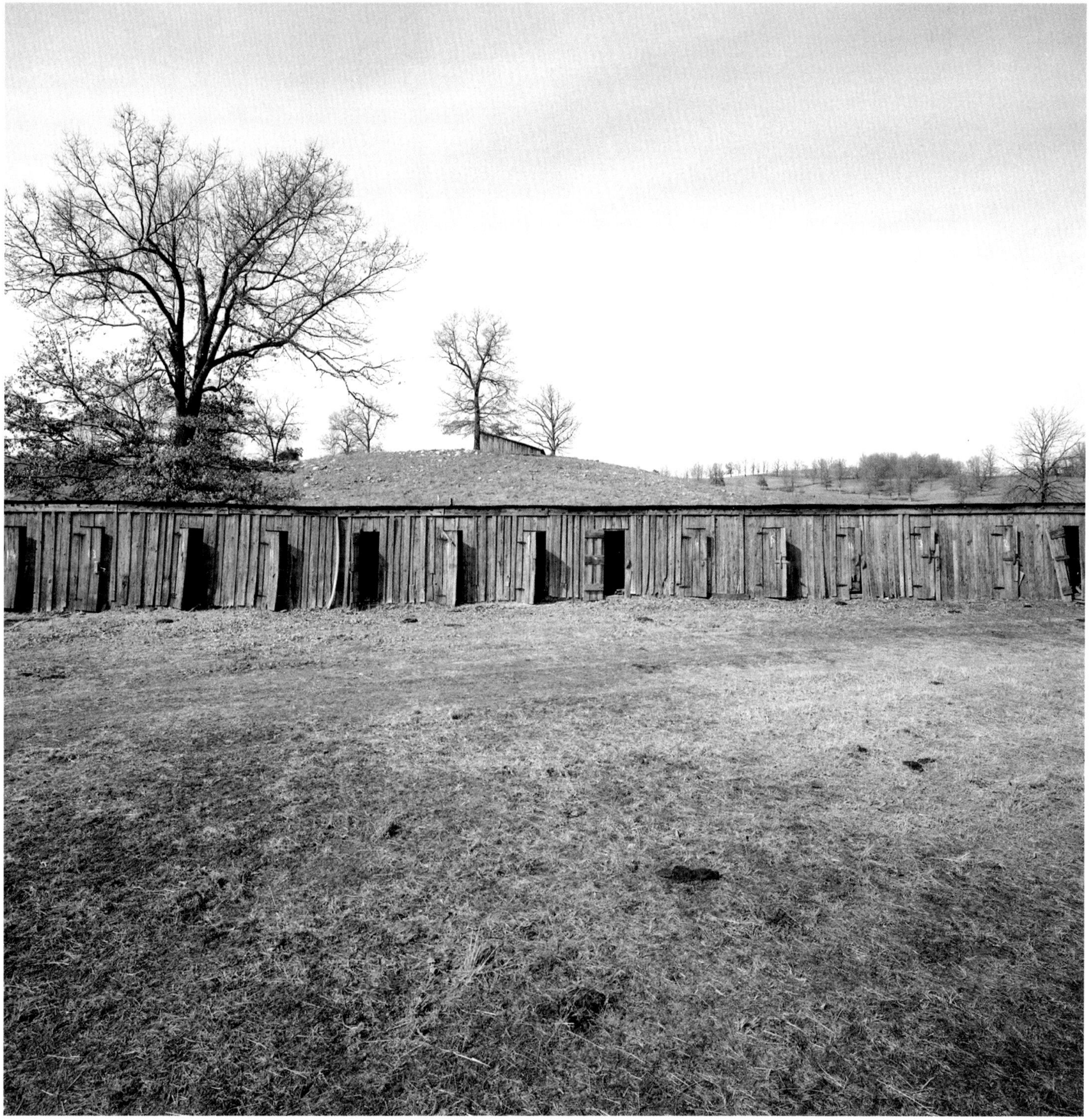

Presumed hog house of box and batten construction
Boone County, Arkansas

When I was a girl, I lived in a house just like that one, on Cornbridge Road, down toward Tollett. That's what we called a sharecropper's house, and that's what I lived in, starting when I was about ten years old. You see, my father died in '45, and then my mother . . . well, she took off for Texas. The children, all five of us, we moved in with my grandpa and grandma. They already had seven children of their own, but they raised us all together in that little house.

We might have been the poorest family around here, but for sure we were the *happiest* family. We were surrounded by cotton fields and peach orchards. I remember Grandpa had a cucumber patch. It was right there in front of the house. He raised those *little tiny* cucumbers, the best kind.

I remember a song that we used to sing in church. It was a song about a beautiful life. Well, we *lived* a beautiful life. Truly, we did. We lived a poor life, but it was a *beautiful* life.

When we were kids, we did some crazy things. I've heard it said that God looks out for fools and children, and he sure must have been looking out for us. Good lord, we did some crazy things. We would swim in the pond with snakes. We would catch the snakes and collect them in cocoa sacks. We would climb up on the roof of the barn and slide off, just for fun. And we would sing. Lord, we were *always* singing.

Grandma would set us down by the fireplace at night to read the Bible, say memory verses, and sing together. We would sing at home and we would sing at church. We would sing on the school bus. Mostly, we would sing church songs, but we would even sing hillbilly songs, too. You know, I'm talking about what you call country and western songs today, but back then we called them *hillbilly* songs. Hank Williams, cheating heart, and all of that. I had such a beautiful childhood. When my daddy died and my momma left, well, my brother and a sister they weren't in love with that, but I told them then, like I tell them now, God gives you all you need and more. Be happy. Just be happy.

I remember one time when a white man came to our church to learn about our music. He wanted to know the songs we sang, where we learned them, and the way we had of singing. Grandma said he liked the way we put the gravy on the music, giving it our own style and spirit. Anyway, this white man, he taught my grandpa to read shape notes. Once he did that, Grandpa could sing all the songs in the books, not just the songs we already knew. Before that, we just sang by ear, singing the songs that our parents and grandparents sang. Then Grandpa taught us to read the shape notes, and after that we could sing so many new songs. But even when we learned new songs, we still put our gravy on the music. That's just the way we like to sing.

I remember we used to eat what we called the clay dirt. Just walking down the road, if we saw some of the clay dirt, we would eat some of it, because that's what we learned from our parents. That's what they had been taught to do, and then of course they taught us. That was just part of country life, and my kids today don't like anything about country life. They despise living in the country. ►

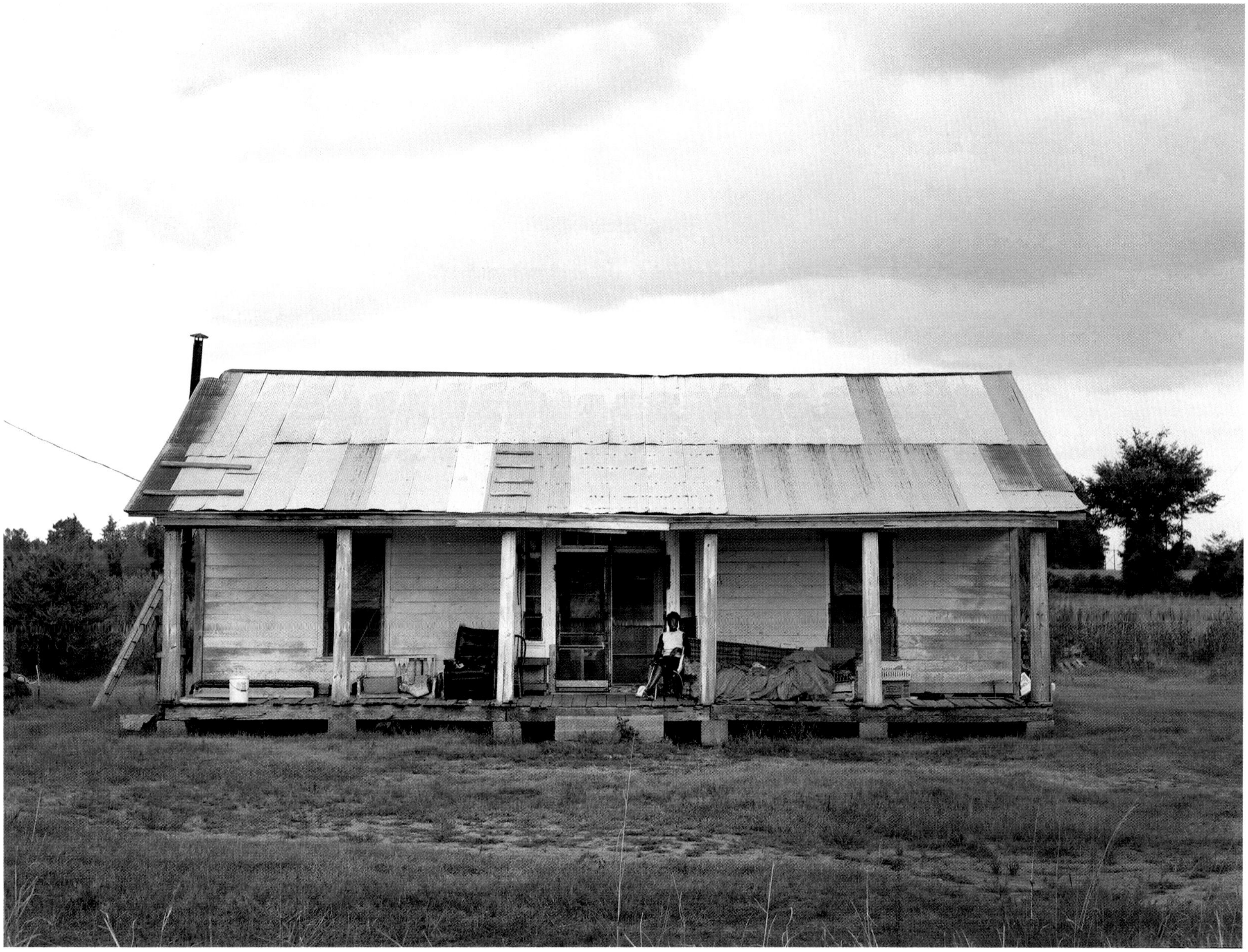

Greek Revival cottage with battered columns
Mineral Springs (Howard County), Arkansas
(no longer standing)

I was the salutatorian of my high school class, class of '58, and I had perfect attendance. Perfect attendance. Can you believe that? You know what else? I could *palm a basketball.* It's true. When I was sixteen years old, I could palm a basketball. I played guard for our basketball team—the Childress Tigers, that was us—and we won all our games. We were state champions my senior year.

I can still palm a basketball.

When I got out of high school, I had two scholarships to choose from. I had a salutatorian scholarship and I had a cosmetology scholarship from a beauty college in Little Rock. I decided on the cosmetology scholarship, and one of my high school teachers, Mrs. Williamson, she took me to Little Rock to go to school. Two years later, I got my degree and started looking for work. But there were no jobs for me, not in Little Rock, not anywhere around here. So I just got on a bus and headed for Chicago, looking for my future.

In Chicago, I worked for Zenith radio for twelve years, making radios and TVs. I got married and had two girls. That was good for a while, but then I had problems with my husband, plus my daughter had gotten in trouble, running with some wild kids in school, so I decided maybe it was time to come back home. So I drew out all my profit sharing money, bought a black and gold '72 Monte Carlo, threw all my stuff in it, and headed back home to Mineral Springs.

With my savings and my profit sharing money, I started buying property. First, I bought that white house over there across the street. Bought that one for seven thousand dollars equity share and rented it out. After that, I bought that lot over there for nine thousand, moved a trailer on it, and put my daughter in it. Next, I bought this house for myself and moved in. Then, I thought to myself, *hold on honey,* you're a single woman, you better *ease* off and *cool* down. But before I quit buying, I bought one more lot. I guess I had plenty of faith and nerve. Then, after I bought all that property, I went looking for a job, because I was out of money.

I took a job at the only place that was hiring, and that was the cement plant. I worked there for fifteen years, until they closed it down for asbestos. That was hard work, *man's* work, hauling bags of cement. When they closed the cement plant, I went to Tyson and worked there for six years. Sometimes I would have three jobs at once, cleaning the school, working in the nursing home, whatever other job there was, I would take it.

I think it all started with my grandma. I would go with her to do cleaning and laundry and ironing. She loved to work, and I loved to be with her, watching and learning from her. To this day, I don't like to be still. I'd rather be working. I like to be moving. If I sit still one day, I just get sore, and nothing gets done.

Helen Harris
Mineral Springs, Arkansas

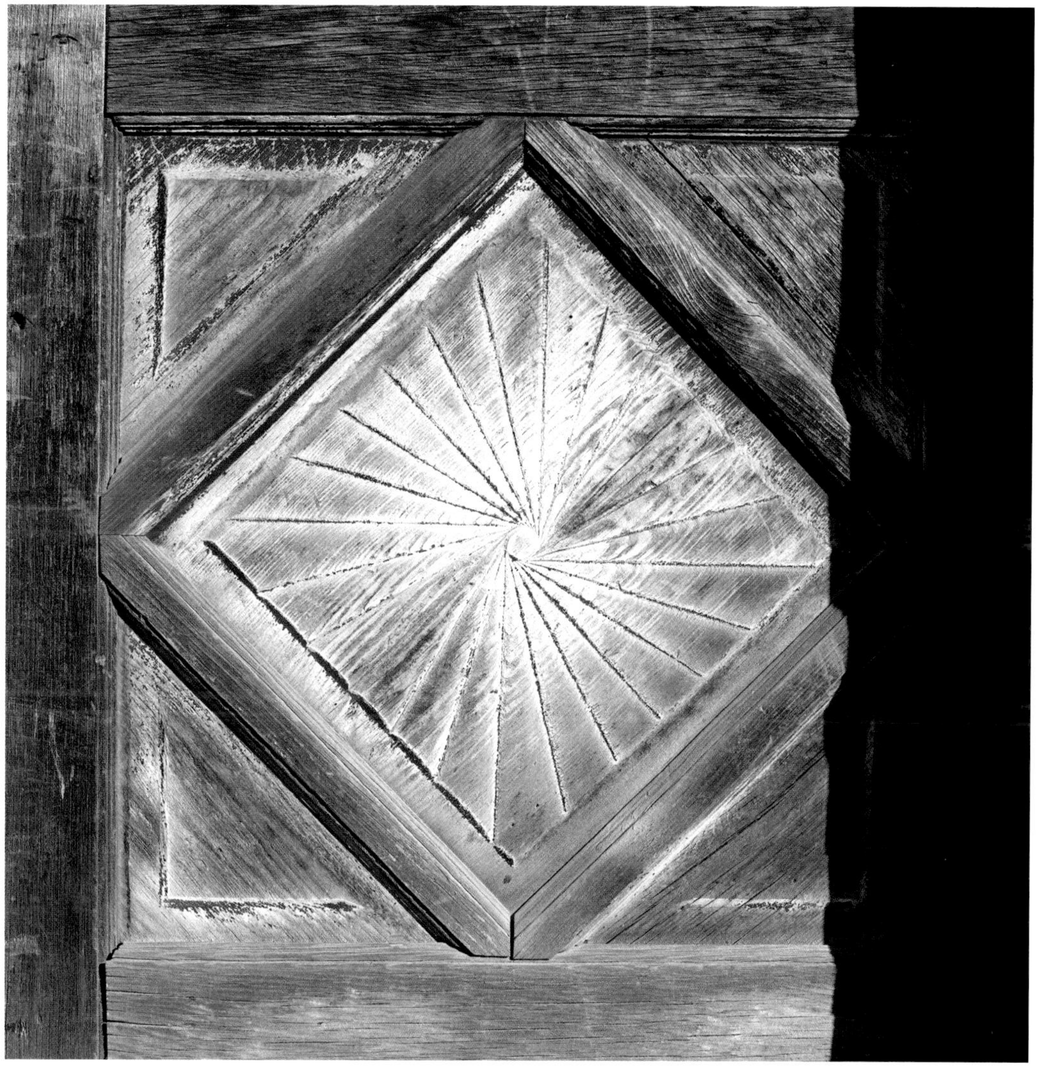

Exterior wood door detail
Dardanelle (Yell County), Arkansas
(no longer standing)

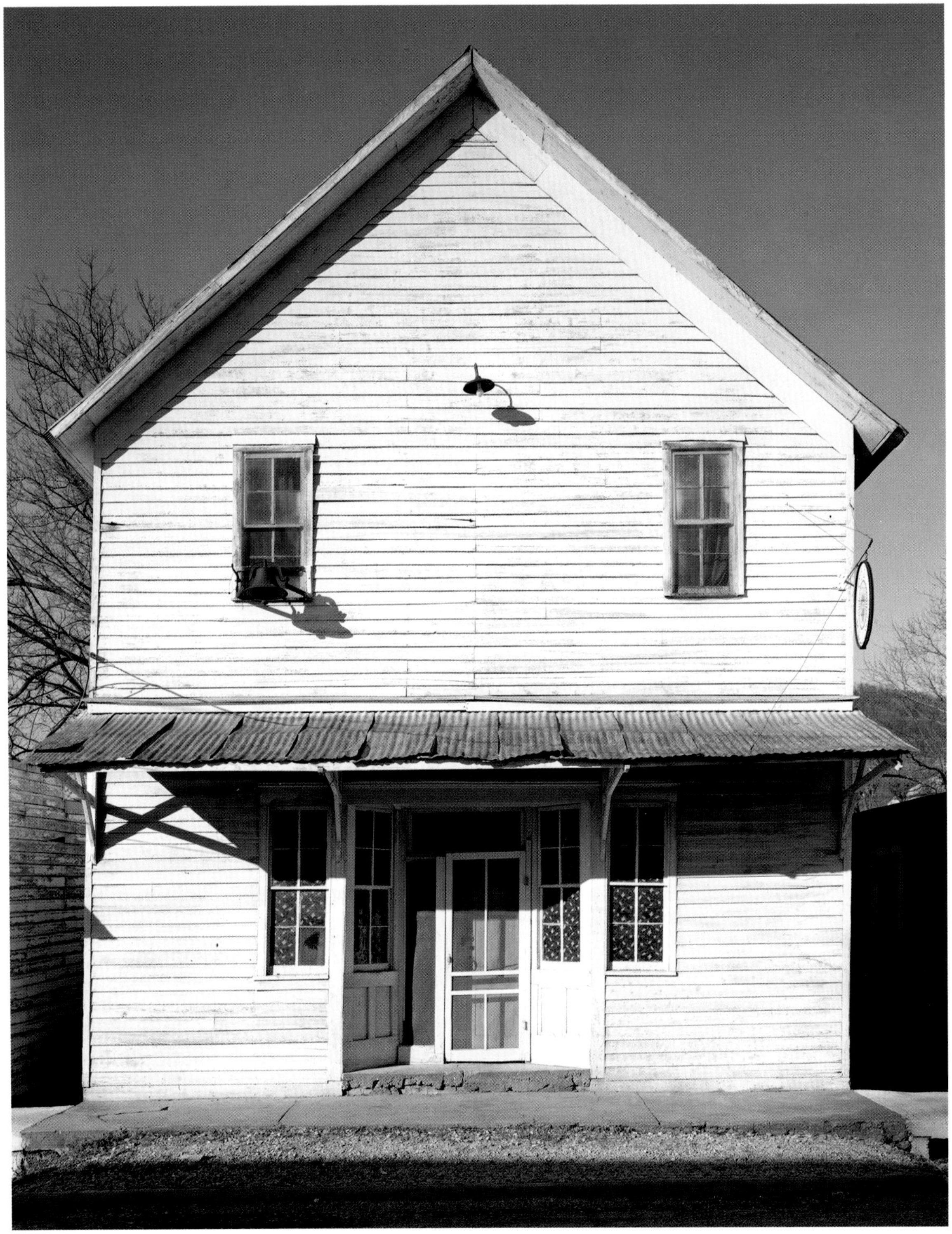

Two-story, wood frame commercial structure with highly peaked roof
Kingston (Madison County), Arkansas

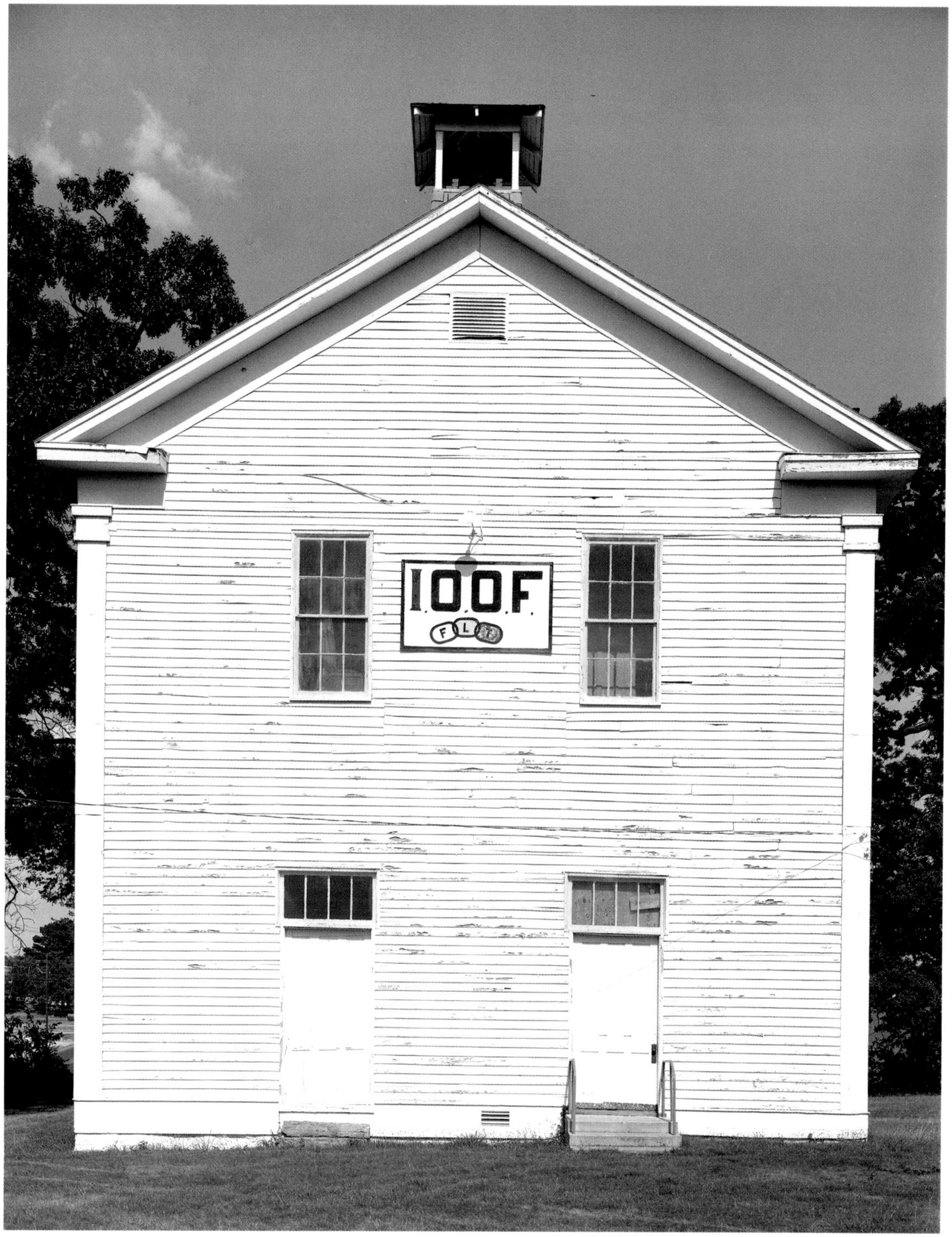

Two-story Odd Fellows lodge with meeting hall above and church sanctuary below
Omaha (Boone County), Arkansas

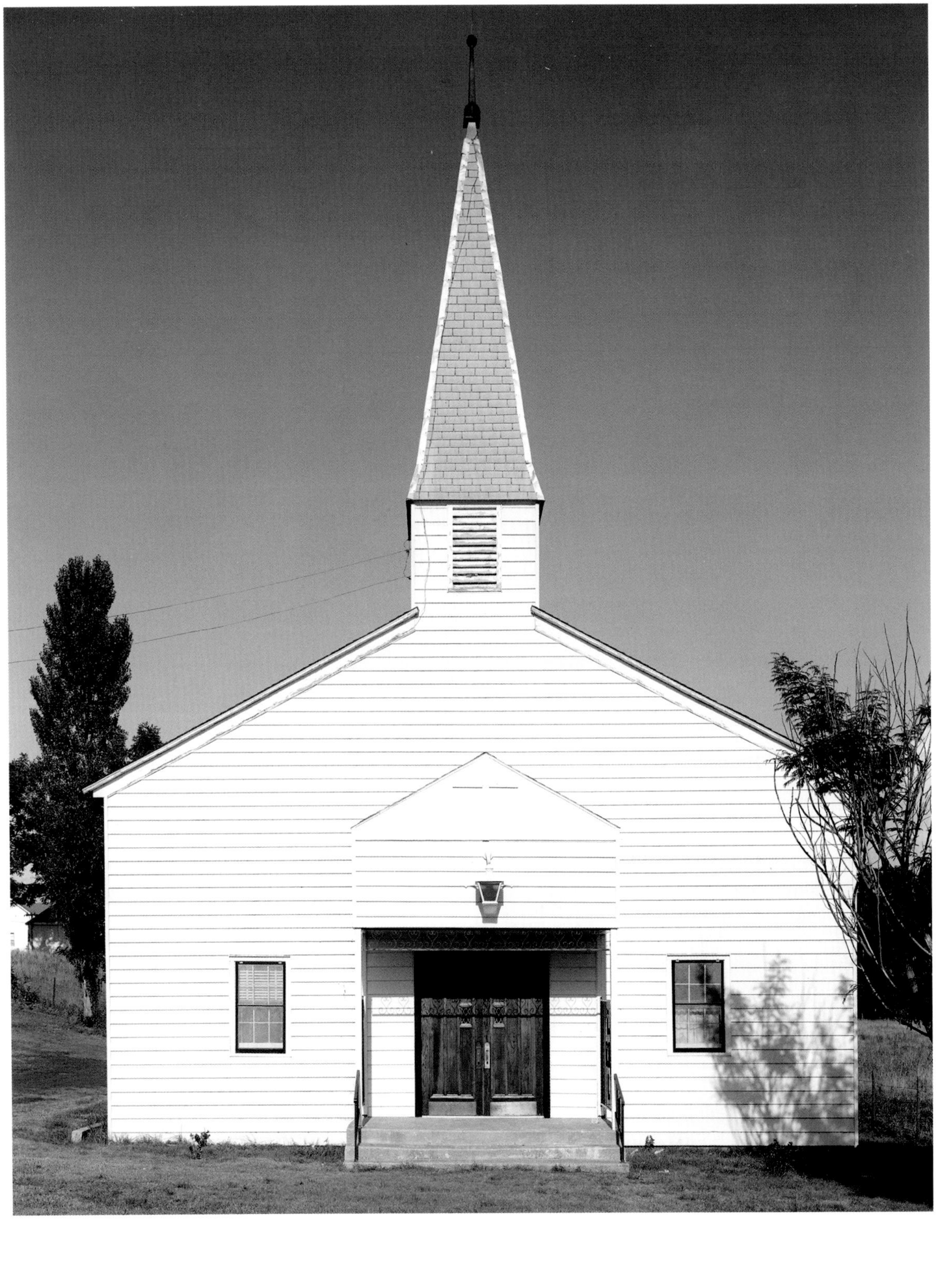

Wood frame church with projecting pedimental entry
Tulip (Dallas County), Arkansas

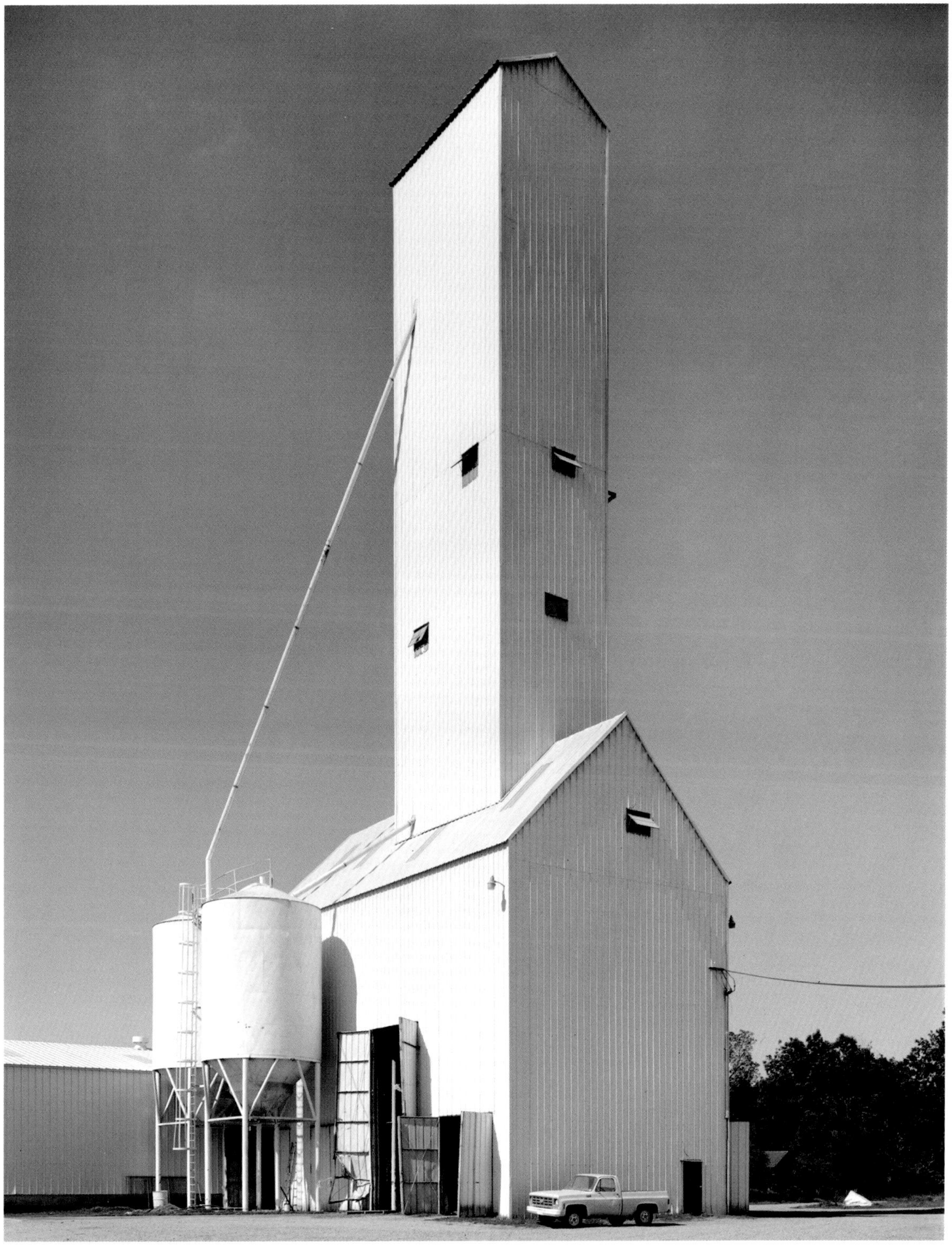

Rice silo with sheet metal siding over wood frame
Arkansas County, Arkansas

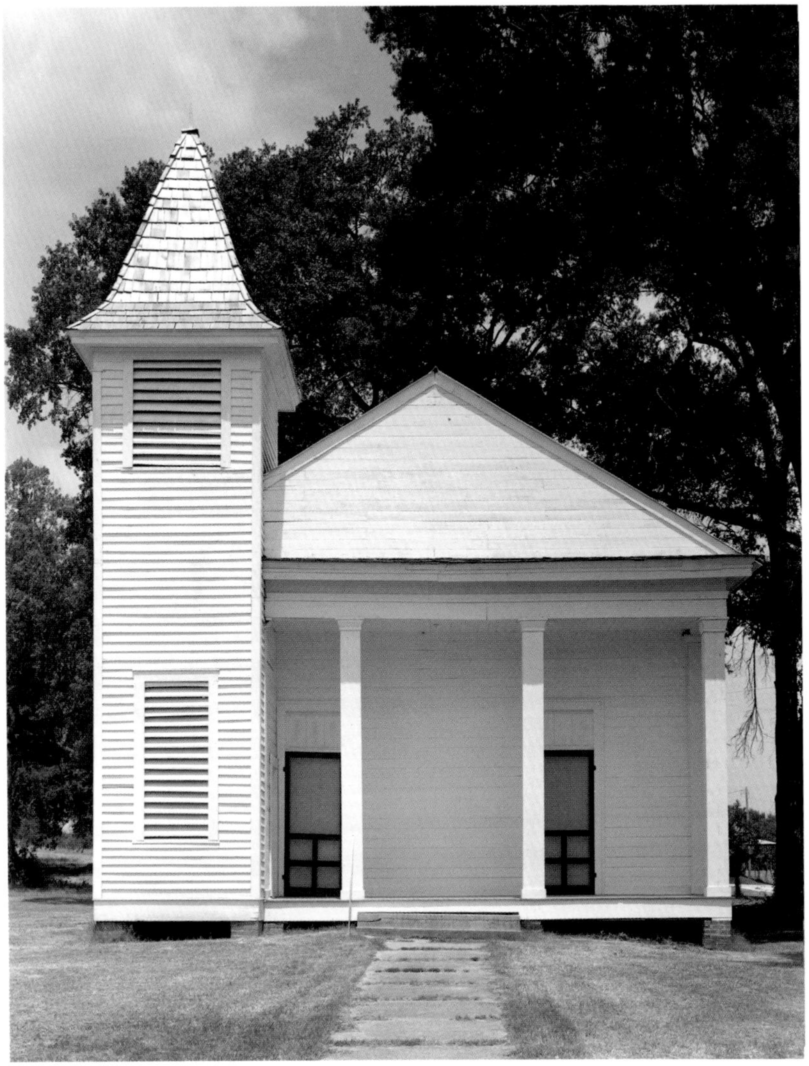

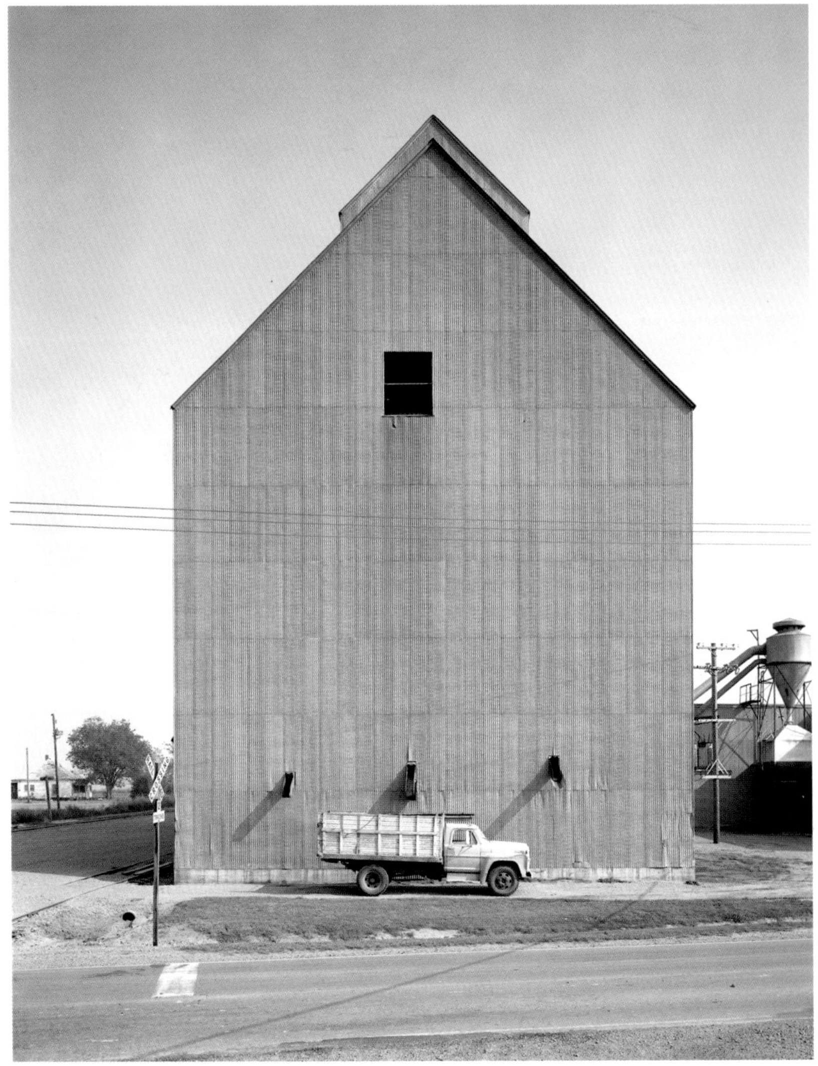

Greek Revival church with flush wood siding and added tower (left)
Columbus (Hempstead County), Arkansas

Rice silo with sheet metal siding over wood frame (right)
Arkansas County, Arkansas

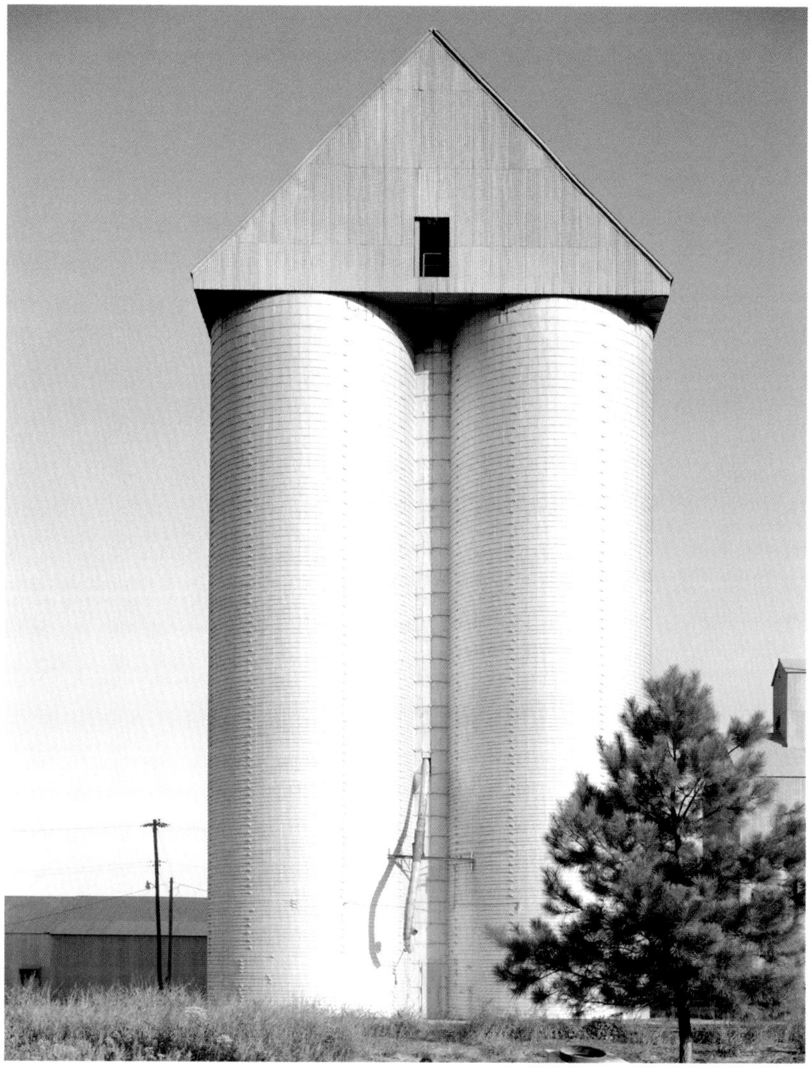

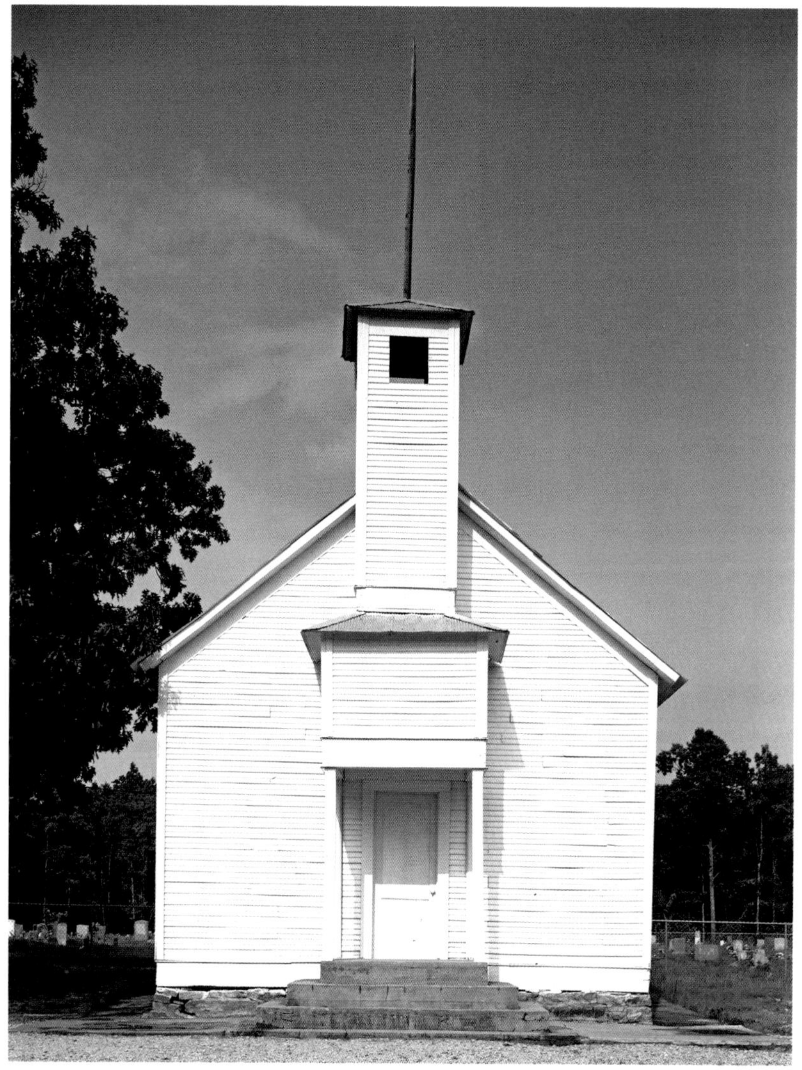

Rice silo with sheet metal siding over wood frame (left)
Arkansas County, Arkansas

Wood frame church with tower mounted on porch in episodes (right)
Newton County, Arkansas

RIVERVIEW HOTEL, THAT'S WHAT THEY USED TO CALL THAT ONE, yes sir, that's what it was, back when it was here. The old theater laid right in there next to the hotel, and then there was a skip in there, and then there was a government building, a *Jap* building is what we called it, that laid in there, too. Some people called it a Jap *camp,* you know. It was a place they put the Japanese people during the war.

So the hotel sat in there between the old theater and a drug store. There was a bank in there, too, but that was all *years* ago, when I was just a kid. The last one I remember living in that hotel was Manny Drydale. He was the last one. Before that, if I'm right about this, Mr. Leo owned that hotel, and he had a woman and child he kept up there. I mean, you know, he was living across town with his wife, but he kept this woman in the hotel. He was, what we call it, "catchin' a draft."

What I remember most about that old hotel is what my momma told me one time. She told me that when she was a young woman there was a fella that lived down the river. He was a fisherman, I think, and he kept a bear. He was supposed to keep that bear chained up, but one day he come into town and that bear come follering him. Some folks took the bear and cooked him right there in that hotel. Momma told me lots of times about those folks cooking that bear. She said that was the first bear she ate, and they fixed it up real good, but she still didn't care much for it. She said it was the last time she would eat bear, no matter how you fix it.

Now, you know, this used to be a *big* old town, back in the day. There was banks and boardinghouses, and hotels. One hotel had a *saloon* with it, all together. There was an opera house and arena. Jack Dempsey even had a big *fight* here. The James boys, they come through. You could say that this was the *main place* around here. Course the only way to get here was to ride your horse in or take the steamboat down the river. There wasn't no roads, least what we call roads today, no real roads coming in. ►

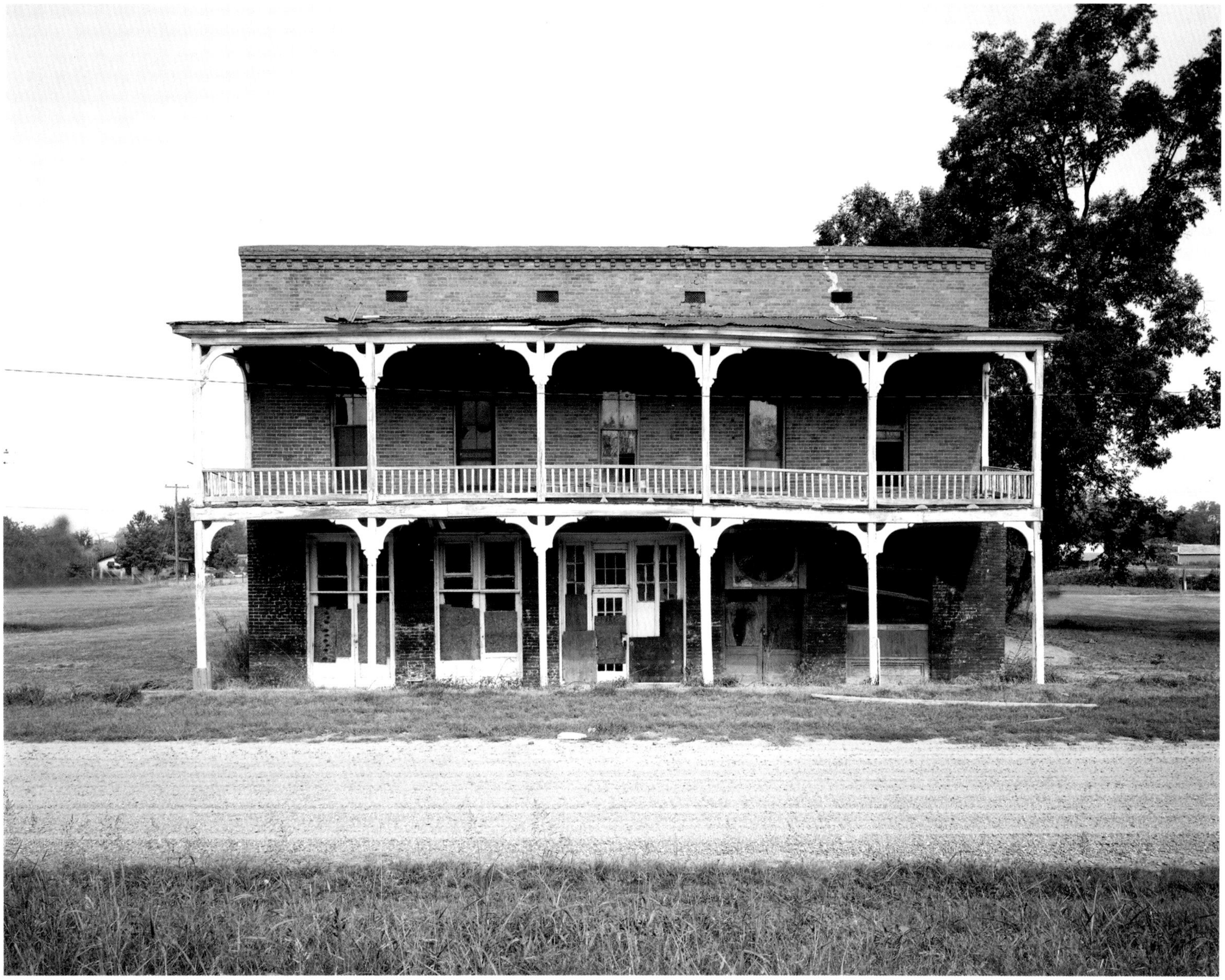

Brick inn with double wooden gallery
Riverview Inn
Arkansas City (Desha County), Arkansas
(demolished)

Back then, Arkansas City sat right on the river, right up *next* to the river. This was a Mississippi River city. But when the big flood of '27 come, the levee broke upstream, and that river cut itself a whole new stream. By the time the floodwater went to falling out, the river was laying two miles east of where it had been. The river just moved itself over. After that, Arkansas City was what you call *landlocked*, and that's what you got still today.

My momma was a young woman when that flood come along, and she had brothers, and they all run their johnboats up and down, all around, picking people off their the roofs of their houses and what all. You know what I mean when I say *johnboat*? Johnboat was a flat bottom kind of boat, had a inboard john motor on it, with a flywheel. You'd crank it up and just putt, putt, putt around. When your john motor hit the max, the governor'd kick in, you'd idle down, and just keep putt, putt, puttin' around.

My daddy used to cut timber upstream. He'd float that timber down the river or load it on his boat. That was what he done. Cut timber. Any way he could. Timberman. That's what he was. He'd cut that timber, float it down, load it on boxcars, and sell it to mills up in Chicago. That's what he done. He come out of Texas and Louisiana, met his first wife in Louisiana, but they couldn't get along, so he come up this way, and this is where he met my momma. She was raised here, up in the woods, up above where the paper mill is now. They had a big track of timber in there, and that's where she was raised. She come out of that timber. Back then they'd call it Napolean's Landing.

The creek that come down from there, that was what we call Cypress Creek, and momma used to take us up there when we was kids. We'd do first one thing and then another, do some fishing, and she would make us lunch. That was her home, Napolean's Landing, so she would take us there from time to time. Above that was Chicot City, and I'm not going to tell you how many people there was up there, but it was a lots of people, and it's all gone now.

There's not a whole lot of nothing going on around here now. Back in the day, we had a railroad coming through here, and we had our own power plant. Big diesel engine sat right over there. Arkansas City was one of the first places in the state with its own power. Back then, I guess you had two thousand people living in Arkansas City, maybe more, but not now. Now the place is *depopulating*. There's no work for *nobody*. What jobs they are, the same hands are working those jobs as have been for years. So I don't know where it's all going, but seems like most of it is in the past.

Myron Case
Arkansas City, Arkansas

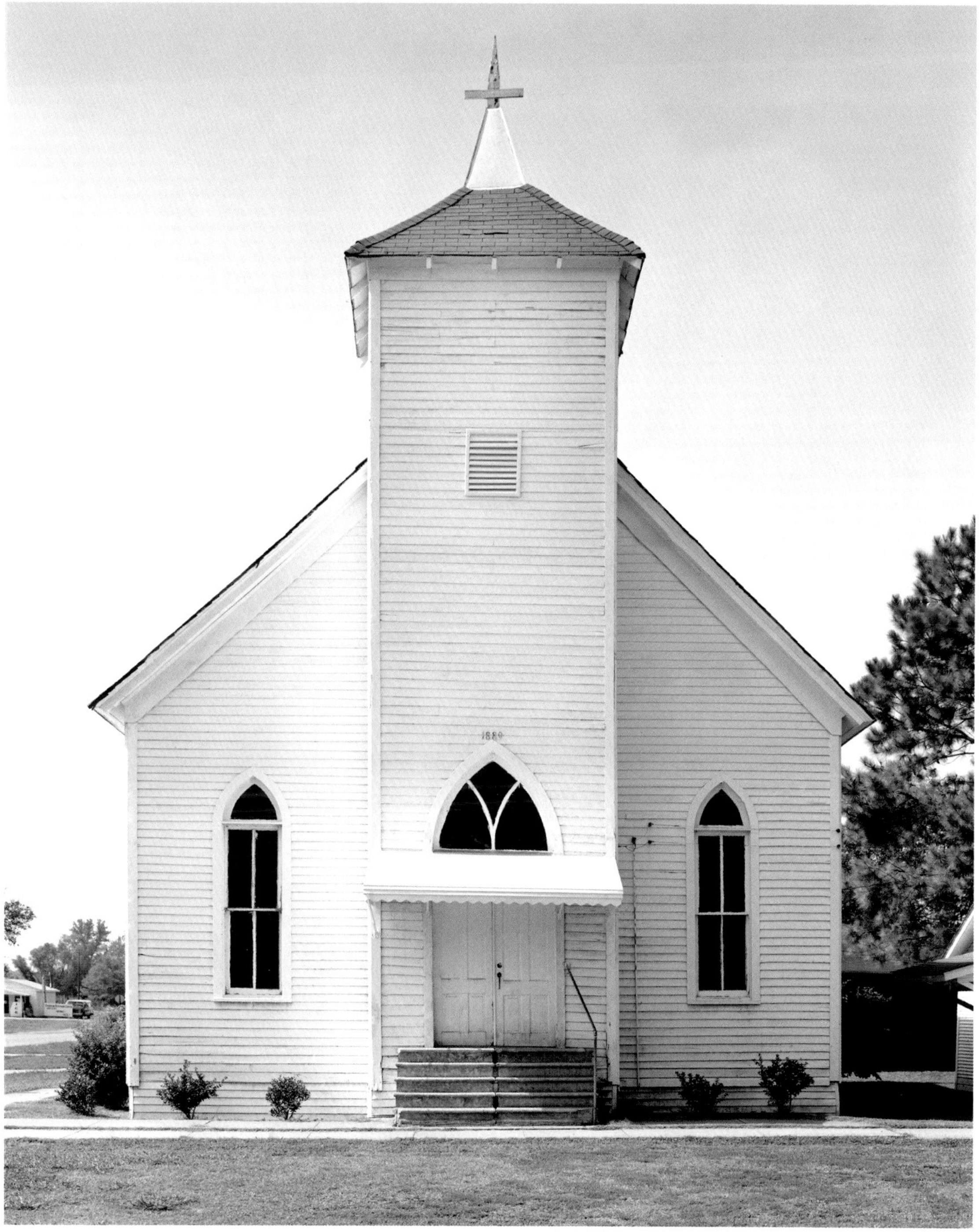

Wood frame church with central tower
Arkansas City (Desha County), Arkansas

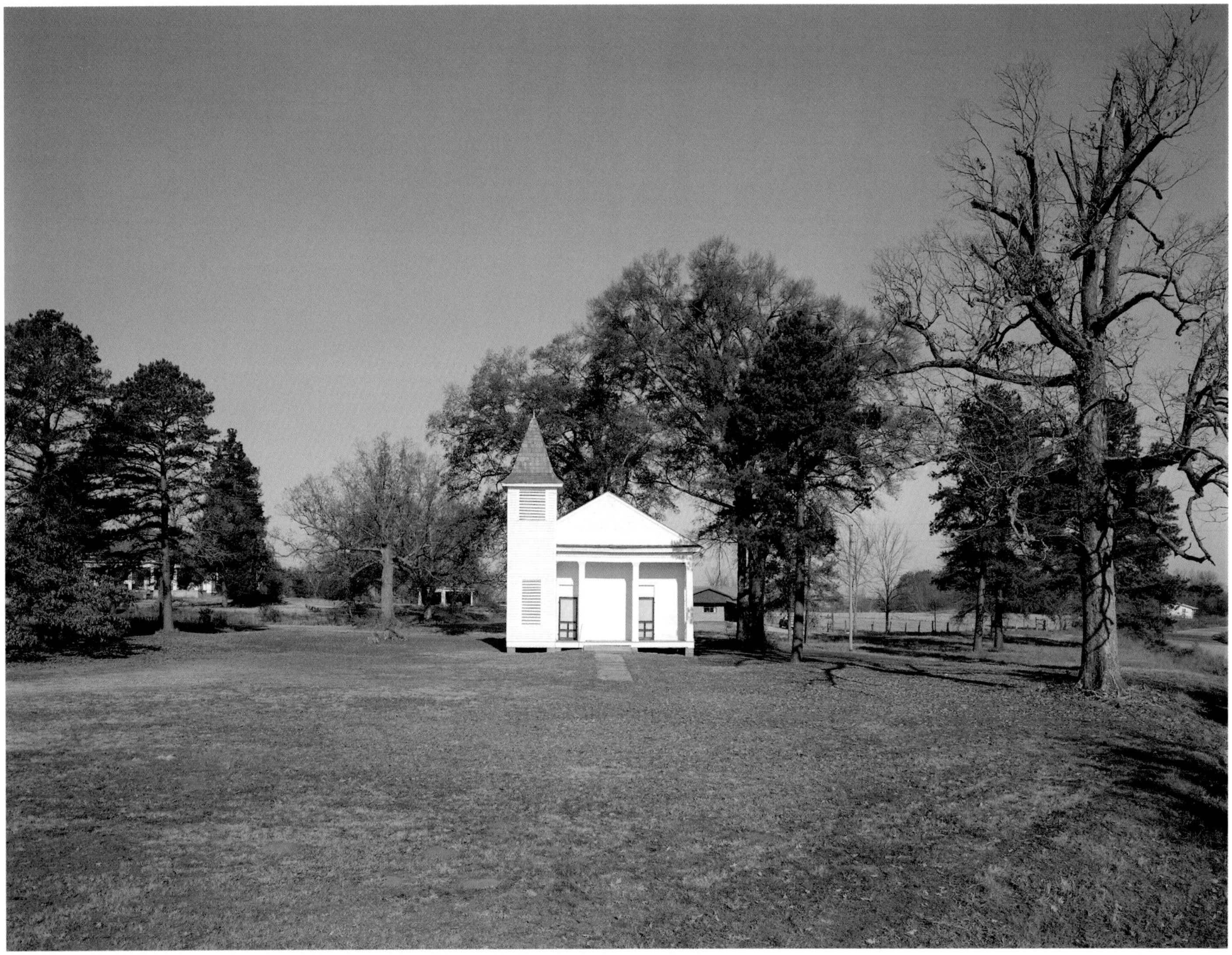

Grrek Revival church with flush wood siding and added tower
Columbus (Hempstead County), Arkansas

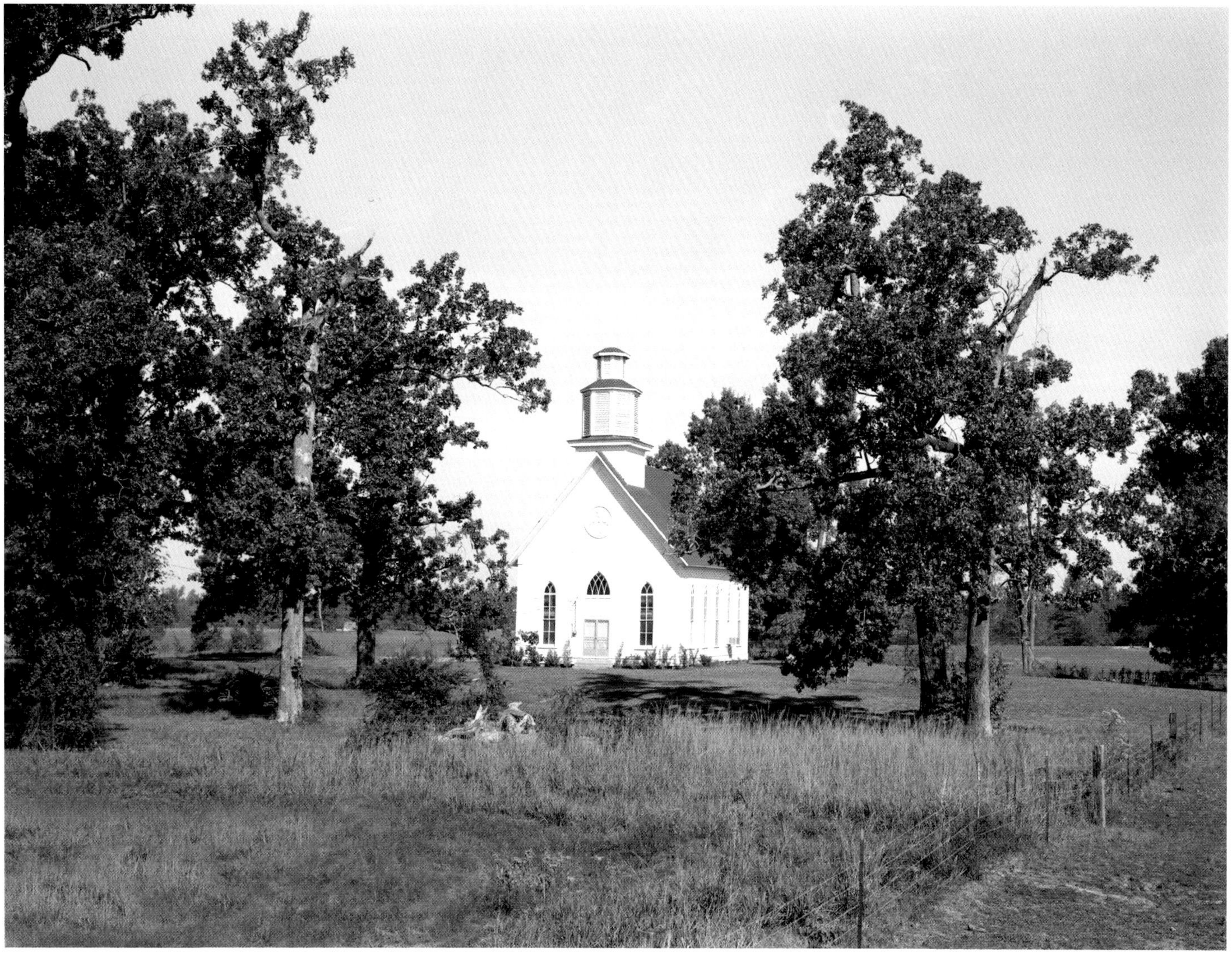

Wood frame church in the manner of architect Richard Upjohn
Selma (Drew County), Arkansas

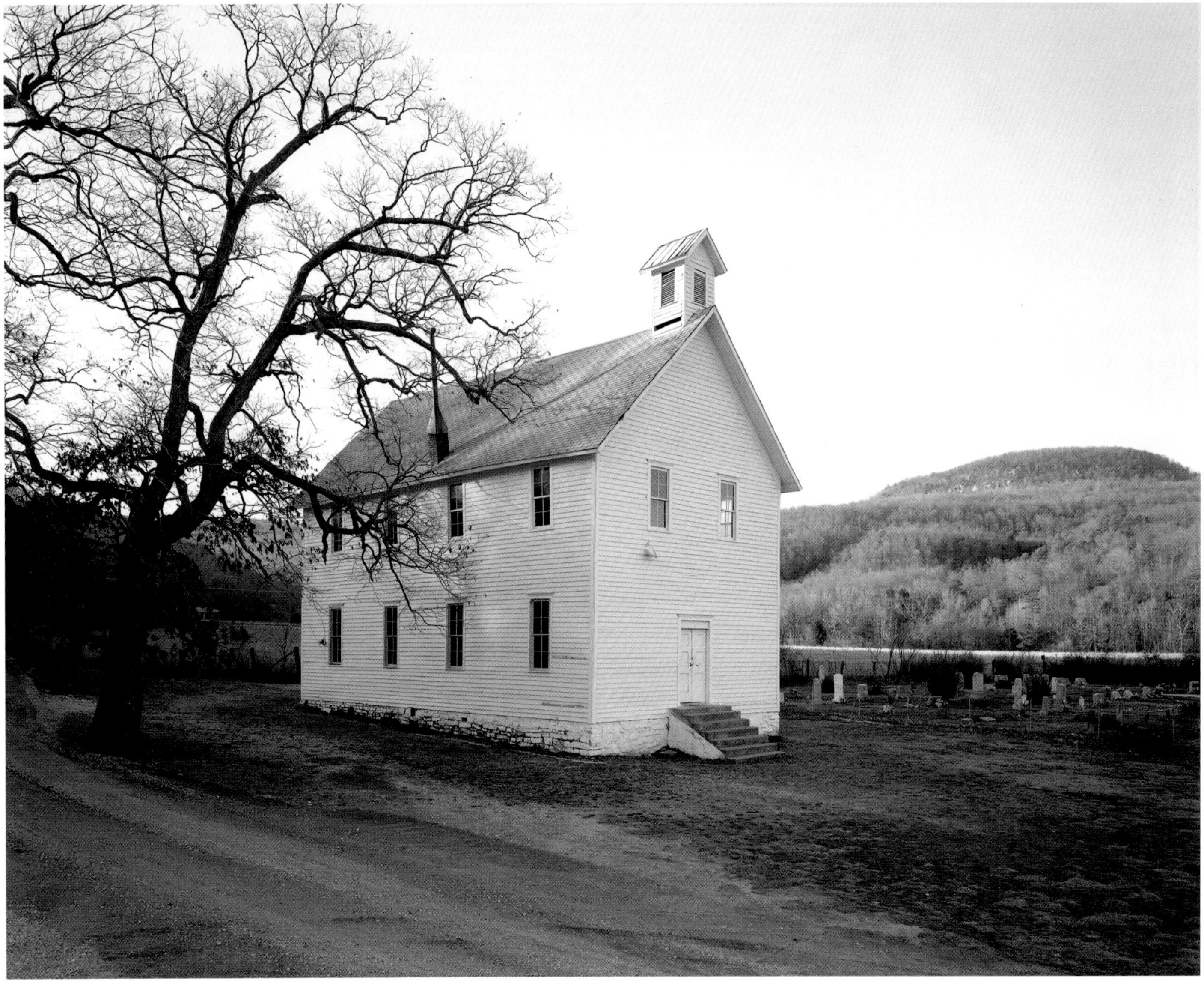

Wood frame church and community center
Boxley Baptist Church
Newton County, Arkansas

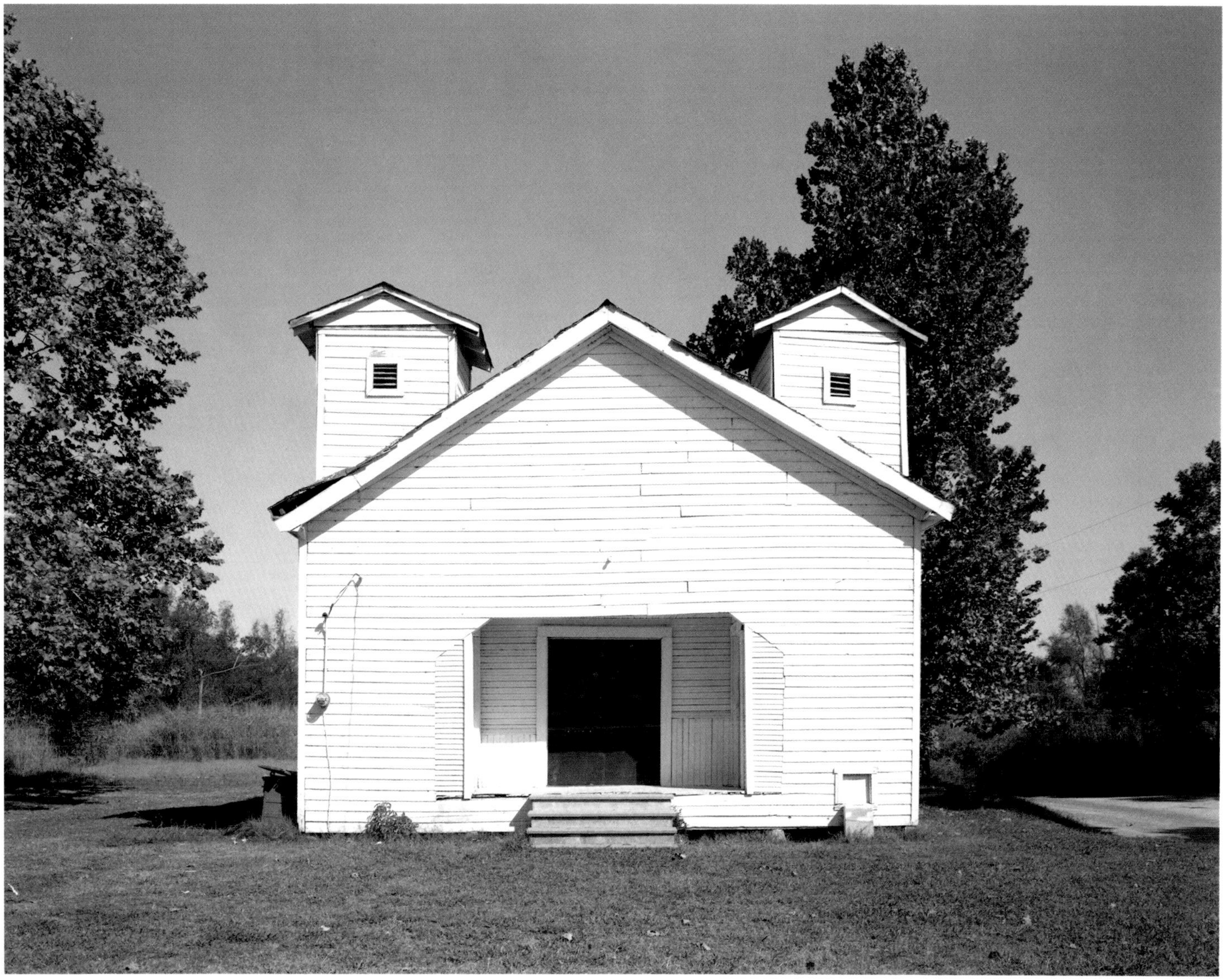

Twin-towered, wood frame church with loggia entrance
Chicot County, Arkansas

WHEN I CAME HERE TO EUDORA, THAT WAS 1967. Now I been in the barber business here for forty-five years. Same location. Before I came, there were five barbers in this town. *White* barbers I'm talking about. Now they all gone, and I'm the only barber cutting hair in Eudora.

Haircut was 75 cents when I came. White or black, same price. Seventy-five cents. We finally got it raised to one dollar. Now, today, we're at ten dollars. But we been stuck at ten dollars for seven years.

That's my shop in the picture, on the right side of the church. And that's my son, Herschel Wynn, standing on the steps of the church. Herschel Wynn left Eudora right out of high school. Went to Fayetteville and graduated from the university. He works as a counselor now. Still living in Fayetteville.

Our pastor, Reverend Tyrone Broomfield, you can see his name over the church door. He was a young man when he came to our church, maybe twenty years old, a fine preacher. When he came to Eudora, we were just a little two-Sunday church. Reverend Broomfield was also preaching in Comitto, a community up outside of Monticello. Broomfield would preach in Comitto the first and third Sundays of each month, and then he would preach here on the second and fourth Sundays.

That picture was taken after Reverend Broomfield left. The AME church had him transferred to a new church, but we kept Broomfield's name up there because we didn't like the new preacher they sent us.

It wasn't long after that I left the AME church and went Baptist.

Eric West
Eudora, Arkansas

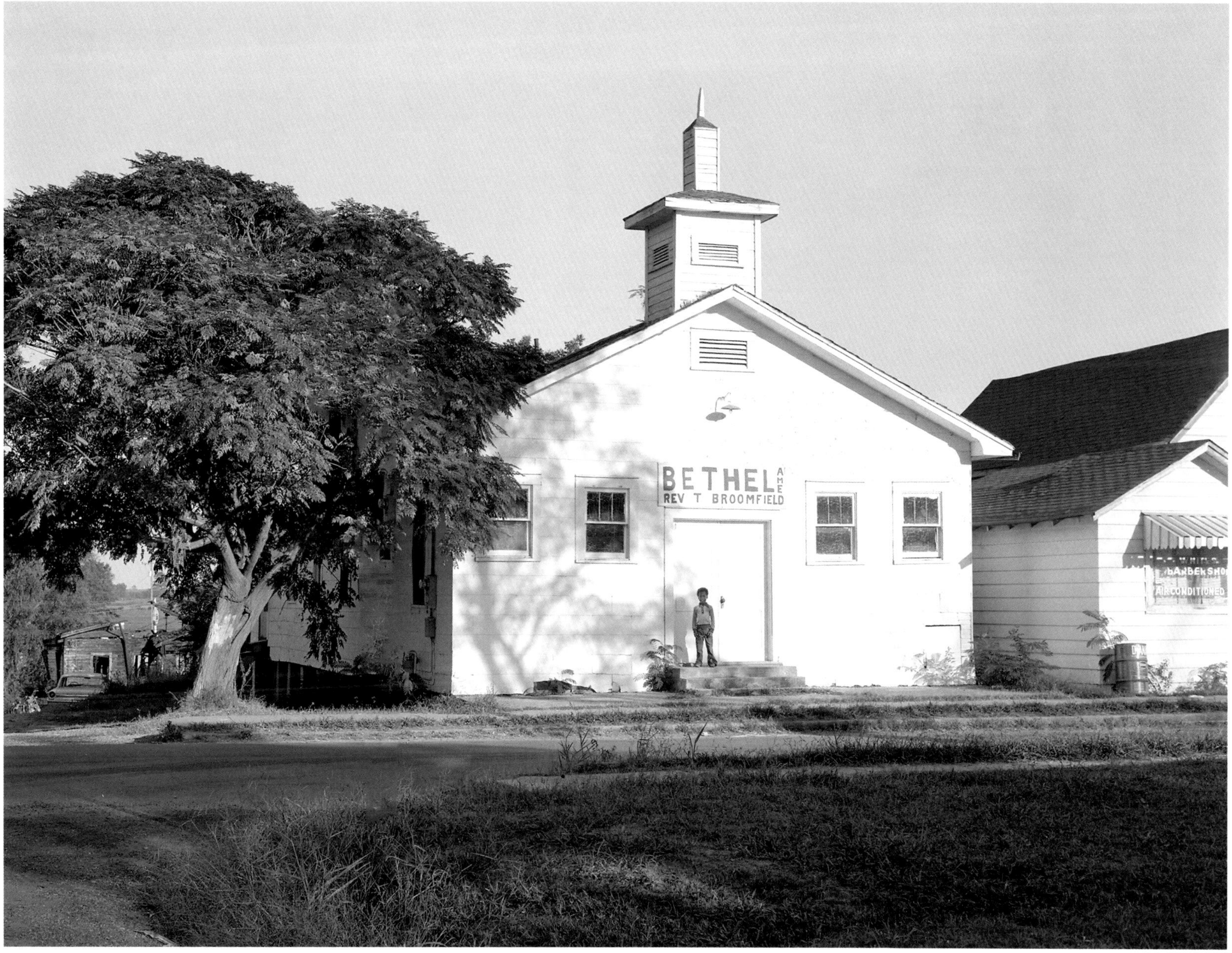

Wood frame church with asbestos siding
Bethel AME Church
Eudora (Chicot County), Arkansas
(no longer standing)

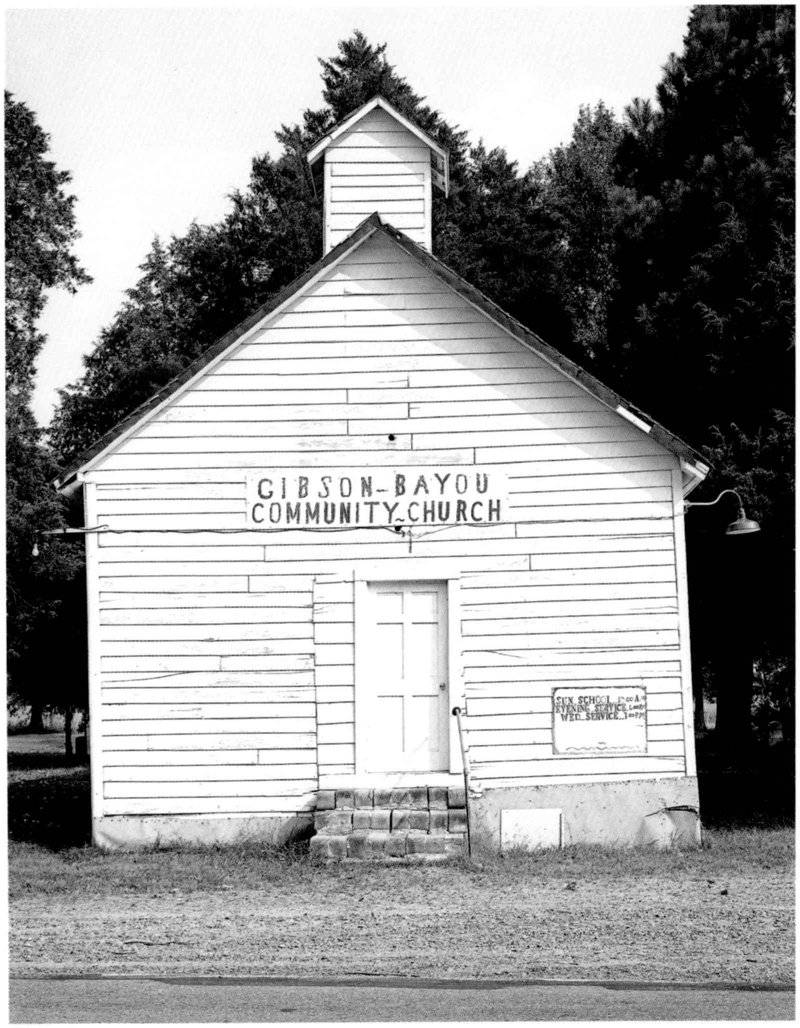

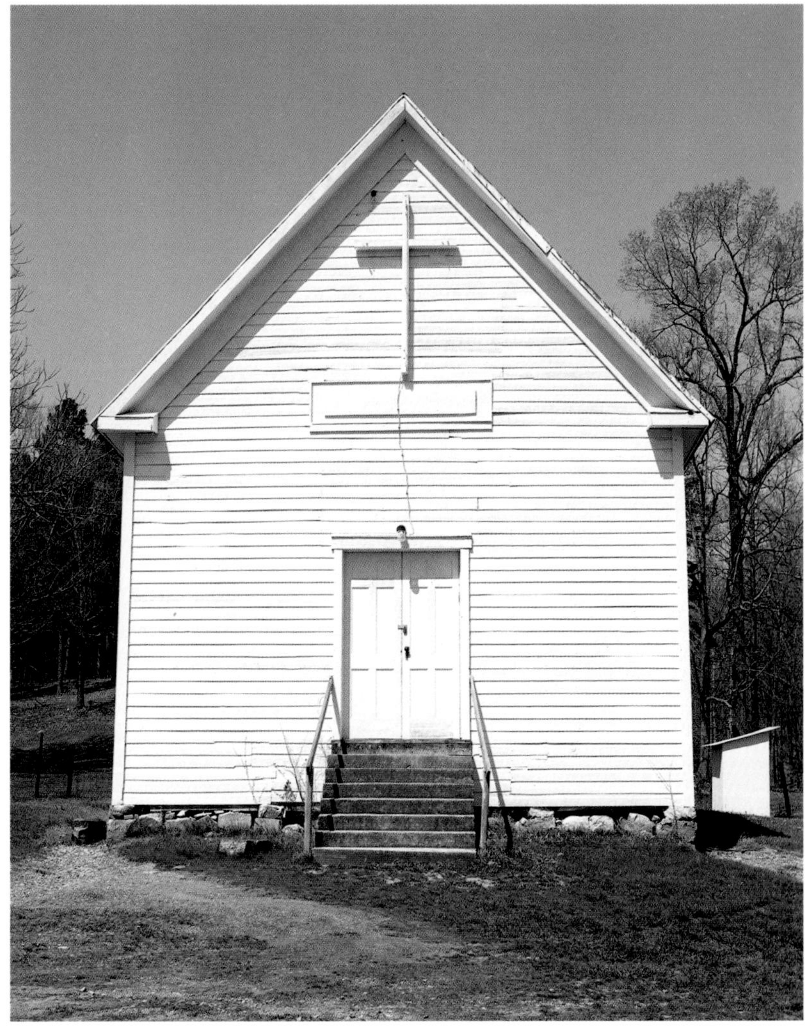

Wood frame church with altered doorway (left)
Crittenden County, Arkansas

Wood frame church with classical panel and peaked gable (right)
Boone County, Arkansas

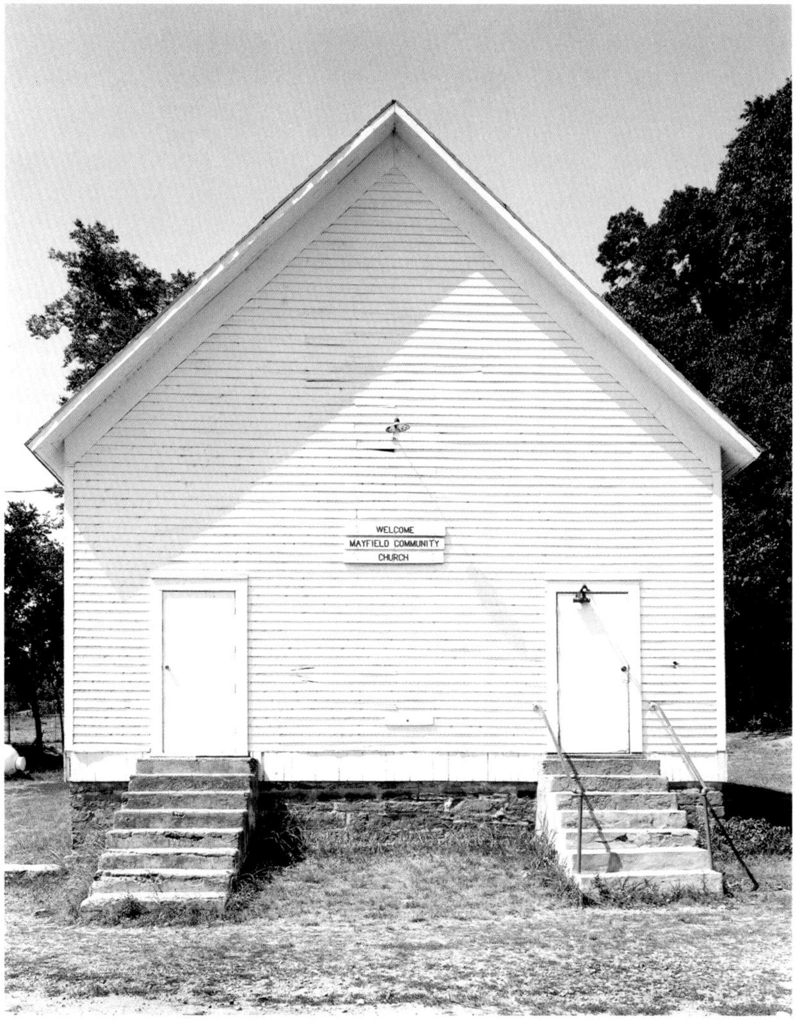

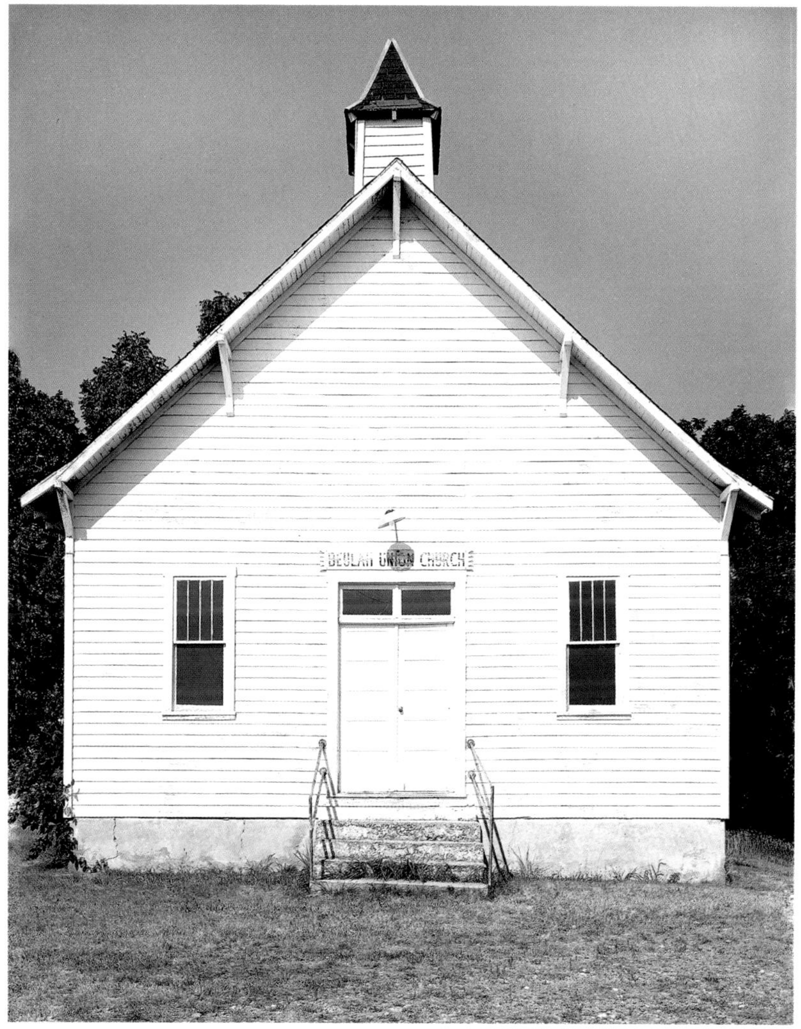

Wood frame church with double entrance (left)
Washington County, Arkansas

Wood frame church with carpenter Gothic bracketed eaves (right)
Carroll County, Arkansas

Upon these structures, light:

. . . each texture in the wood, like those of bone, is distinct to the eye as a razor: each nail-head is distinct: each seam and split; and each slight warping; each random knot and knothole: and in each board, as lovely a music as a contour map and unique as a thumbprint, its grain, which was its living strength, and these wild creeks cut off stiff across by saws; and moving nearer, the close-laid arcs and shadows even of those tearing wheels: and this, more poor and plain than bone, more naked and noble than sternest Doric, more rich and more variant than watered silk, is the fabric and the stature of a house.

James Agee
from *Let Us Now Praise Famous Men*

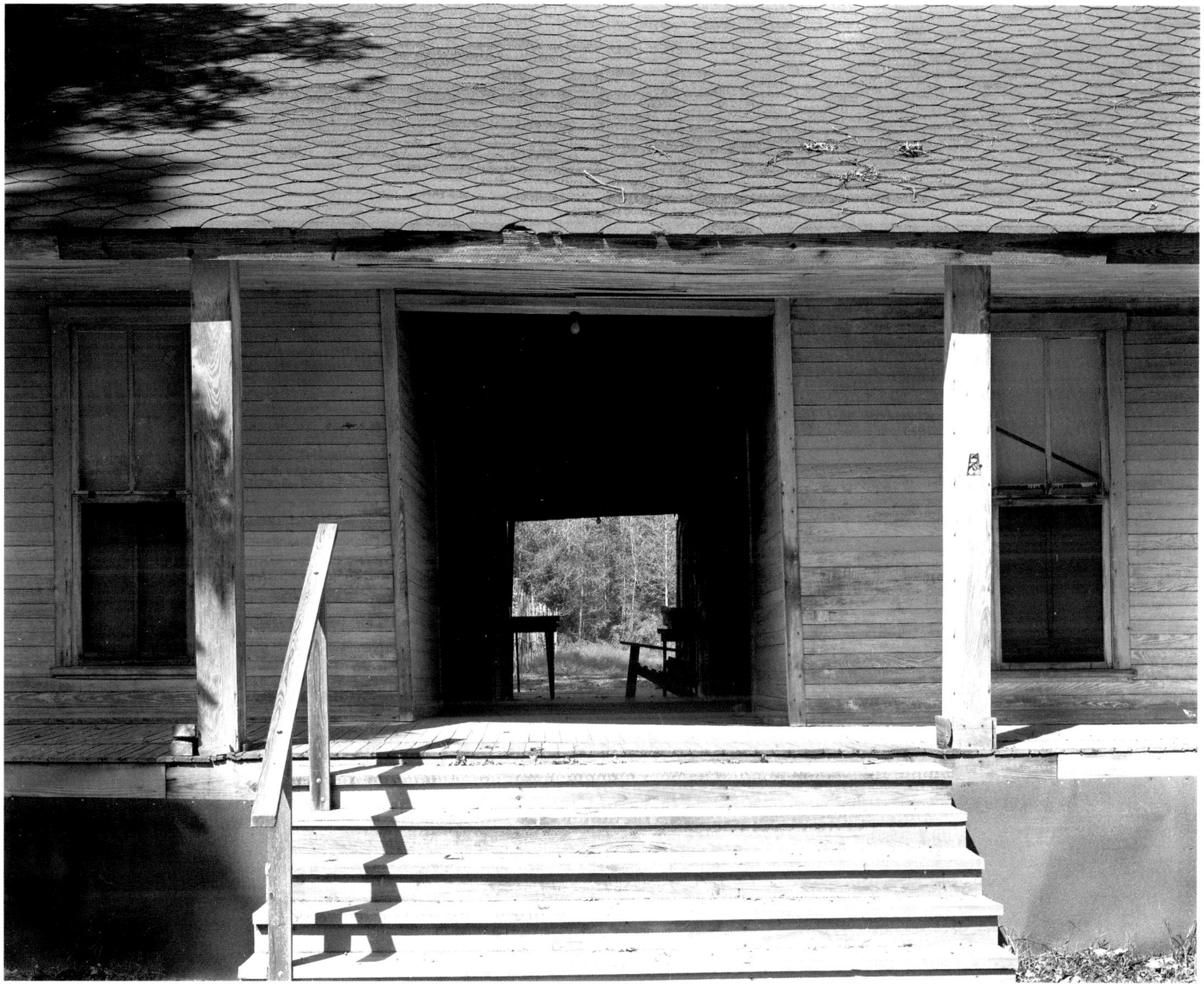

Wood frame dogtrot house
Hempstead County, Arkansas

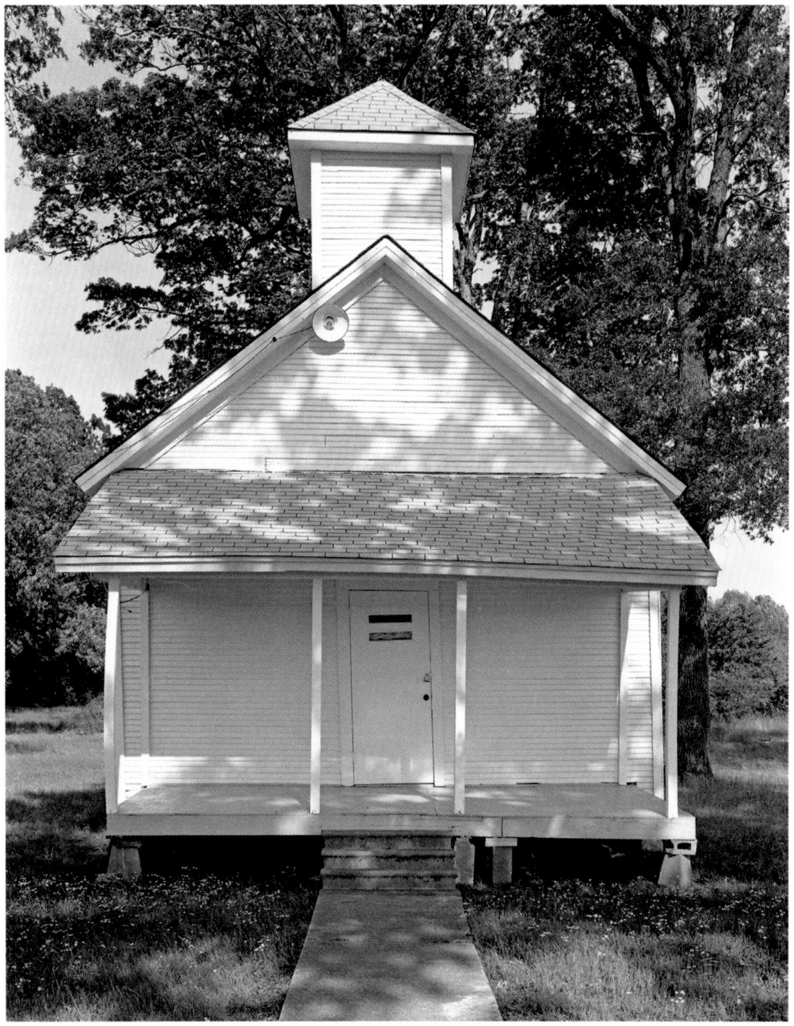

Wood frame church with central tower
Monroe County, Arkansas

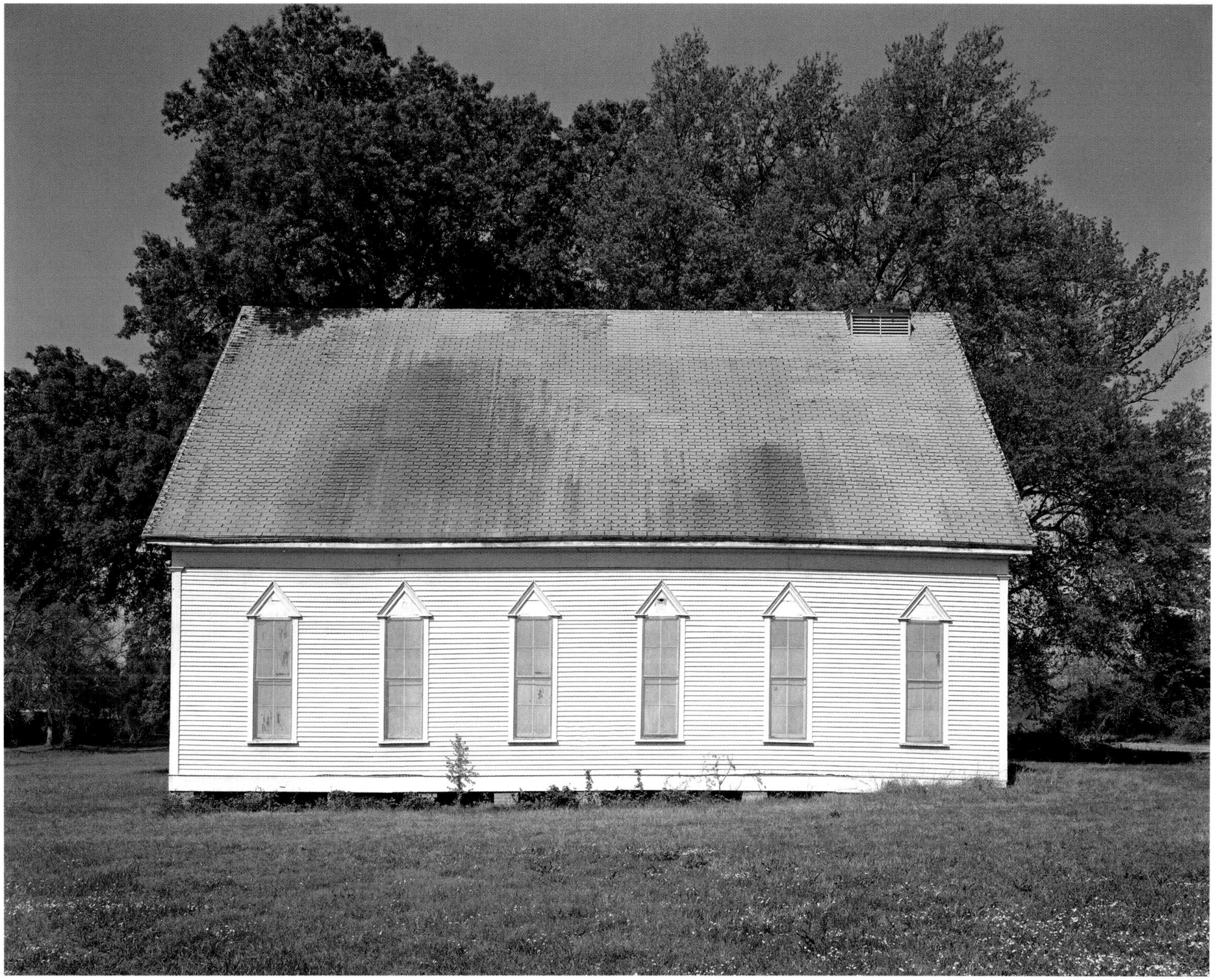

Wood frame church
Ozan (Howard County), Arkansas
(relocated)

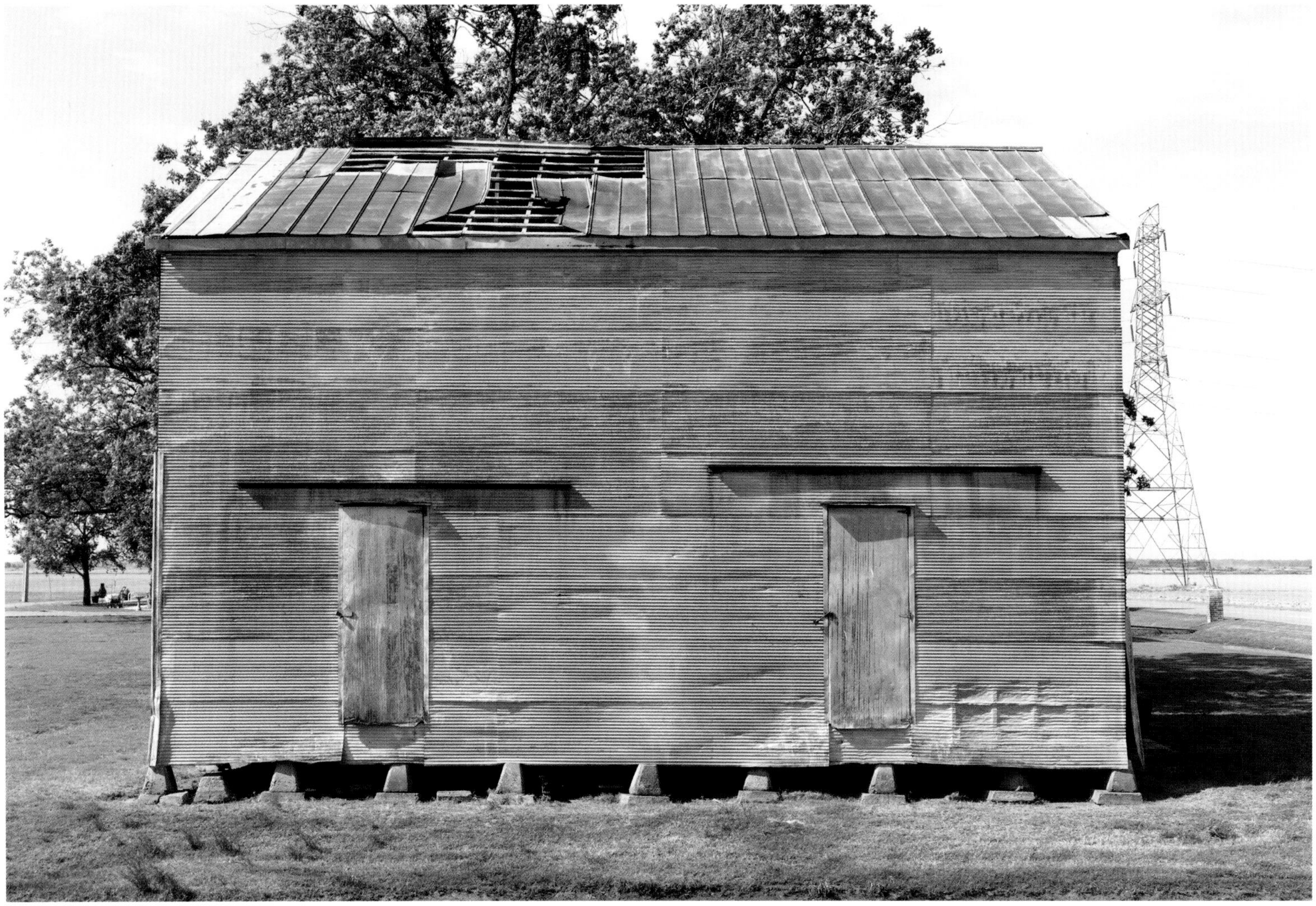

Two-story farm building with v-crimped metal roofing and corrugated metal siding
Dewitt (Arkansas County), Arkansas

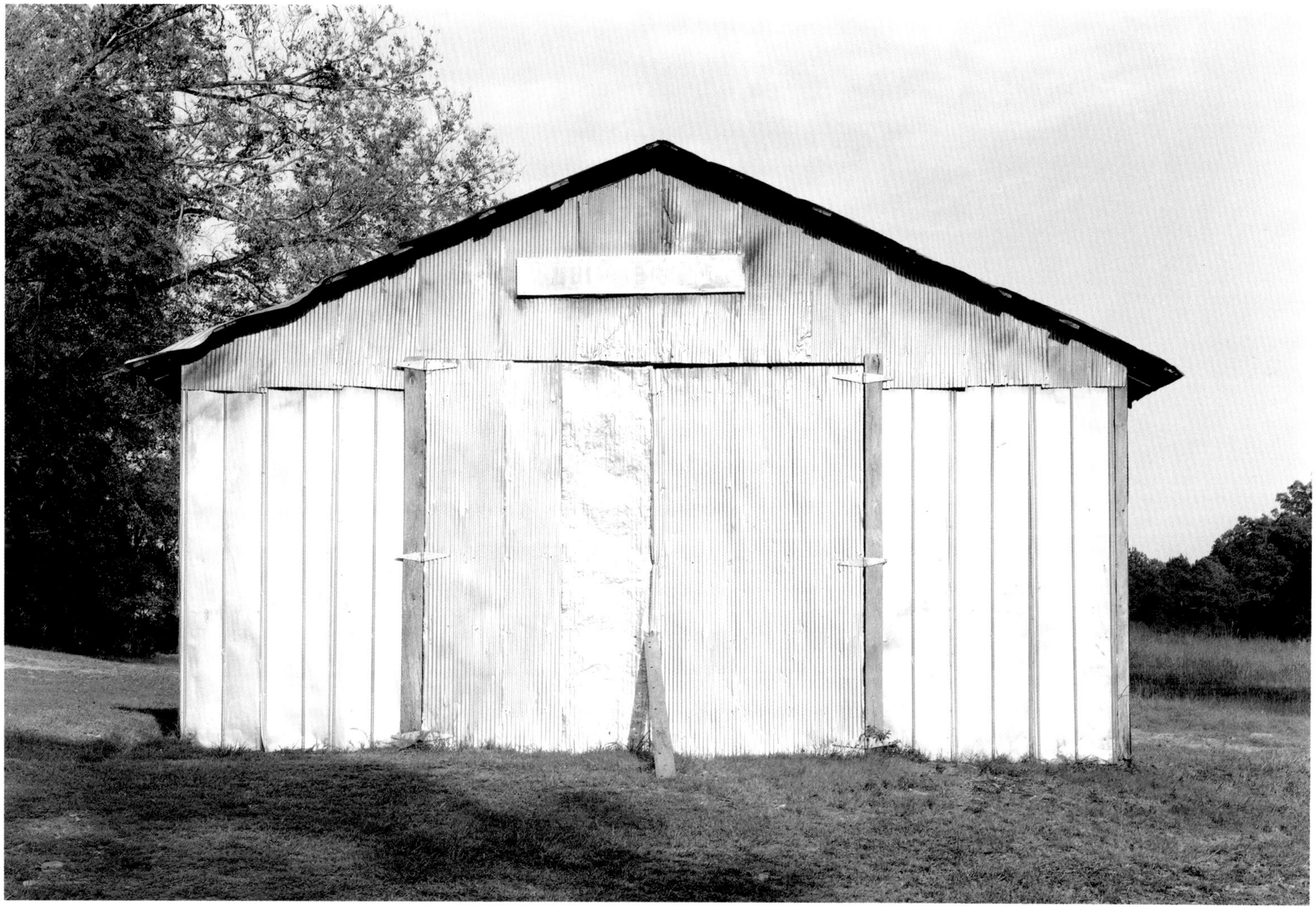

Tractor-repair garage with v-crimped tin over wood frame
Pike County, Arkansas

THAT OLD BUILDING STOOD THERE ON THE SIDE OF THE ROAD. It was just west of town, out toward Ulm. It must have stood there for least a hundred years.

Most people thought of that building as a *store*. That's because when my momma and daddy—Matilda and Floyd Huggs—when they bought the place from the Porter family, the Porters were operating it as a store, and my family kept it as a store. But before that, it had been a lodge, a bar, a saloon, and who knows what else. I'm telling you now, if the walls of that old place could have talked, they could have told some *hair*-raising stories. I mean, just *look at it.* What does it look like to you? Don't it look like a old western saloon? What do *you* think went on in those rooms upstairs?

But like I said, my mom and dad, they kept it as a grocery store. Up front, just inside the front door, was a kid's dream come true. It was a candy counter with about a million kinds of candy, all sitting inside a glass case. To the other side of the candy, my mom had a meat counter, or what you call a *sandwich* counter. The truckers would pull off the highway and stop for lunch. My mom would make 'em all a sandwich. There was a big, wide space in front of the store where they could park their trucks while they'd come in and eat.

I remember we used to have two kinds of people coming through town that you don't see much anymore. Hobos and gypsies. The hobos would jump off the trains and come up to the store asking for free food. They wasn't really no problem, they just wanted something to eat, and my momma would usually give 'em something. But the gypsies was a real problem. They'd come along in a caravan of old trucks, big *families* of gypsies. They'd come in the store all at once. While you was talking to one of 'em, others would be stealing you blind, working as a team. My dad got to where, when he'd see the gypsies coming, he'd only let one of them in the store at a time.

Now look at the *name* on the store, and I can tell you a story about that. My family name started out being Hug. Just *H-u-g. Hug.* But the right way to say it was "Huoog," like a man named Hugh, but with a "g" stuck on the end. My daddy's grandma and grandpa came here to Arkansas with that name. They came from Switzerland in a covered wagon, and they met Wild Bill Hickok on the way. They settled here in Roe, Arkansas, but nobody here could say the family name right. So my granddaddy, my daddy Floyd's daddy, somewhere in his lifetime, his name caught an extra "g" on the end. Then it was *H-u-g-g,* with *two* g's on the end, and people started saying "hug." Same as you grab somebody and *hug 'em*. After that, the family name was Hugg. Two g's. Now look at my name. *Huggs*. Where the *hell* did that "s" come from? Nobody can say, but it got tagged on there somewhere down the line. You'd think that a family's name would stay the same, but *no,* it don't, and my name, Huggs, is proof of that.

Ricky Huggs
Roe, Arkansas

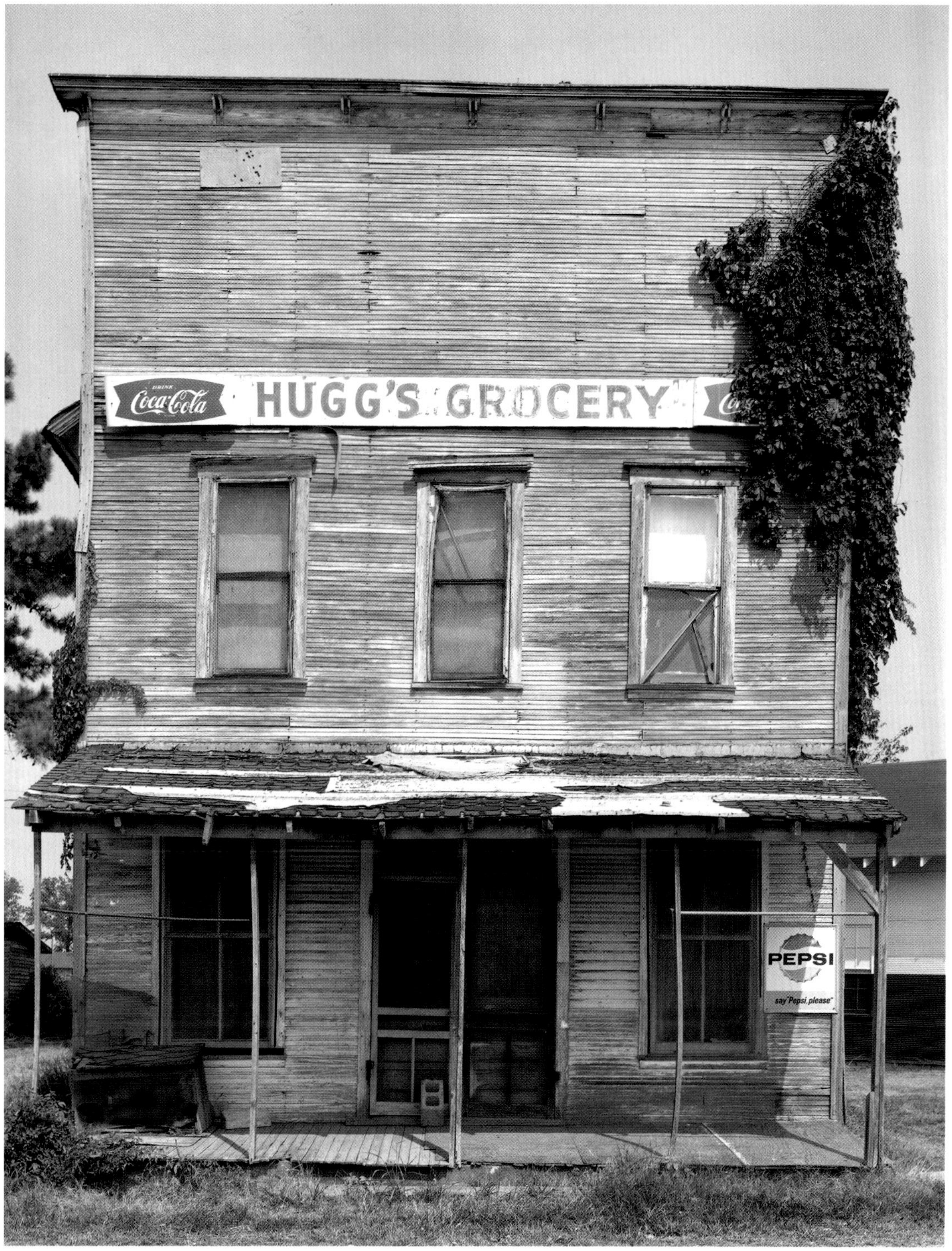

Two-story commercial structure sheathed in drop siding, third floor implied with bracketed false front
Hugg's Grocery
Roe (Monroe County), Arkansas
(demolished)

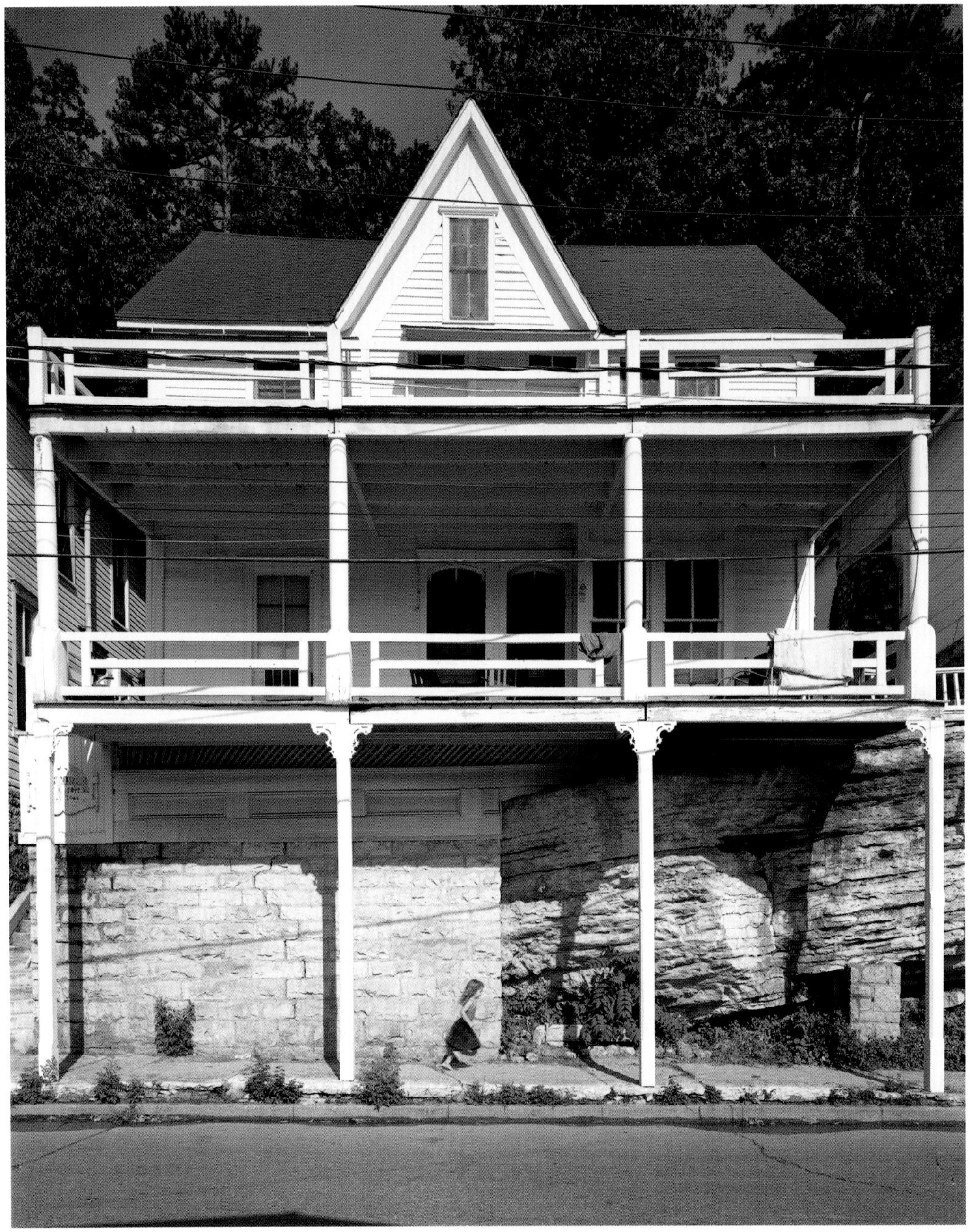

American Gothic residence with stilted porch
Eureka Springs (Carroll County), Arkansas

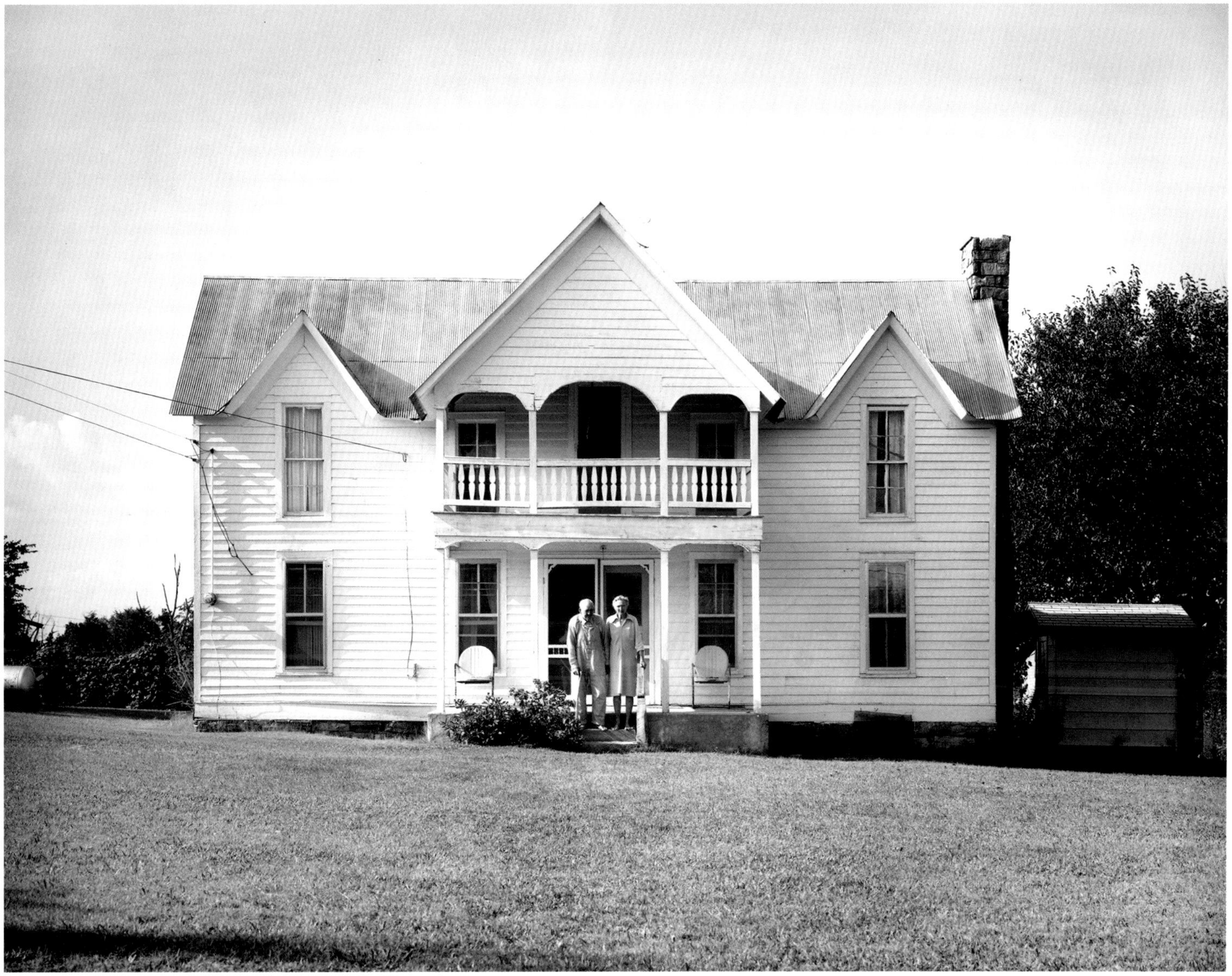

American Gothic residence with added porch
Salem (Fulton County), Arkansas

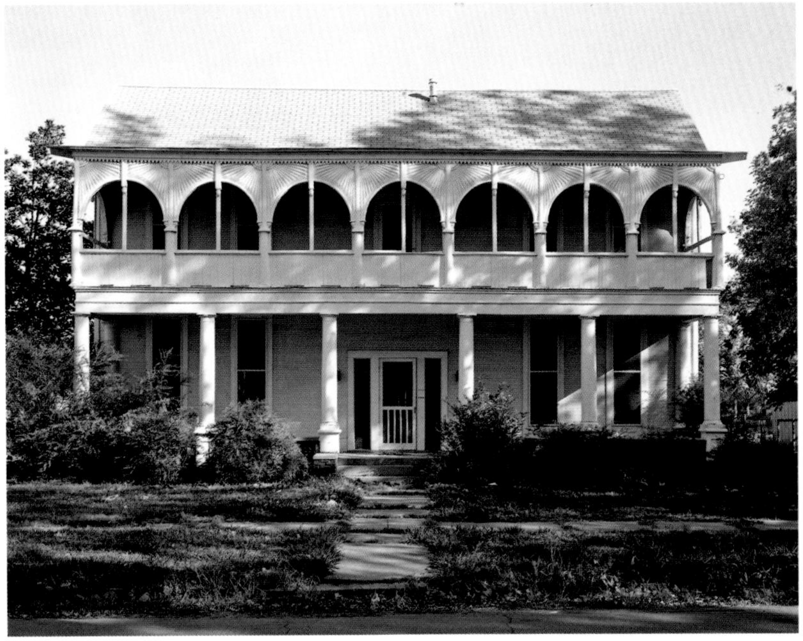

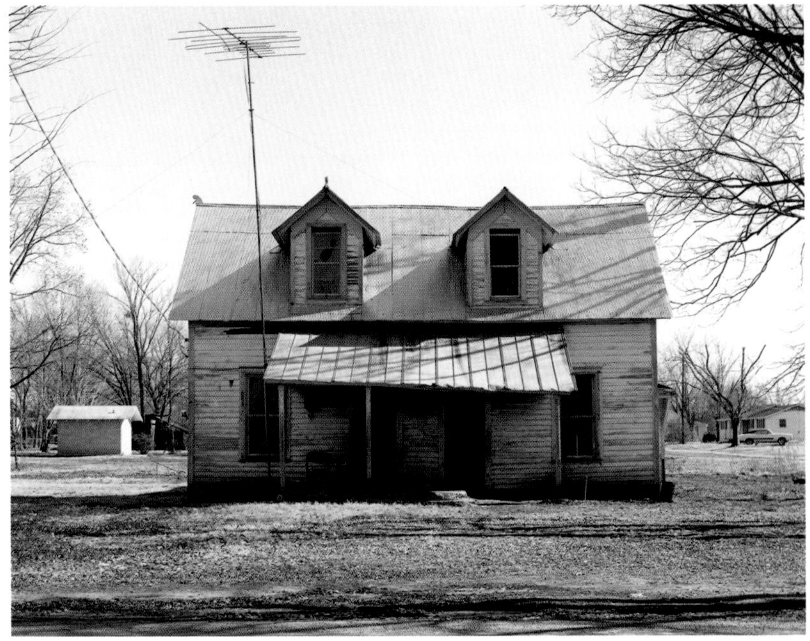

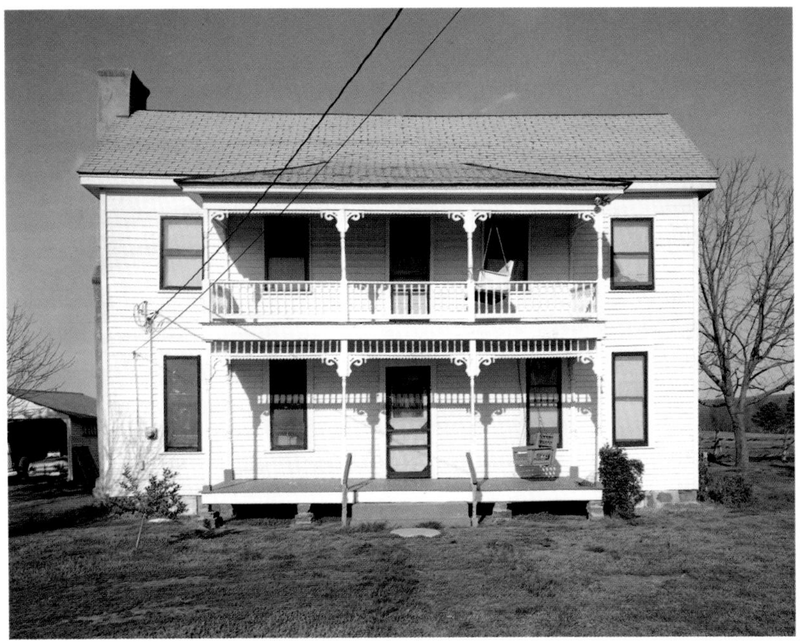

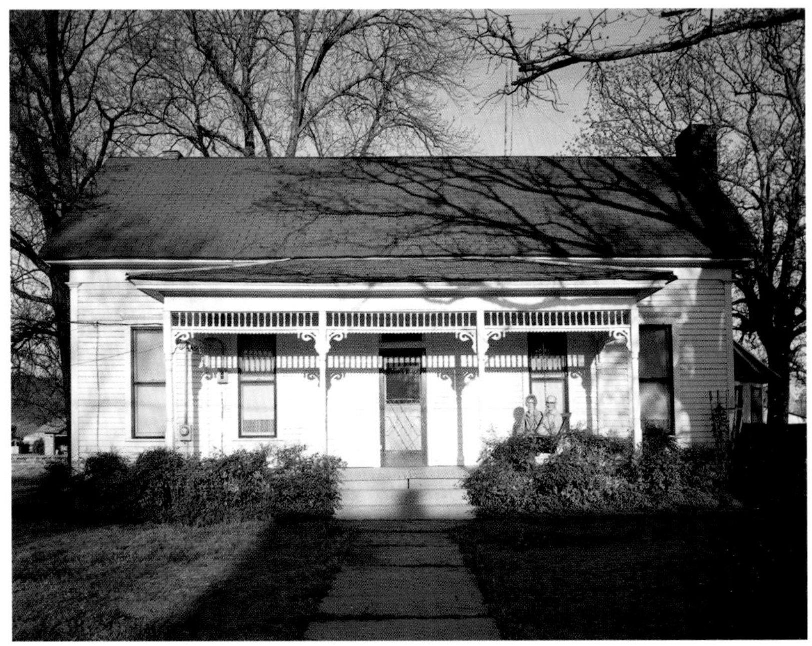

Raised basement house with arcaded second floor gallery, London (Loanoke County), Arkansas (upper left);
Wood frame double house with dormer windows, Ola (Yell County), Arkansas (upper right);
Two-story wood frame farm house with double-stacked Queen Anne porch, Ulm (Prairie County), Arkansas (lower left);
Wood frame Queen Anne cottage, Paris (Logan County), Arkansas (lower right).

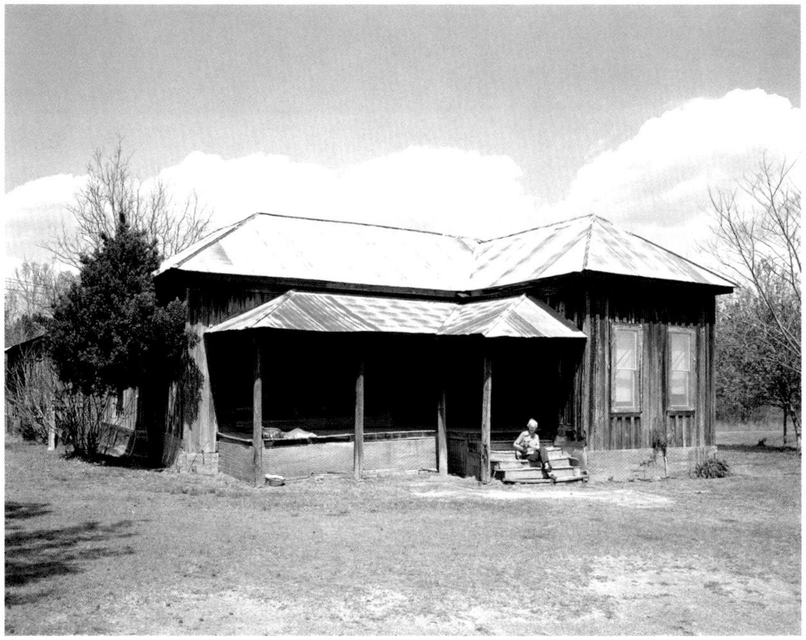

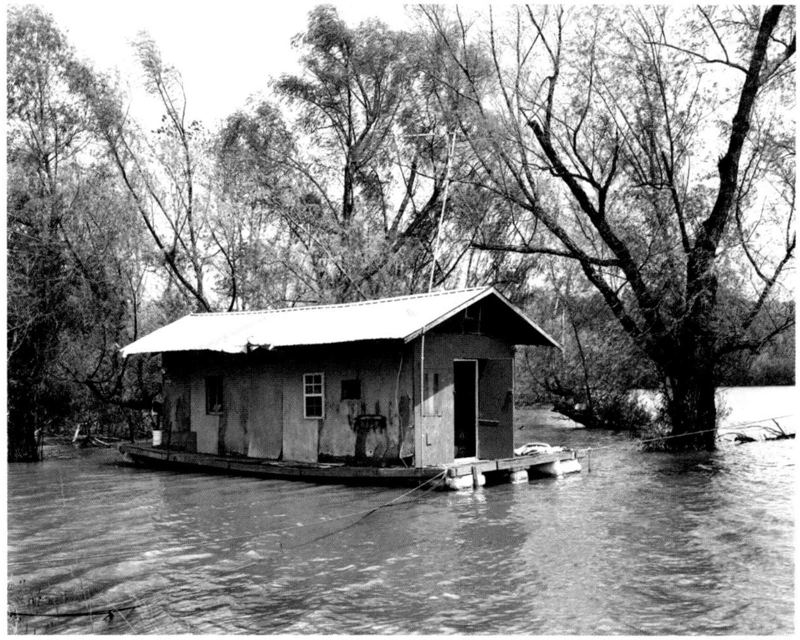

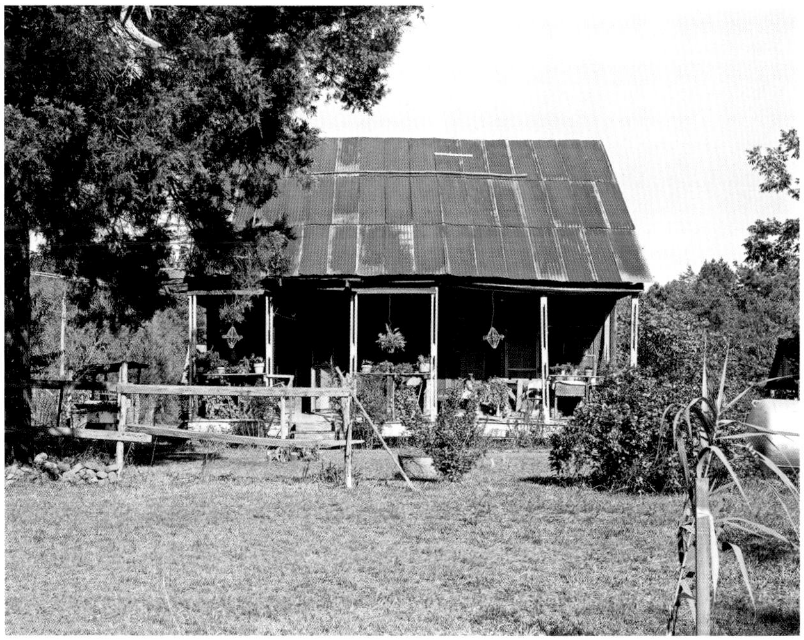

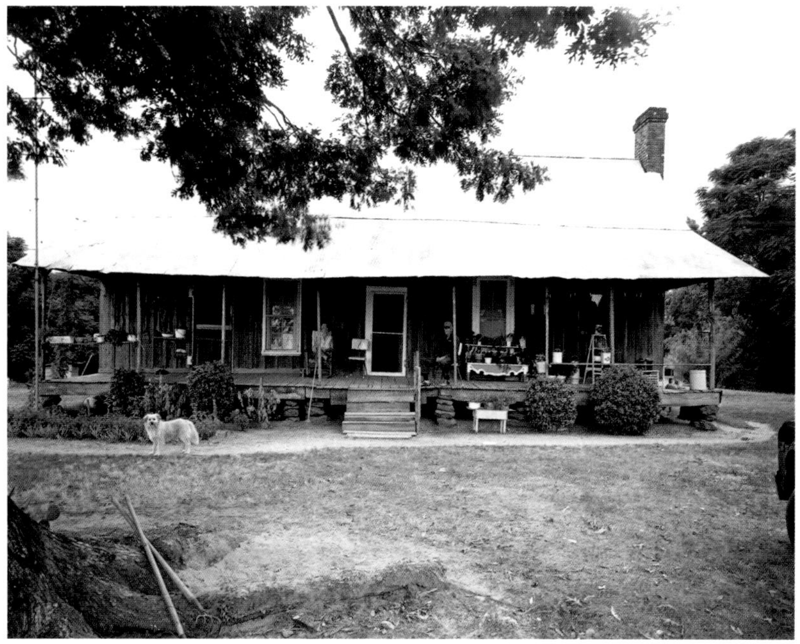

*L-shaped cottage with box and batten sheathing and porch cut back, Clyde (Washington County), Arkansas (upper left);
Shotgun houseboat, White River, De Valls Bluff (Prairie County), Arkansas (upper right);
Double pen house, wood frame or covered log, Sevier County, Arkansas (lower left);
One-story house, box and batten construction and filled-in dogtrot, Howard County, Arkansas (lower right).*

I WAS ABOUT FIVE YEARS OLD when my family lived in that building.

We lived in the front corner apartment, up on this end of the building. That would have been about 1970, and by then it was already sort of a raggedy place, but I just loved it because I could ride my tricycle up and down the long hallways. Down at this end, on the first floor, was a dentist's office. That was Dr. Nobey's office, and next to that was the Delta Clinic. There was a doctor there in the clinic and a couple of beds. Most of the older folks in this town were born in the Delta Clinic.

I remember how I would stand in the corner window of our apartment in the evening time, waiting and watching for my daddy to come home from work. I would stand there, in that tall window on the corner, looking for him. Daddy worked in the rice fields down by Stuttgart, and his ride would drop him off on the next corner. Every evening he would come walking down the street, waving at me up in the window. Seeing the picture of the building makes me want to cry, just remembering Daddy coming down the street every evening, waving at me, and me wanting him to come home and pick me up and hug me.

I'm told that hotel had a lot of history. I think it was called the Clarendon Hotel before I lived there. But some of the older folks in town called it the New South Inn, and I think that was its original name. By the time we lived there, the second floor was all turned into apartments, and the downstairs had a skating rink and a café and a place they called "The 8-Ball." Girls didn't go in "The 8-Ball." It was strictly a place for boys. They'd go in there and shoot pool, gamble, and drink beer, and who knows what else. The men in this town will tell you they grew up in "The 8-Ball."

I've heard many stories about how the people of Clarendon rode out the flood of '27 up on the second floor and on the roof of the old hotel. People stayed up there for weeks, waiting for the floodwaters to fall back. My momma told me that there was a lady who cooked every evening on the roof of the hotel, and people would come paddling up on boats to get something to eat.

I remember Fred's Dollar Store was in there between the "The 8-Ball" and the café for a while, but all that just played out, and the building sat empty for a long time. Finally, the roof fell in, and they had to tear it down. This little town just didn't have the money to take proper care of that building, so it's gone now.

Wendy Smith
Clarendon, Arkansas

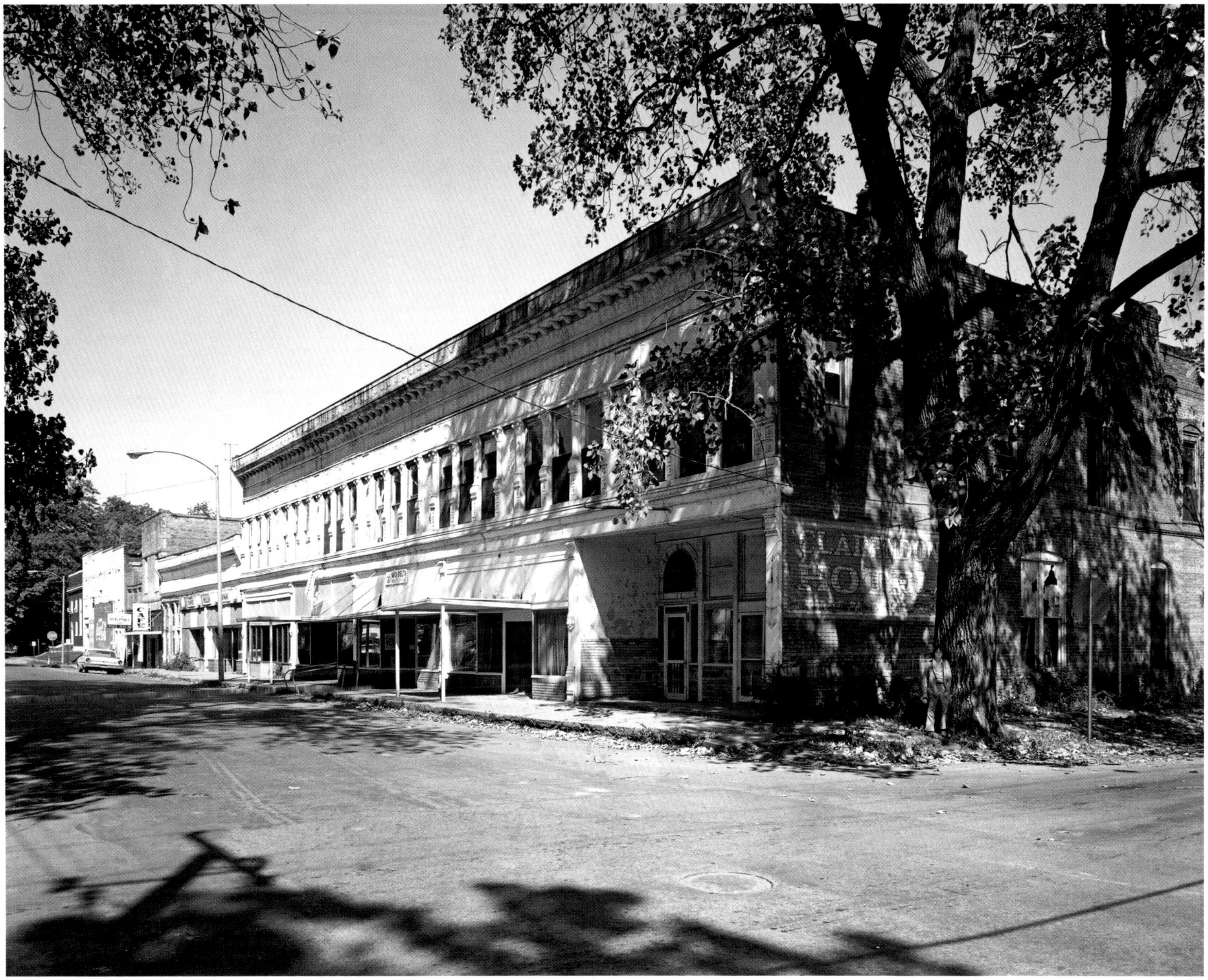

Grand hotel, brick construction with Renaissance Revival details
New South Inn
Clarendon (Monroe County), Arkansas
(demolished)

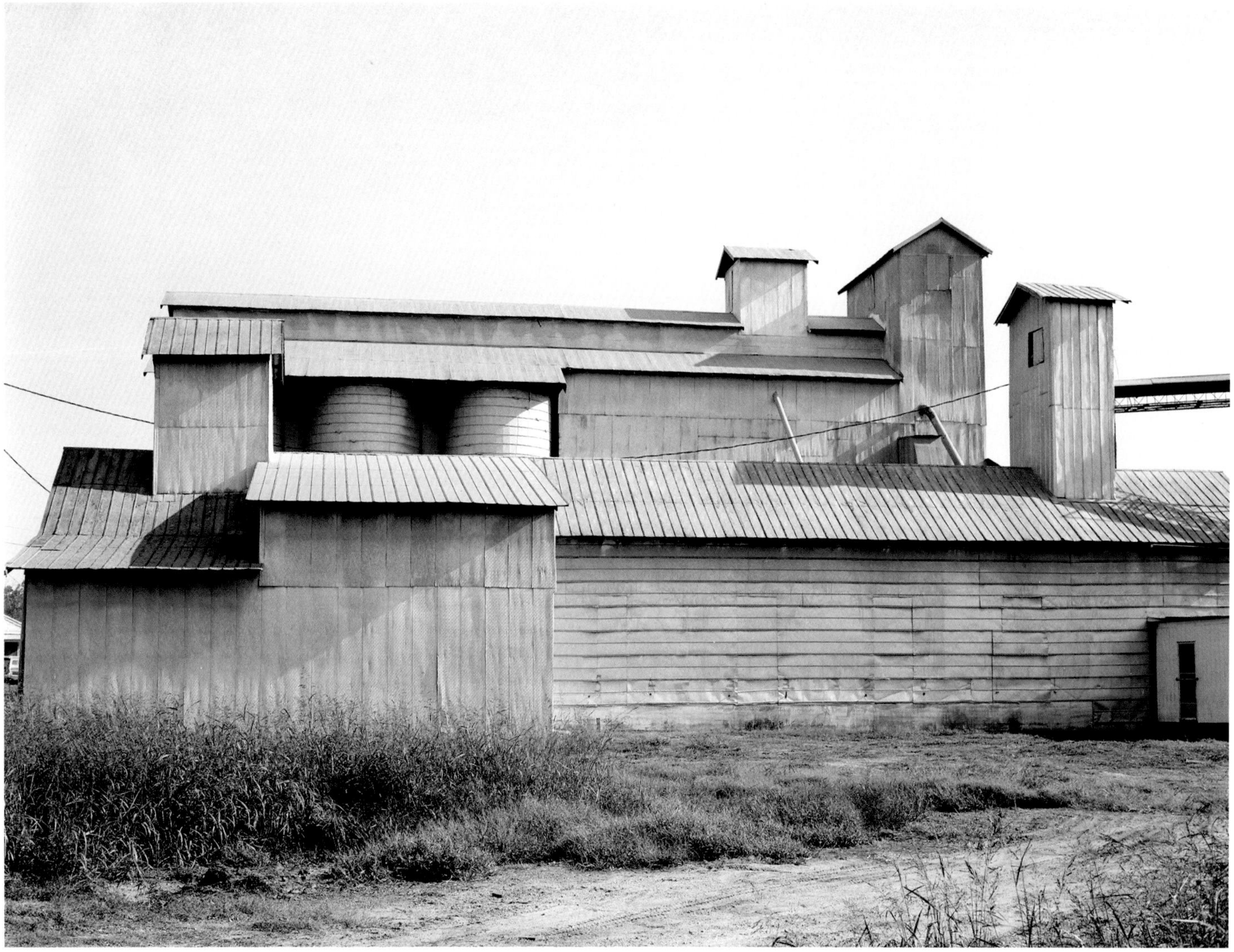

Rice mills and silos, sheet metal over wood frame
Arkansas County, Arkansas

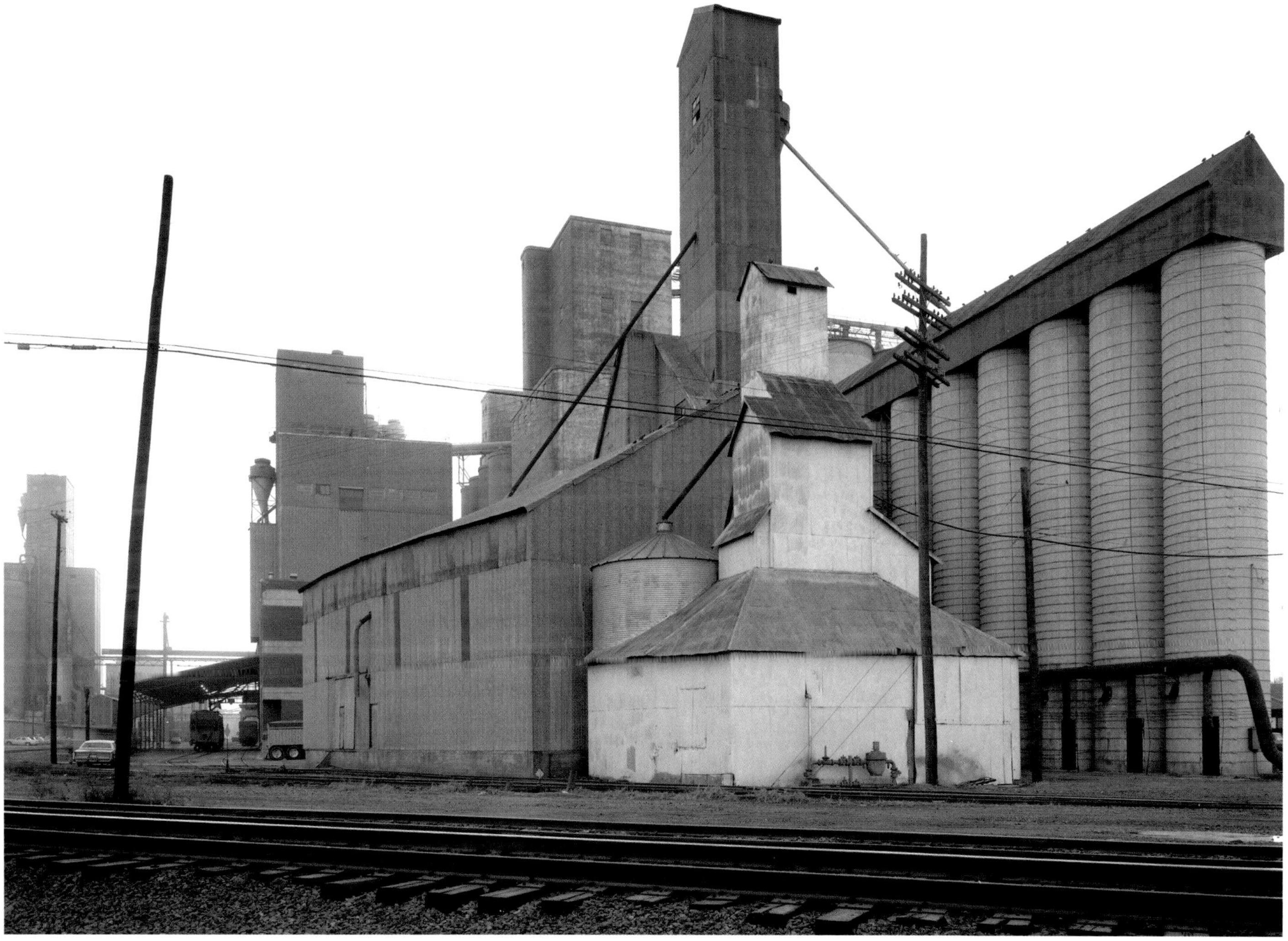

Rice mills and silos, sheet metal over wood frame
Arkansas County, Arkansas

What we now call the Grand Prairie started around Carlisle, up north of Stuttgart, and it ran all the way down through Wellford and down to Gillett. The tall grass stood everywhere, as far as a man could see, and it must have been a magnificent thing to see. Here and there, scattered out among all the tall grass, you would find a clump of trees, and they called those *islands.* So when you come across towns like Snake Island or Lost Island today, that's how they came to be called islands.

My granddaddy came here from Ohio, right after the Reverend Adam Buerkle came with the first settlers. Buerkle had been searching for the perfect spot to start a colony of fellow Germans and set up a branch of his church. The story is that when he first saw the beautiful Grand Prairie, Buerkle knew he had found the right place. It must have been quite a sight back then, mile after mile of tall grass, so tall in places that it stood over the head of a man on horseback. Then, when Buerkle found the old pre-Civil War Gum Pond Plantation for sale, he bought all 7,700 acres of it and started moving his family and his followers down here.

By 1879, my granddaddy had settled here. My dad would tell me the story about how they would have to go over to Carlisle to get supplies because that was the closest store. So they would hitch up the oxen to their wagon and take off for Carlisle to get a barrel of flour and whatever else they needed. That was a trip of about thirty miles, so it would take them a day to get there and a day to get back. My dad was the oldest child, and he would go with my granddad in the wagon. He told me how the wolves would run alongside the wagon, out in the tall grass. They could hear them out there in the grass, and they would get glimpses of them, running along with the wagon. They carried a gun, of course, but the wolves never gave them any real problem. ►

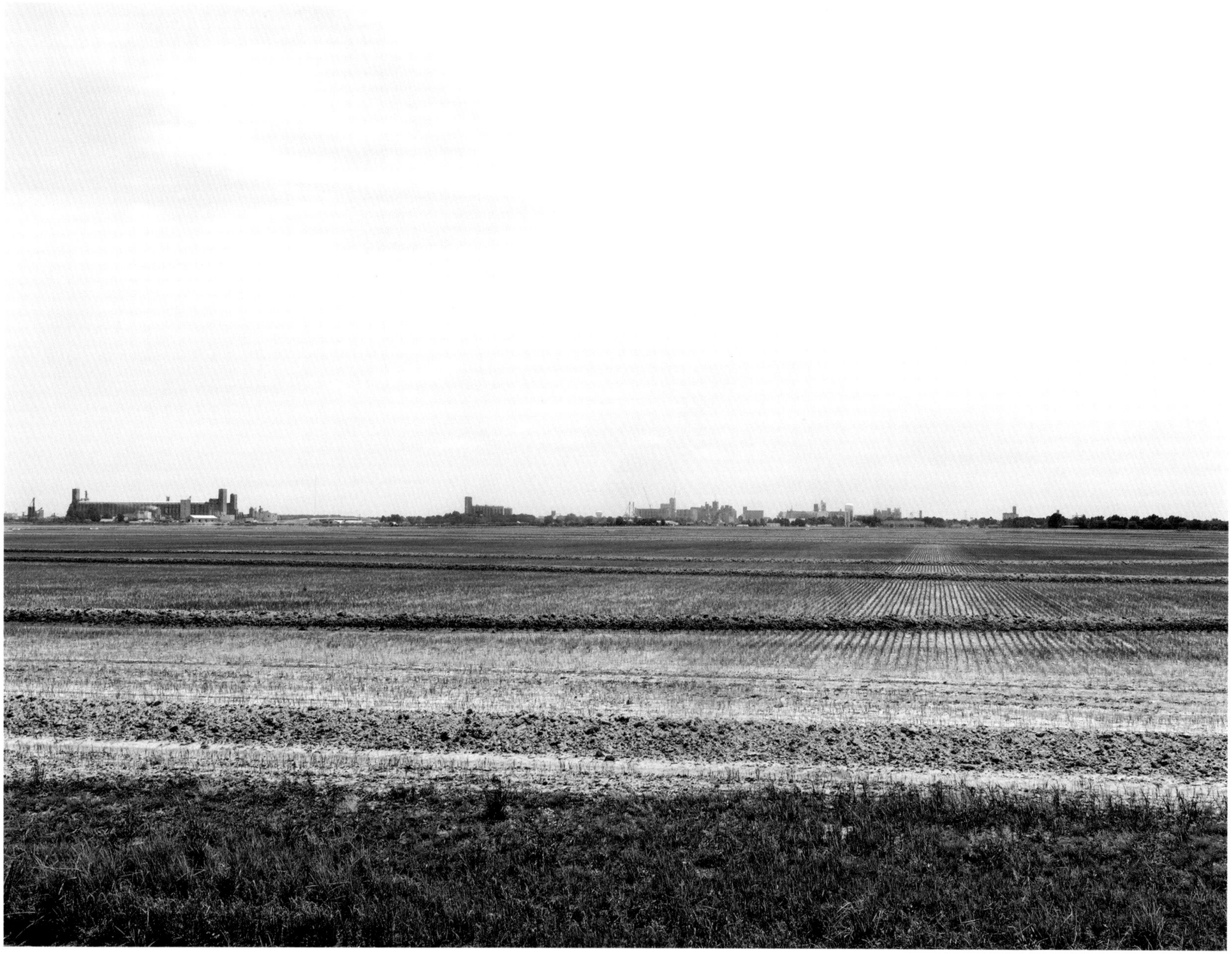

Stuttgart (Arkansas County), Arkansas, and the Grand Prairie

Stuttgart got started out there at Gum Pond when Reverend Buerkle built his big house on the site of the old plantation. In 1889, Buerkle was named the first postmaster out there, and that's when he gave it the name Stuttgart, after his old hometown in Germany. When the railroad came through, Buerkle built a little shack close to the tracks and hung up a sign saying Stuttgart. That was on the west side of what is Main Street today, and that's how Stuttgart came to be where it is.

In the early days, hay from the tall grass was the main crop, and it provided the income around here. Then it was hay and cattle. In the 1880s and '90s there were efforts to industrialize Stuttgart. They started factories and mills and all kinds of plants. They even had *two newspapers,* one in English and the other in German, but the place really took off when they brought rice here as a cash crop. Rice was a boon and a lifesaver for the farmers. It brought hundreds of new families from the North and Midwest, and it also brought a whole lot of ducks and geese and people that like to hunt them. By the early part of the 20th century, Stuttgart was truly the duck and rice capital of the world.

All that success came at a cost. That beautiful Grand Prairie that brought Reverend Buerkle and his people here, it's gone now. The tall grass and the flowers and the wild animals are all gone, and what you have now are rice fields.

Bill Mott, Jr.
Stuttgart, Arkansas

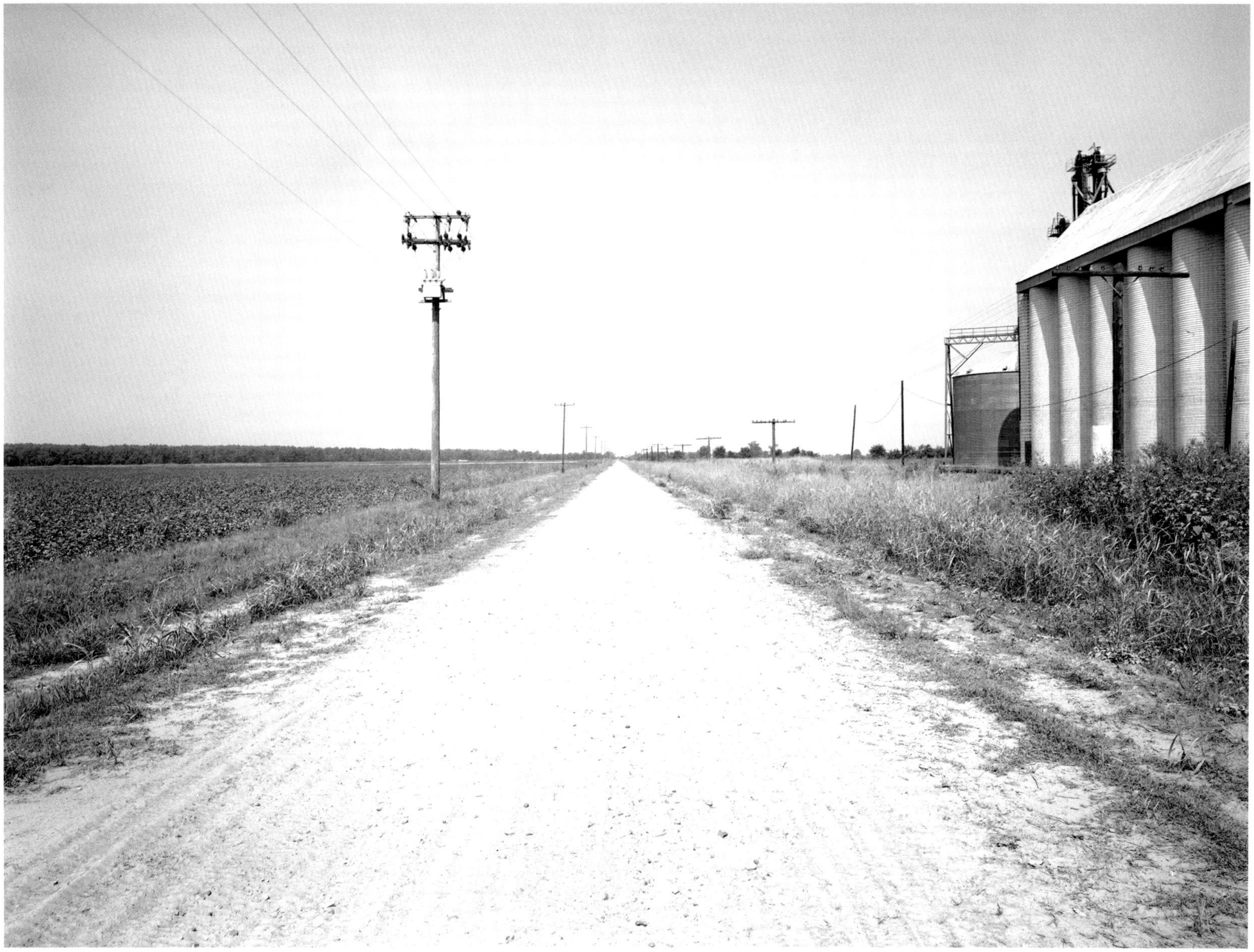

Gravel road, rice fields, and silo
Arkansas County, Arkansas

THERE USED TO BE A HINDU MAN that came through town about twice a year. You'd know he was here in town because you would see him standing around down on Main Street. He wore those balloon-type pants and a turban and a vest. He would stay down around downtown and people would go to him and he would operate on people's toes. He would do it back in the alley there behind Main Street. He would cut on people's toes when they had a problem — ingrown toenails or whatever —and he must have been good at it because a lot of people went to him and I never knew anybody that didn't speak highly of his work.

Where he came from, and where he went, I have no idea. But the last time I saw that Hindu man around town, that must have been in the '50s.

Then you had the two sisters, Miss Birdie and Miss Blossom Brierton. That was in the '30s and the '40s. They lived out of town, right where the Stuttgart High School is now. You would see them come walking along Main Street, walking into town to sell the jams and jellies they made. They lived modestly, but they had a lot of dignity. They didn't drive, 'cause they didn't own a car, so they would make their way wherever they went on foot. They mostly kept to themselves, and they dressed a little different, always wearing long dresses. They might have been Quakers, I'm not sure, or maybe Seventh Day Adventists. Whatever they were, people had a lot of respect for them. They were thought of as fine Christian women.

Miss Birdie worked on people's feet, too. Bill Cells told me one time that he couldn't hardly walk. Miss Birdie told him to come out to her place and she would take care of him, and she did. Bill went out to her place, and she made a poultice and put wraps on his feet, and he walked away fine.

Joy White
Stuttgart, Arkansas

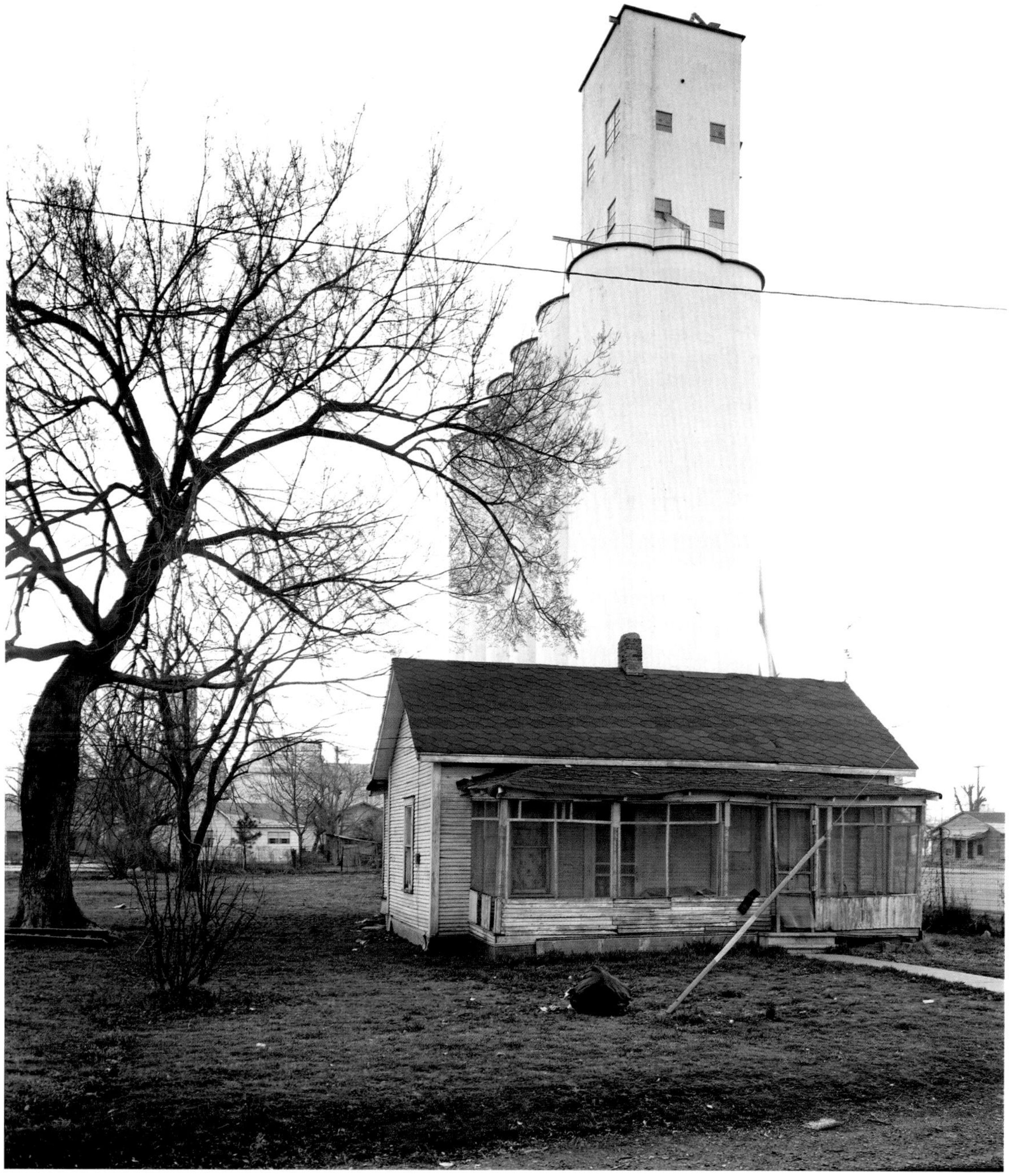

Rice silo and wood frame double cottage with Queen Anne columns
Stuttgart (Arkansas County), Arkansas

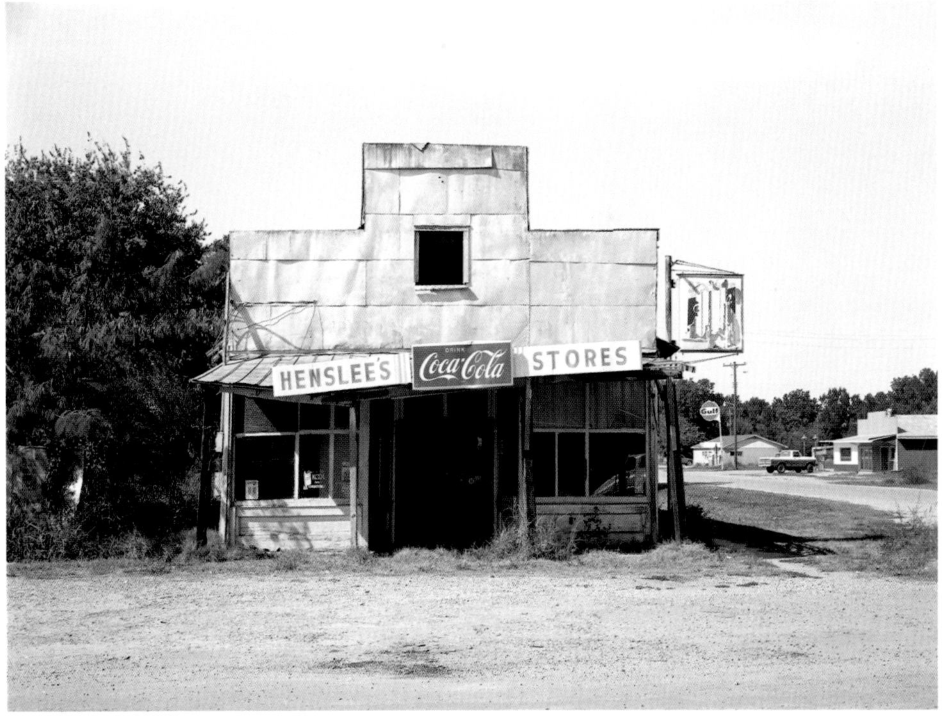

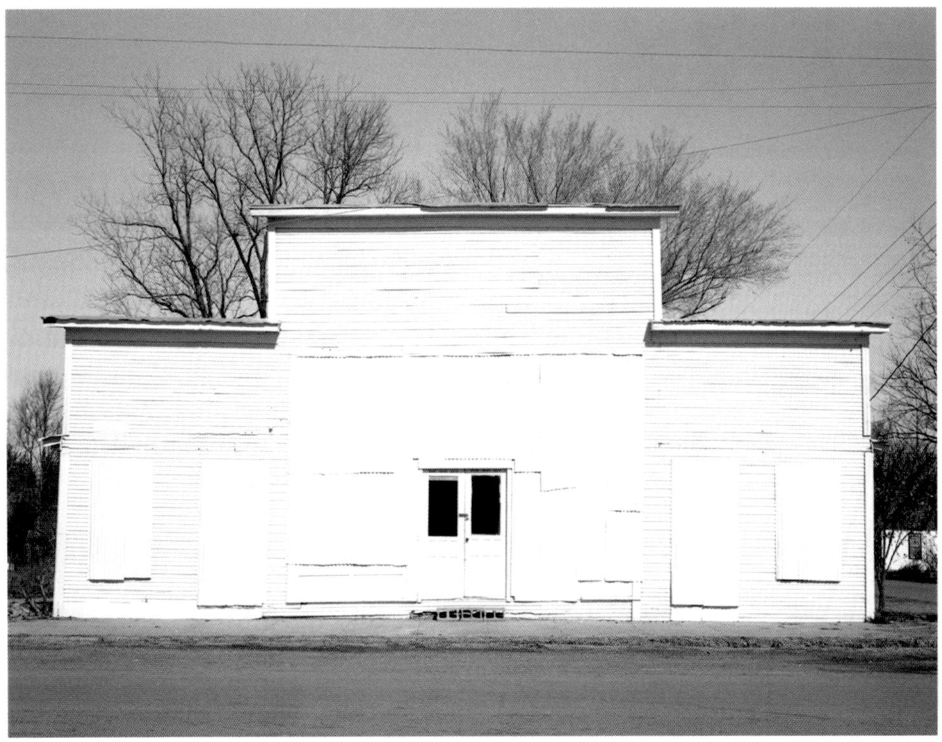

Corrugated metal commercial structure with false front (above)
Desha County, Arkansas (no longer standing)

Corrugated metal commercial structure with false front (below)
Ola (Yell County), Arkansas (no longer standing)

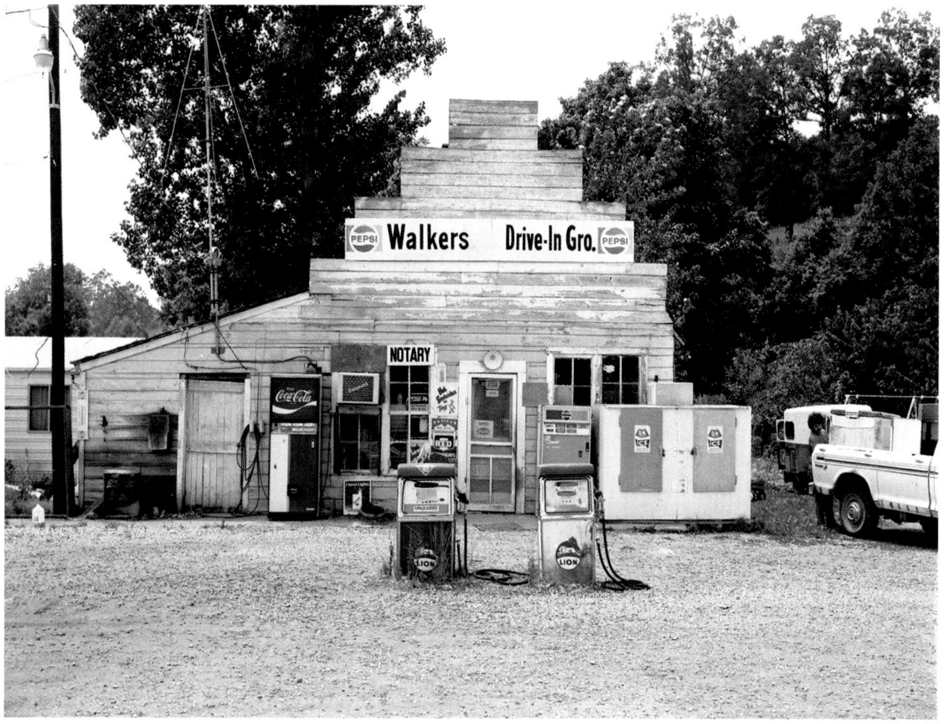

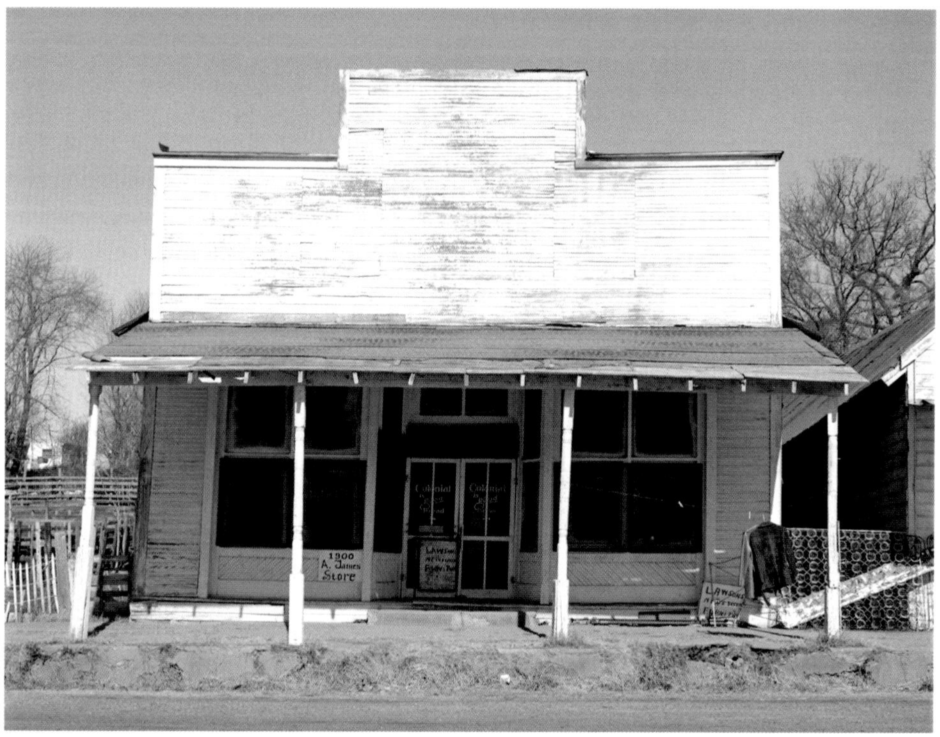

Wood frame commercial structure with false front (above)
Madison County, Arkansas (no longer standing)

Wood frame commercial structure with false front (below)
Ola (Yell County), Arkansas

THIS IS THE NATHAN STORE, at least that's how it is generally known, the Nathan Store of Nathan, Arkansas. It's gone now, but it was a true gem of southern American architecture. In fact, however, there was more than one store in Nathan, so we should properly refer to this as the *Floyd Store*, the *S. N. Floyd Store* of Nathan, Arkansas. That would be more accurate and true, for this store was built and operated by Syrinius Nimrod Floyd. Most folks called him S. N., but to those of us who knew him, he was Uncle Bud.

Now let's look at this beautiful store. The crown is just perfect. I call it the crown. Others might call it a façade or a false front. Whatever you call it, this one is just *superb*. The proportions are elegant, and it serves the purpose, of course, of making the store look more impressive. Notice that you have an ordinary shed roof, a gable roof, but that common roof is hidden by the storefront.

The design of the store is typical for this time and place. Doubtless, Syrinius had seen and studied a number of stores, and you might say he *borrowed* from what he had seen, as he designed and planned his store. Then, of course, he had to have a good knowledge of what you could do with local materials. He had no choice but to work with local materials because there was no railroad coming through Nathan, no way to get materials from the outside. But the woods, of course, were full of fine pine timber, and that was what he used, pine that was milled in the nearby Stevens Mill. And of course he had four sons to help him put up the store, and he had neighbors as well, who would have pitched in and helped. The store is constructed of vertical board and batten. One by twelve board and one by four batten. The store is completely symmetrical. Notice the steep roof of sheet metal. Notice the windows, six over sixes.

The Floyd Store stood for eighty to ninety years. But remember, these buildings—the Floyd Store, the Westbrook Store—were made of lumber, nailed together on the spot. No bricks and mortar. No steel. It's a wonder that they lasted as long as they did. By the time you took this picture in 1983, Uncle Bud was long gone. Aunt Mollie lived a bit longer. Eventually, she moved into Nashville to live with her son, Milwee, and I believe she died in 1948. That boy on the bicycle in your picture, I believe that's one of the Westfahl kids. I think his name is Steve. And I bet that's his brother standing on the porch. They have moved away, too.

First, let me tell you about my family on my mother's side, the Parkers, and I'm going to surprise you, because it's quite a story. It was just after the turn of the century, 1905 to be exact, and the Parkers were part of that huge migration in this country from the east toward the west. Burton and Margaret Parker, along with their nine children, came from Charlotte, North Carolina. They traveled by train all the way from Charlotte to Bonham, Texas, just south of the Red River, and that's where they started their farm, in Bonham, Texas. But right away, Uncle Burt didn't like farming there, so he got on his horse and said to his wife and kids, "I am going to Arkansas to find us another farm." And so he rode all the way over to Arkansas—to Martha, Arkansas, to be exact—to visit some friends, the Shuffields, who had also come from North Carolina. And they told Uncle Burt that there was a nice farm for sale over in Pike County. So he got on his horse ►

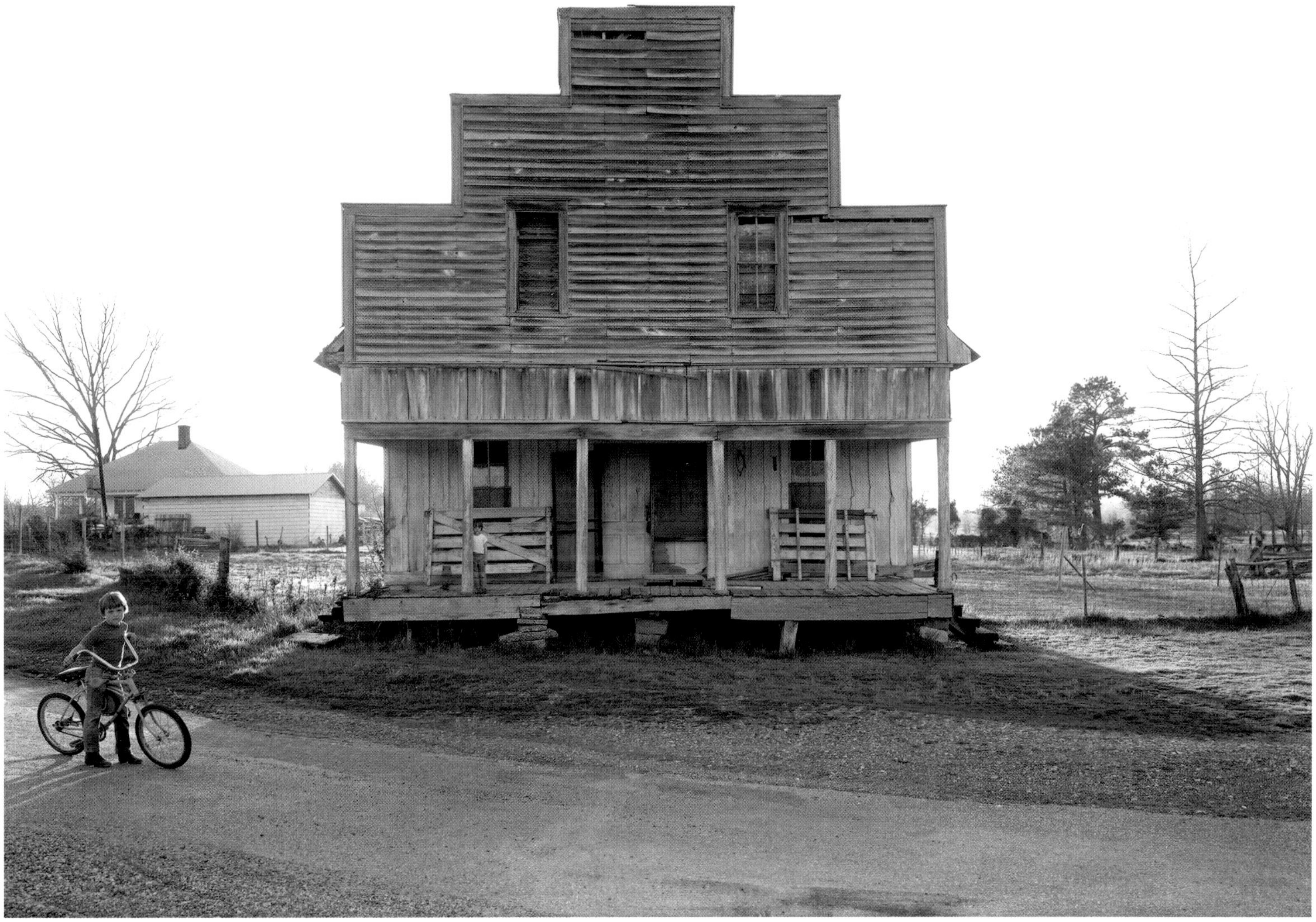

One-story wood frame store building with false front and dummy windows
The Floyd Store
Nathan (Pike County), Arkansas
(no longer standing)

again and rode over and found a Mr. Dixon, who sure enough had a 375-acre farm for sale. Uncle Burt bought that farm on the site, right there on the Muddy Fork Creek. Then, he got on his horse and rode back to Texas and said, "Kids, get all the crops picked, because we're going to Arkansas." Which they did do. And that's the short story of how the Parkers got to Nathan, Arkansas.

Now my family on my *father's* side, the Westbrooks, they came from South Carolina, but they came much earlier. You see, on my father's side, I am a *fifth generation* Arkansan because the Westbrooks came to Arkansas in 1832. On my father's side, they were all farmers. Of course a few of them were blacksmiths and other tradesmen as well, since they needed those skills to survive.

Now the Floyds, the family of Syrinius Nimrod Floyd, who built this store, they all came from Georgia. The patriarch of that family was Jasper Floyd, and he lived right up the lane from this store. Now by 1910 you had quite a thriving community here in Nathan. You had a cotton gin and a sawmill. You had two stores, the Floyd Store and the Westbrook Store, which was operated by my family, and you had a thriving Church of Christ. Just down the road from Nathan, between Corinth and Highland, was the World's Largest Peach Orchard, that was the name of the orchard, and they advertised *one million* peach trees in that one orchard.

Nathan would have been a very tight-knit community back in its day. One of Jasper Floyd's sons, Anthony Floyd, called Boss, *Uncle Boss* we called him, married my aunt, Lelia Frances Westbrook. My mother's sister married Joe Floyd. My father's sister, Ella Mae, married yet another Floyd boy. His name was Milwee. Two of the Crawford girls married two more Floyd boys, so you had a community filled with *double first cousins*, a very tight community, to say the least.

The store, of course, is gone. It continued to deteriorate over the years, the way old buildings invariably do, and then one night a big storm just *took* it. I don't know what year that was, and I don't suppose there's any reliable record of what year we lost that beautiful store.

But now I'm going to *surprise* you again. When the Floyds came to Arkansas from Georgia, they brought something with them. They brought a little tree, a little sapling of a yellow poplar tree, and they planted it in their yard. The Floyds are all gone from Nathan, what's left of Nathan, and so are the Parkers and the Westbrooks. The Polks are gone, too, as well as the Crawfords. All those people are gone, and the stores and the sawmill and the cotton gin, they're all gone, too. But that tree is still there, and today it's so big that you and I together couldn't get our arms around the trunk of it. It may be over a hundred feet tall, and it's a glorious thing to see in the springtime. Every spring it blooms, and all its bright yellow blossoms are quite something to behold. Perhaps you can photograph that tree the next time you are passing through Nathan. It would be worth a special trip, just to get a picture of that beautiful tree.

Parker Westbrook
Nashville, Arkansas

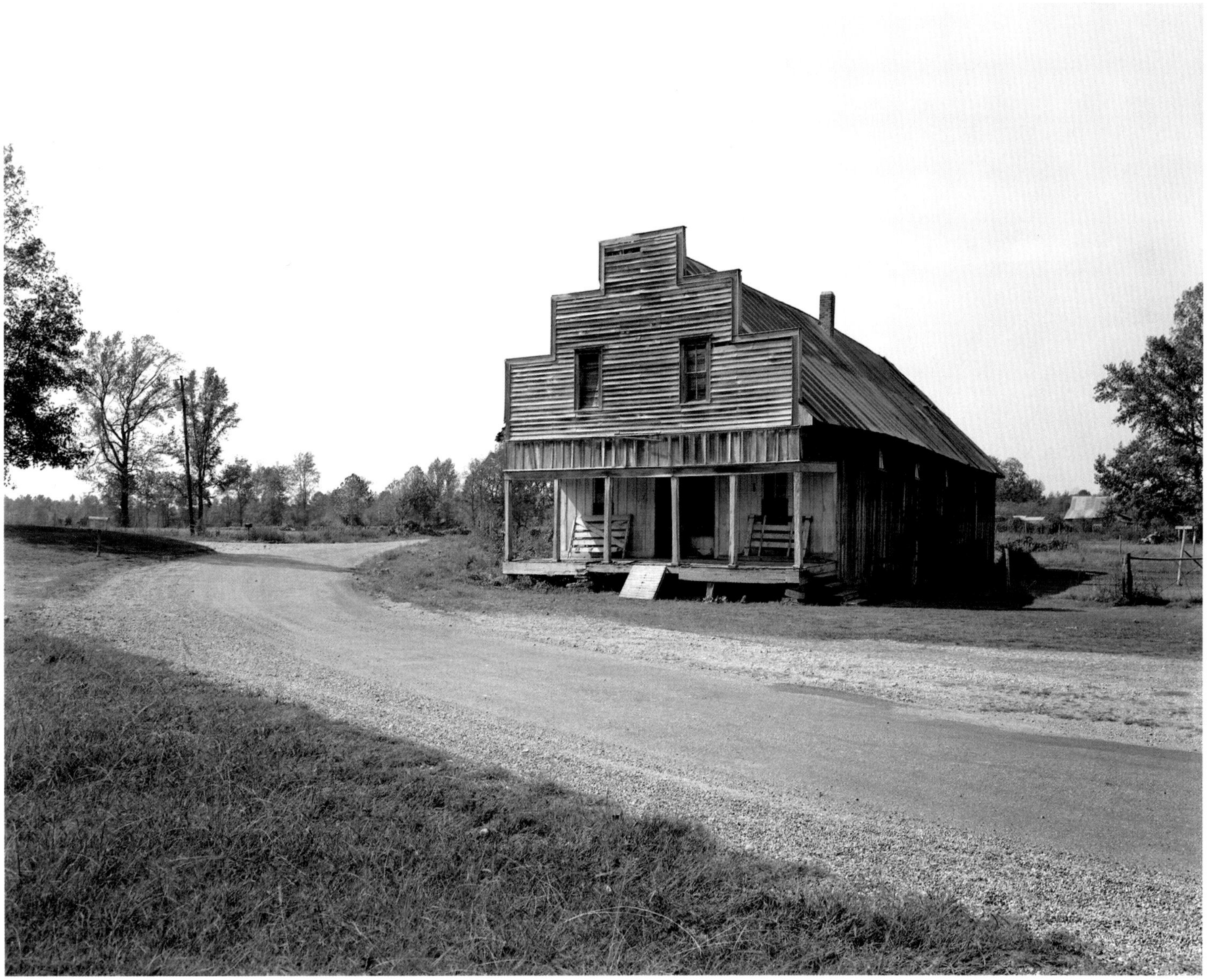

Gum Tree Road and the Floyd Store
Nathan (Pike County), Arkansas
(no longer standing)

THAT BUILDING RIGHT THERE, THE ONE WITH THE FEED SIGN out front, that was our store. My husband Bill and me, we sold feed out of there. I bet I was in that store when you took that picture. See there, how the front door is open. I bet I'm in there right now.

Our main store, where we sold most everything—gas and fertilizer, fabric and thread, food and all the rest—that's the store down the street, under the DX sign. Me and Bill, we operated that store for thirty-five years, minus one month. From nineteen and fifty-eight until nineteen and ninety-four. *This* place, the feed store, it started out as Boydston's drug store, and that's what it was for years, just a small town drugstore. It stayed that way until Boydston hung himself with a venetian blind cord. That took Boydston out of the picture and left the building vacant, so we took over the place.

I can tell you almost for sure who built all these buildings. It would have been Smith Bradshaw. For sure he built the lodge hall, the Odd Fellows hall right there on the left. We know that for sure. And for sure he built the bank. We got his plans for both of those. He built the little hospital up on the hill, too. It's a church building now, but he built it as a little nine-bed hospital. And he built the two-story house out past the cemetery. And he was a casket builder, too, Bradshaw was.

He lived out on what they call Bradshaw Mountain. He had two brothers that lived out there with him, and they all had big families. I think there was thirty-seven Bradshaws lived out there at one time. Nowadays, there's not a one person in Madison County that holds the Bradshaw name. Not one single Bradshaw is left around here.

I was born in Kingston, at least right outside it. We lived on a farm five miles out of town. My mom and pop had bad luck right from the start. Their first child got whooping cough and died. Then I was born, and they spoiled me rotten. My momma said I would hold my breath until I got whatever I wanted. Hold my breath until I was blue in the face and they thought sure I would die. On top of that, my daddy got appendicitis and he almost died. He was in bed in Berryville for twenty-five days. He got over that, and next year he got an abscess on his leg and it like to rotted off. So we didn't have a crop at all in '40 or '41. You might say we were just hanging on until nineteen and fifty, just barely getting by every year until '50, and that's when Daddy got a forest ranger job and we moved to Kingston. That's when things got better.

Bill and me got married in '54, but there wasn't any work around here, so we packed it up and went to California, worked hard and saved like a couple of misers. Bill worked building houses, and I had a job in an abstract office. After four years, we came back here with our savings—two thousand and four hundred dollars—bought this house, bought a truck, and borrowed every penny that the bank would lend us. We bought half interest in that store there and went to work running it. I kept the store and Bill did the trucking. He went out into Missouri most every day—up to Springfield, Joplin, or Aurora—for a truckload of feed or fertilizer or something else to sell. ►

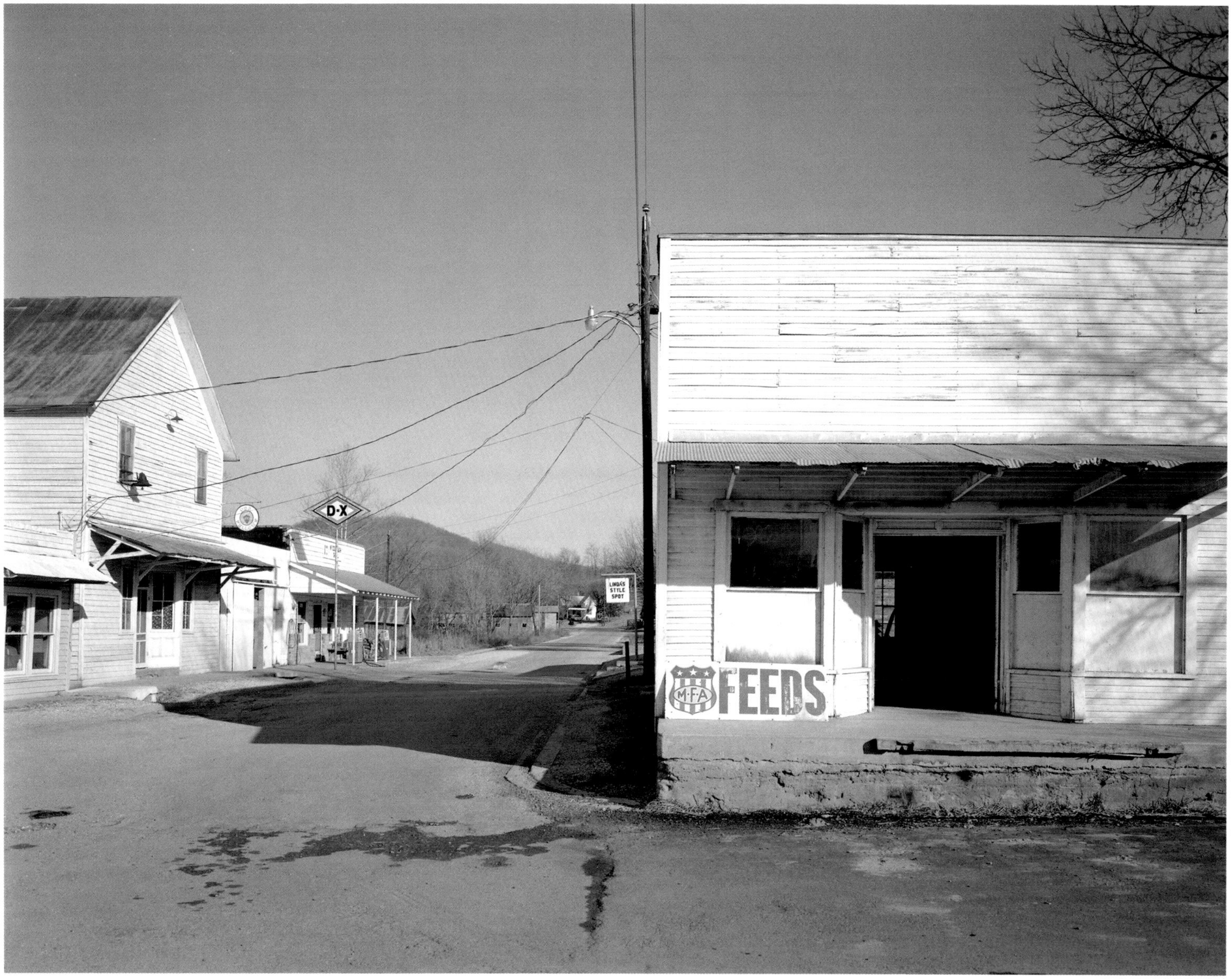

Wood frame commercial buildings on Arkansas Highway 21 through Kingston (Madison County), Arkansas

It was an old country store like you don't see any more. Back then people would come in and sit and talk for hours. We had two benches and people would sit on those benches all day and socialize and tell stories. The only regret I have about running that store is that I didn't make pictures of everybody that came in and didn't write down all the stories they were telling.

Now some folks might get the idea that Kingston is a boring place with nothing going on, but that's not right. We definitely have our share of excitement. One day, I was going in the back door of the store to load feed, and this boy came by with an old shotgun on his shoulder. It was a cold, snowy day in the winter and I had my work to do, so I didn't think anything about it. And what time I was loading feed on the porch, Hugh Bunch came out the front of his store and hollered at me, "*They robbing the bank.*" That boy with the shotgun had gone in the bank and held it up.

Right next door to the bank is the café, and that café has seen its share of trouble, too. One of the Bowen boys got in it with Clyde Hicks, and Clyde shot and killed him right there in the door to the café. Clyde shot him over twenty-three dollars that the boy said Clyde owed him. The Bowen boys were all at church that morning, and one way or another that one boy got in his head it was time for Clyde to pay him, so he came down and found Clyde in the café. Clyde took offense and shot the boy dead on the spot. Then the Bowen boy's *daddy* came down hunting for Clyde, to take revenge. The Bowen boy's daddy took a shot at Clyde and hit him, shot up Clyde's truck real bad, put a whole lot of bullet holes in the back of Clyde's truck, but Clyde got away. Nobody's forgot about that little deal.

Then we had all the shady trouble that they called the *Whitewater* deal. Remember that fellow McDougal that was in business with the Clintons back then? Well, his deal was he bought the Kingston Bank. Then he cleaned up the whole town and painted all the buildings. He was going to put Kingston on the map. Thousands of people came here one weekend. There were cameras on the roof of the bank and a hot air balloon and I don't know what all. Then, before you know it, it all went bust. Greenforest took our bank. Next thing we knew, they took away our school and made it part of the Jasper school district. I don't know *who* thinks that works. We were getting along fine. We had a good school and had thousands of dollars in our bank, then Jasper got us and all our money.

The lodge hall and the stores, the bank building, the *heart of Kingston*, is still here. Smith Bradshaw is long gone, and nobody is going to build any more buildings like he did, but we still have the heart of the town he built. For now, we still got our town.

Charlene Grigg
Kingston, Arkansas

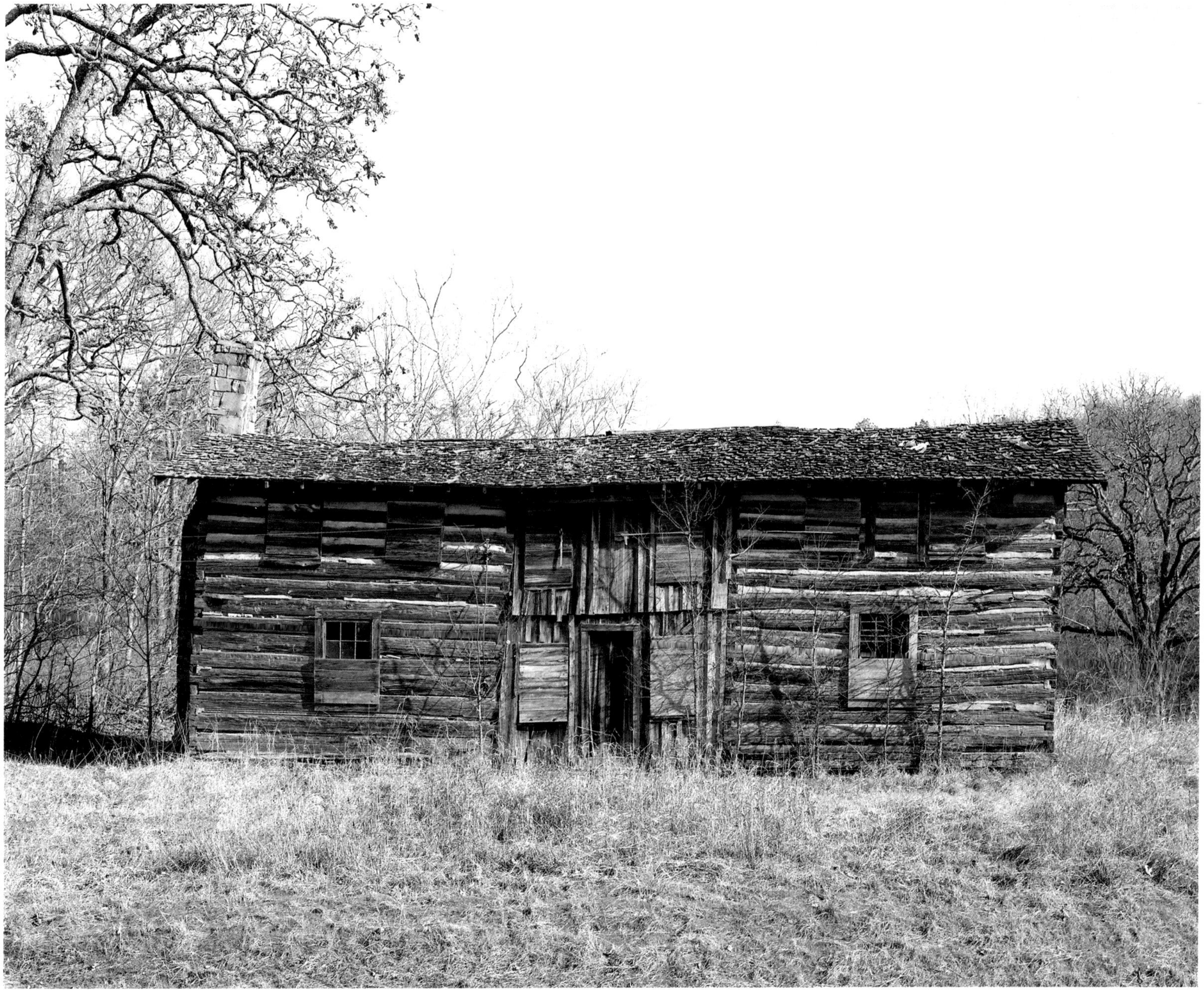

IN THE 1950S, WHEN I WAS A TEENAGER growing up here in Batesville, Tex Ritter came to town and did a show at the Melba Theater. I went with my friends and watched him sing all his famous songs, right there on the stage at the Melba Theater. I remember how he brought his horse up on the stage to do tricks. That horse could count to ten, and he could even answer questions, shaking his head to say no or nodding to say yes.

That was my time here in Batesville—the '40s and the '50s—and those were wonderful times. The Melba and the Landers, the other theater in town, were the center of our social lives. The only other thing for teenagers to do was to go out to the Rainbow Drive-In. The biggest thing, back in those days, was when one of the theaters had a musical show. I saw *Annie Get Your Gun* at the Melba. They had magic shows and talent shows and beauty contests, all on the stage at the Melba. Fridays and Saturdays they had what they called Owl Nights. Those were the late movies that started at ten o'clock and went to midnight. That was very late for us to be out in those days. They even had CinemaScope. I saw Richard Burton in *The Robe* in CinemaScope, right here in Batesville in the Melba Theater.

Right behind where the Melba Theater stands, that was where my great-grandfather set up his tin shop. That leads us into quite a story, a true story that tells like a romantic novel. The story begins with my great-grandfather, Adolphus Baker, who joined the British Army when he was a young man. That would have been in the 1840s, and he worked his way up, until eventually he became a bodyguard for Queen Victoria. It was while he was working at Buckingham Place that he noticed a beautiful woman by the name of Francis Leale. She caught his eye, and it was love at first sight. By all accounts, Francis was quite a remarkable woman, of aristocratic birth, a descendant of Count Leale, the Italian nobleman. By the time my great-grandfather laid eyes on her, she had already been around the world as a missionary for the Church of England. She had spent years with the Aborigines in Australia, and she had ridden camels across the deserts of Arabia. ►

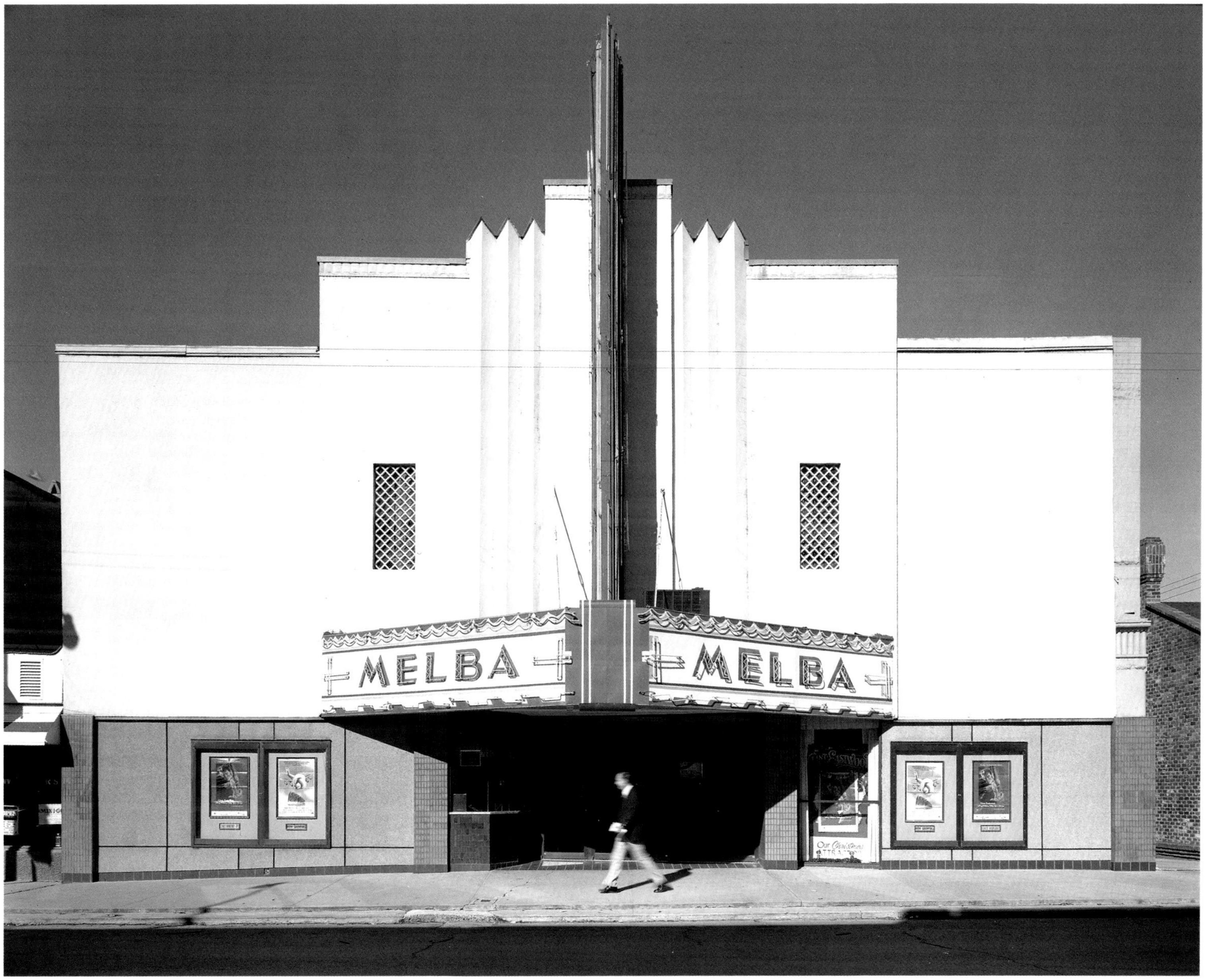

Art deco movie palace faced in stucco
Melba Theater
Batesville (Independence County), Arkansas

They fell in love, but her parents disapproved. They considered my great-grandfather to be a common soldier, and they would not give their blessing to the marriage. So the couple eloped, and her family disowned her.

The crazy part, the part I cannot begin to explain, is how they ended up here in Batesville. We know that he opened his tin shop, right behind where the Melba Theater stands today. But god only knows how they got from London to Batesville, Arkansas. But they did. And by the time they got here, they had two children. I never knew my great-grandparents, but their daughter, my grandmother Bertha Baker, taught me to drink tea, and she told me their story many times.

I'm sure that I inherited my great-grandmother's urge to travel. Right after I got out of high school, I left Batesville for California. I got married, and we traveled for over forty years. My husband was a brilliant man, a scientist and an engineer, one of those people with an IQ of about 250. He worked for the space program. First we lived in California, at the Vandenberg Air Force Base, where he worked. We moved all around, and eventually we lived in Florida, when he worked at the Kennedy Space Center. When he finally retired, we moved back here to Batesville. That was in 2002. He died in 2005.

I think a lot about my great-grandmother, Francis, how she traveled to foreign lands as a missionary, how she married and somehow found her way here, with the love of her life, half a world away from where she started. From Buckingham Palace to Batesville, Arkansas. Then I think about myself, traveling all of my life from one place to another with my husband.

We wander all around the world, some of us, pulled by our need for love and adventure. Then, as often as not, we return to where we started, older, wiser, but with so much of our life behind us.

Gail Harley
Batesville, Arkansas

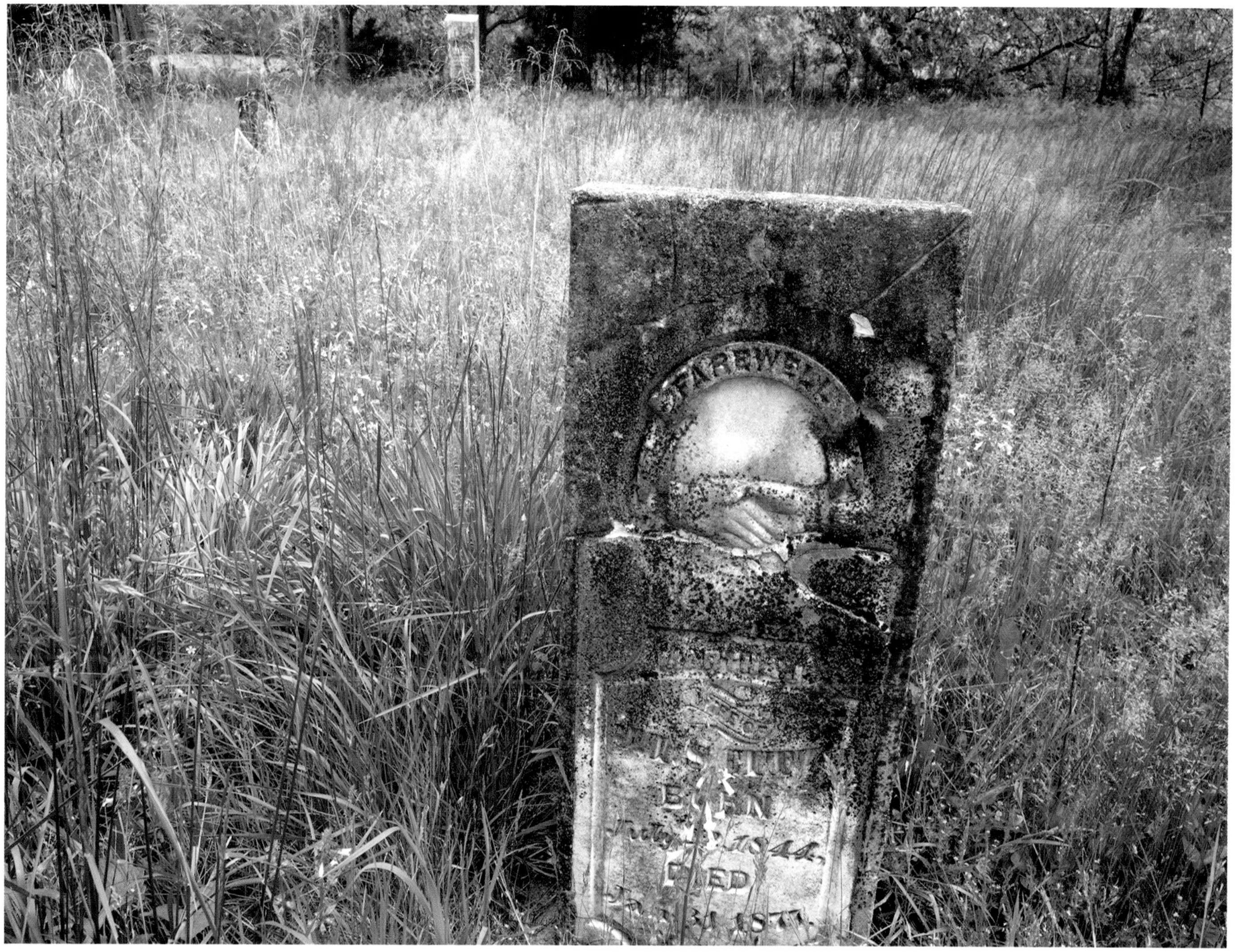

Tombstone
Snead Family Cemetery
Osage (Benton County), Arkansas

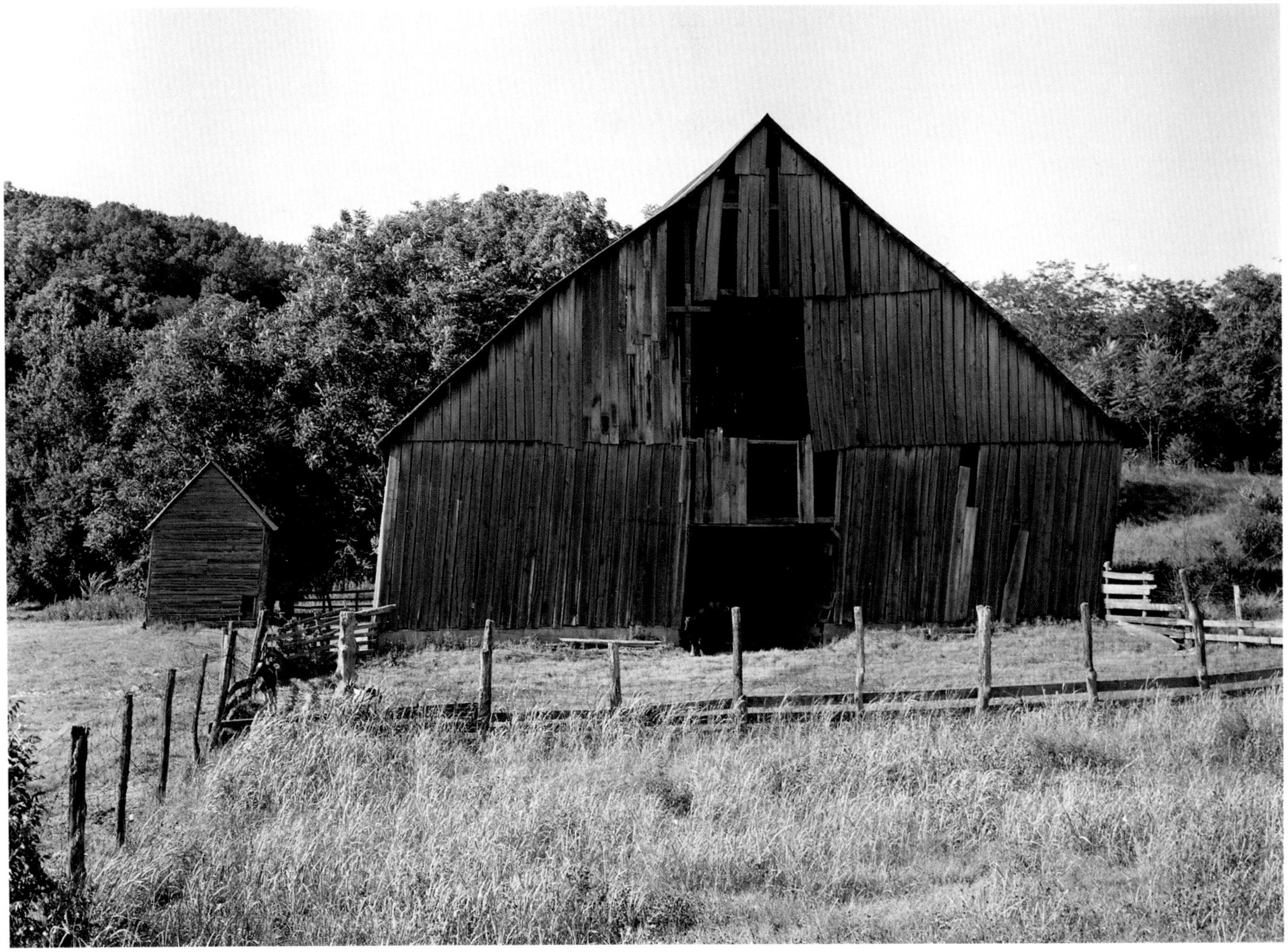

Wood frame barn with high loft and secondary building
Franklin County, Arkansas

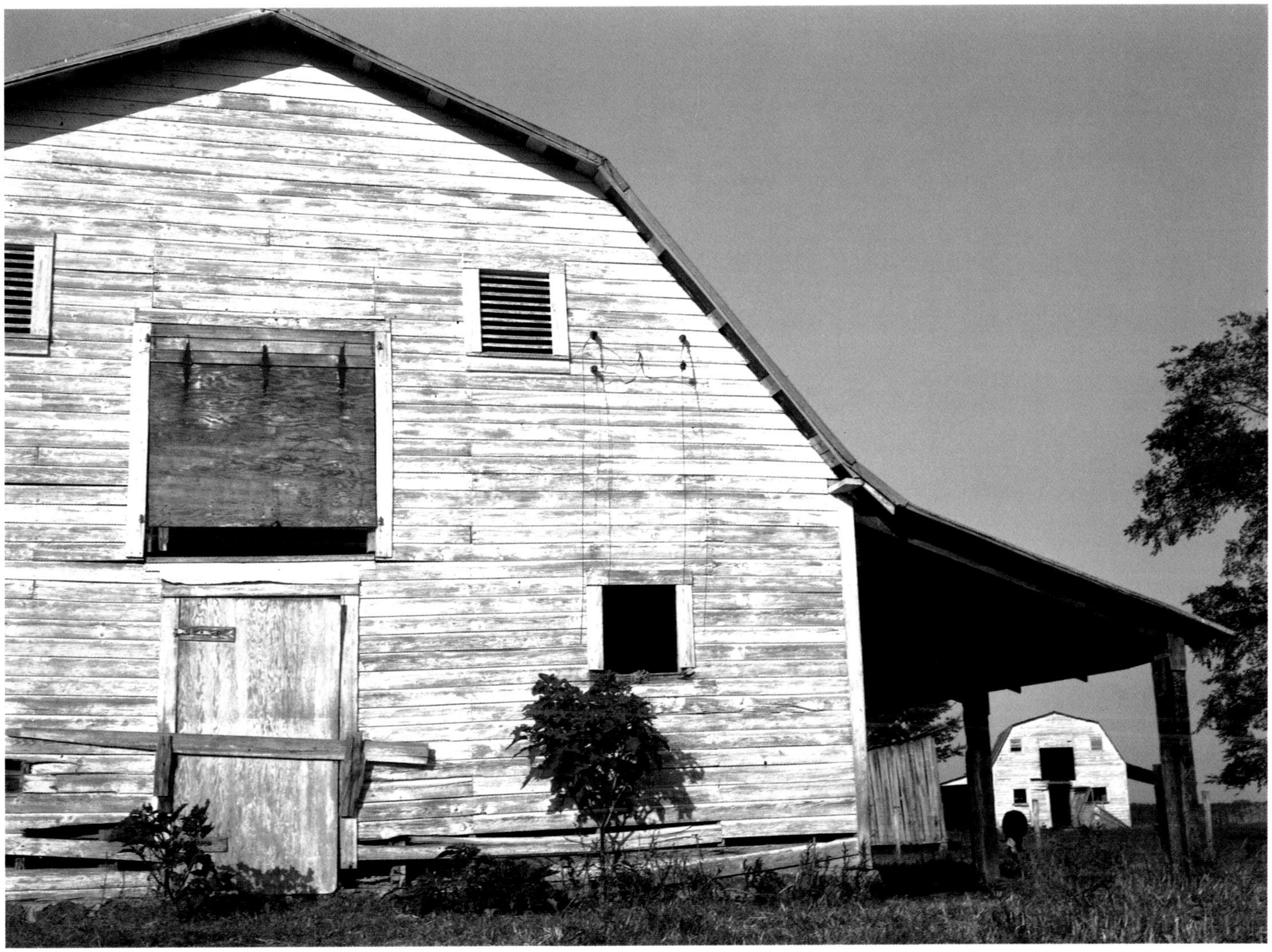

Wood frame barns with Dutch roofs
White County, Arkansas

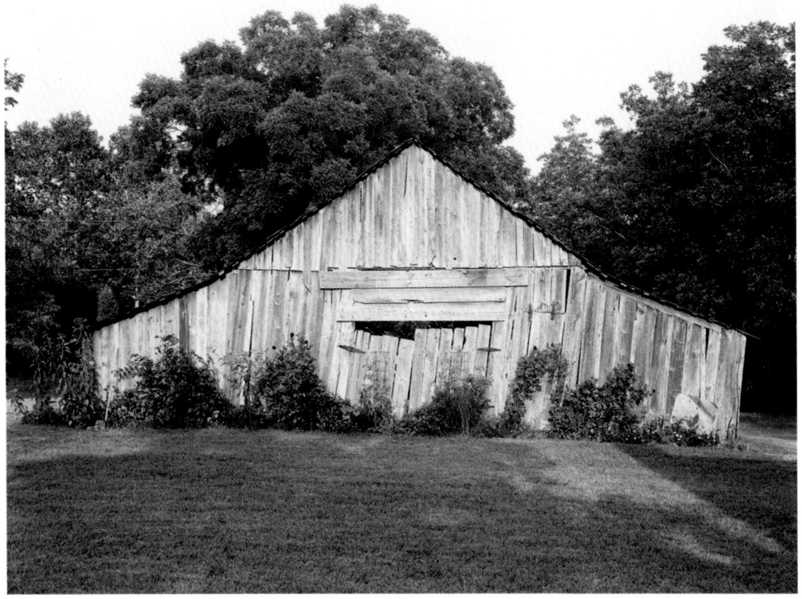
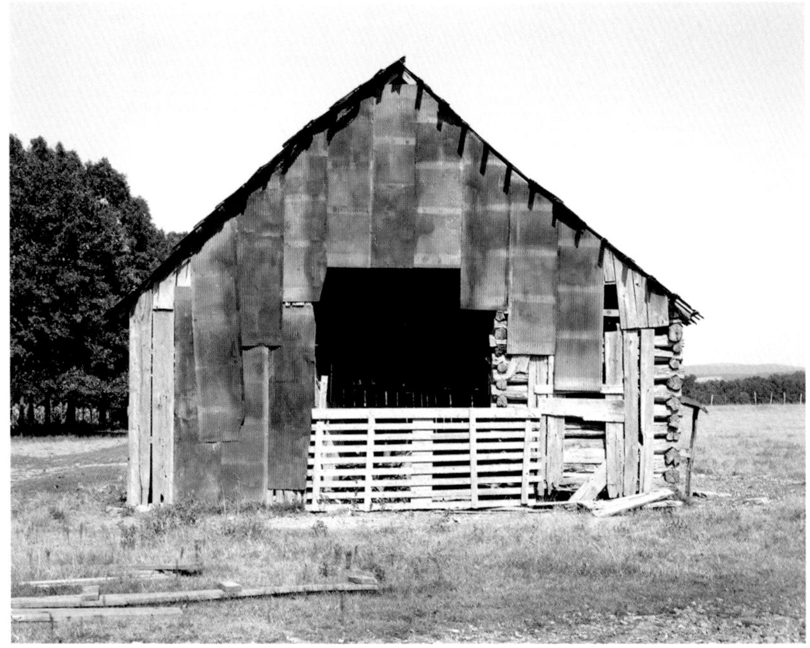
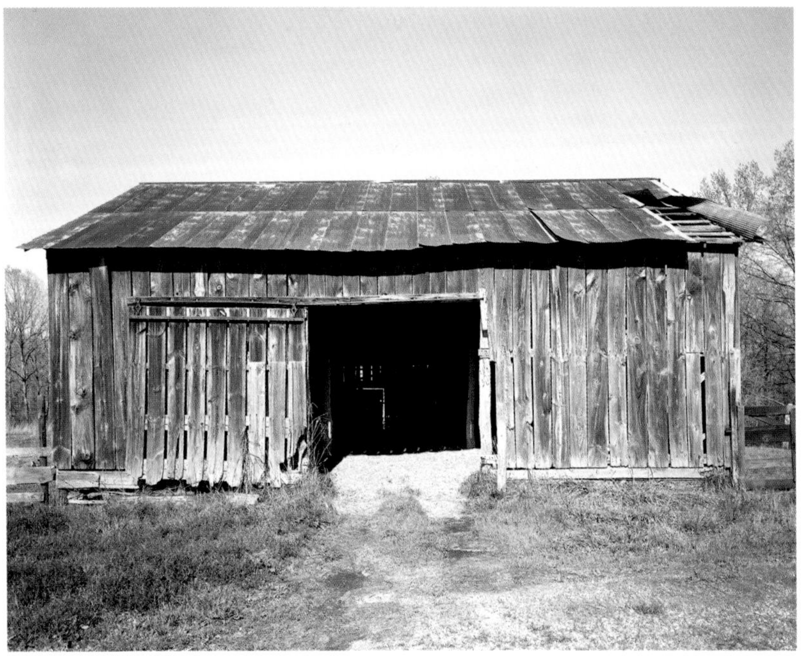
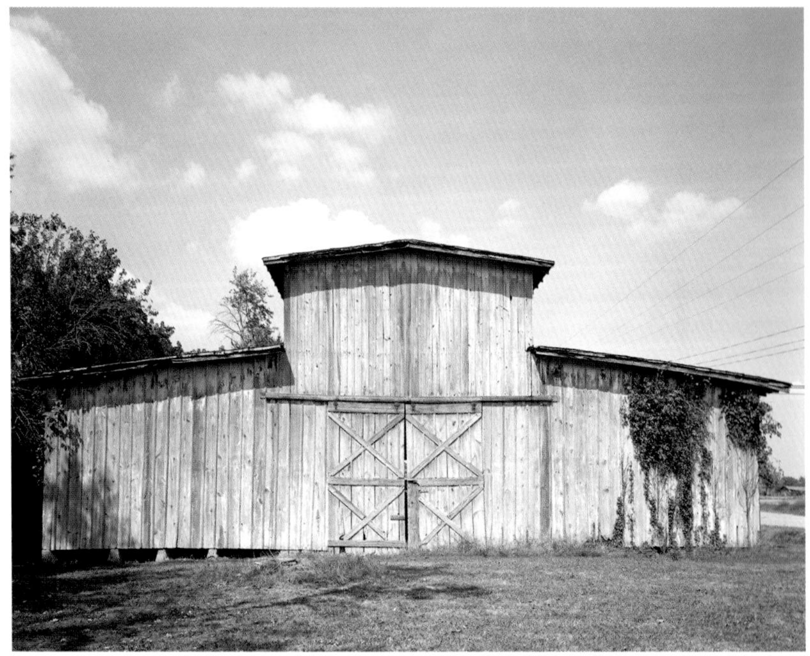

Wood frame, vertical board barn with sheds, Nashville (Howard County), Arkansas (upper left);
Log barn sheathed in boards and corrugated metal, Boone County, Arkansas (upper right);
Wood frame tobacco barn, Howard County, Arkansas (lower left);
Wood frame specialty barn of unknown purpose, Calhoun County, Arkansas (lower right).

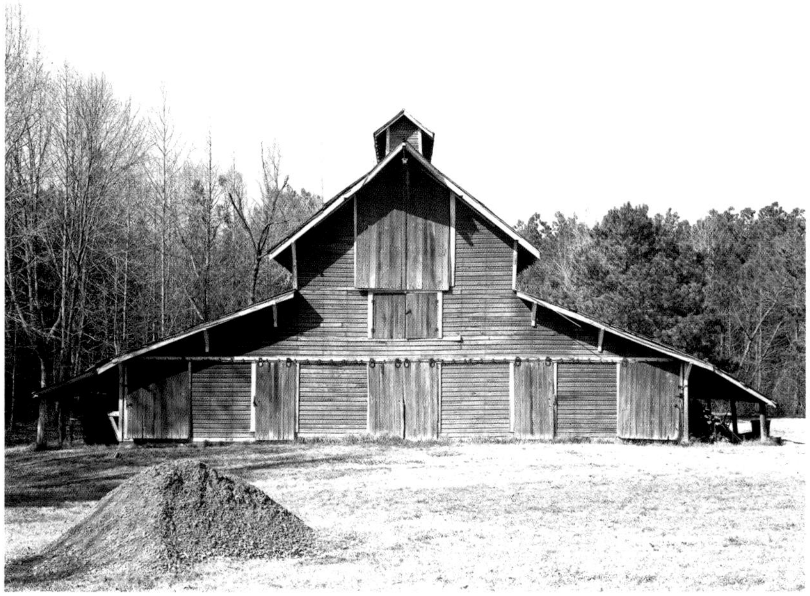

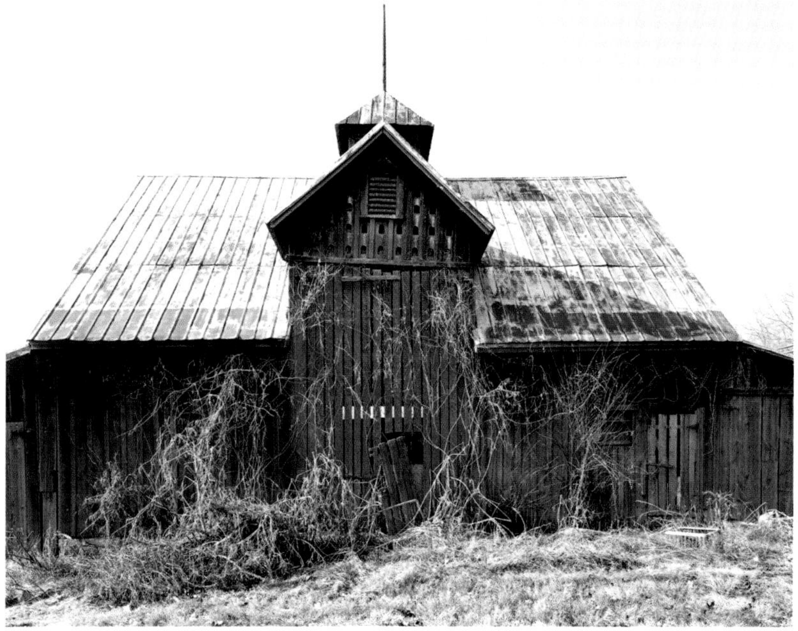

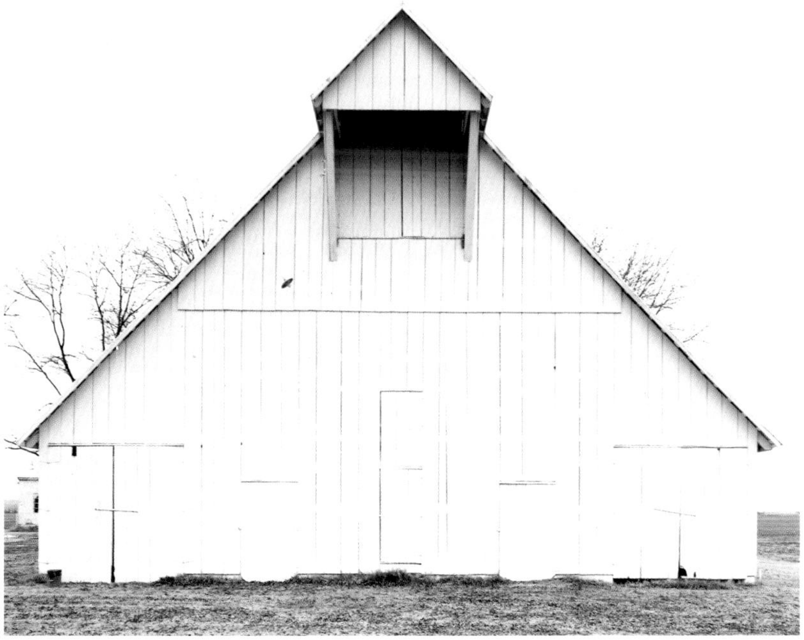

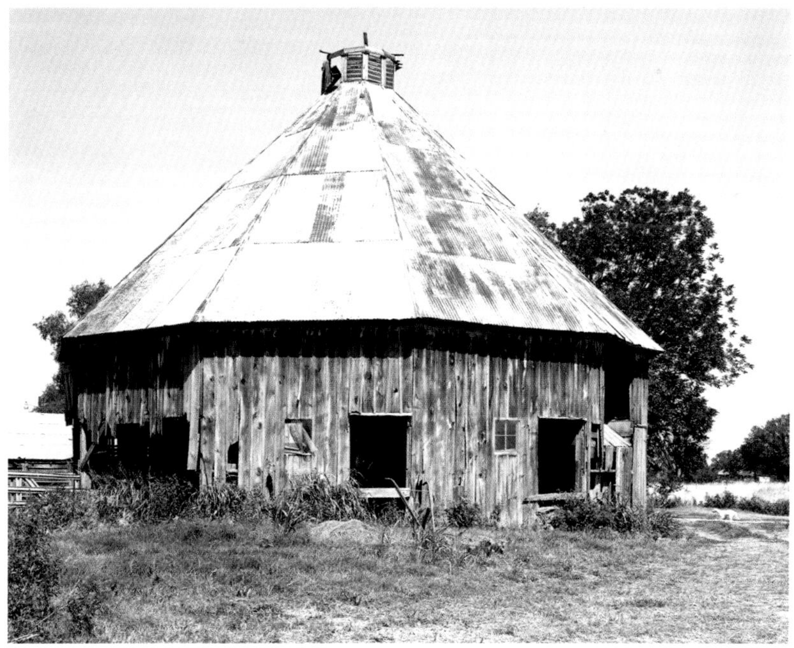

Wood frame barn with side sheds and ventilated loft, Montgomery County, Arkansas (upper left);
Wood frame barn with added bay containing pigeon house, Perry County, Arkansas (upper right);
Wood frame horse barn with sheltered entry into hay loft, Arkansas County, Arkansas (lower left);
Wood frame octagonal barn with later corrugated metal roof, Washington County, Arkansas (lower right).

My father was one of the men who built the town of Forester, Arkansas, and when I say he built it, I mean he actually *built that town.* In 1929, my father was working as the superintendent of schools in Murphreesboro, Arkansas. He was also the football coach, baseball coach, basketball coach, and the school bus driver. My father was a *big* man. He had been an athlete in college, and he was physically big and quite strong. But he was a *quiet* man, too, a sort of retiring fellow. He was also quite a skilled carpenter, and I guess the word had gotten around about all his skills and the kind of man he was known to be.

While he was superintendent of schools in Murphreesboro, my dad was contacted by a man named T. W. Rosborough. Rosborough had purchased a vast tract of virgin timberland in a remote area of Scott County in the Ouachita Mountains, and he had a plan to build a sawmill there. But before he could build a sawmill, he had to have a town there, a town where all the millworkers and their families could live. Rosborough offered my dad a job as the foreman of the carpenters who would go up there and build his sawmill town.

Dad told Rosborough that he already had a good job, but Rosborough said, "I'll pay you half as much again, and you'll be the head of the carpenters. You'll build this town from the git-go." I suspect that Rosborough's offer had plenty of appeal to my father, so he took the job, and he spent the winter of '29 to '30 building the town that came to be known as Forester, Arkansas.

After they got the town built, they started building the sawmill, and they had it up and running by early 1931. That mill became the largest mill in the state of Arkansas. I've read that the lumber shed alone measured over a thousand feet long. As the mill prospered, the town grew, and by 1940 the population of Forester was over 1,300. In the beginning, the men did the logging entirely with mule teams and wagons. Even after they had logging trucks, they used the mules to load the logs on the trucks. And let me tell you, *that was something to see.*

They worked just as hard as the mules. For the most part, they saw their families only on Sundays. They would be up in the morning and gone to work before dawn, and they wouldn't be home until after dark. There was no leisure time, none, except on Sundays. But Forester was a great place for a kid to grow up. My first job, when I was a kid, was getting up at four in the morning and shaking the clinkers down on the bottom of our coal stove. Then I'd go out and get a new bucket of coals for the stove. When I'd done that, I could come back and get in bed and sleep until breakfast. ►

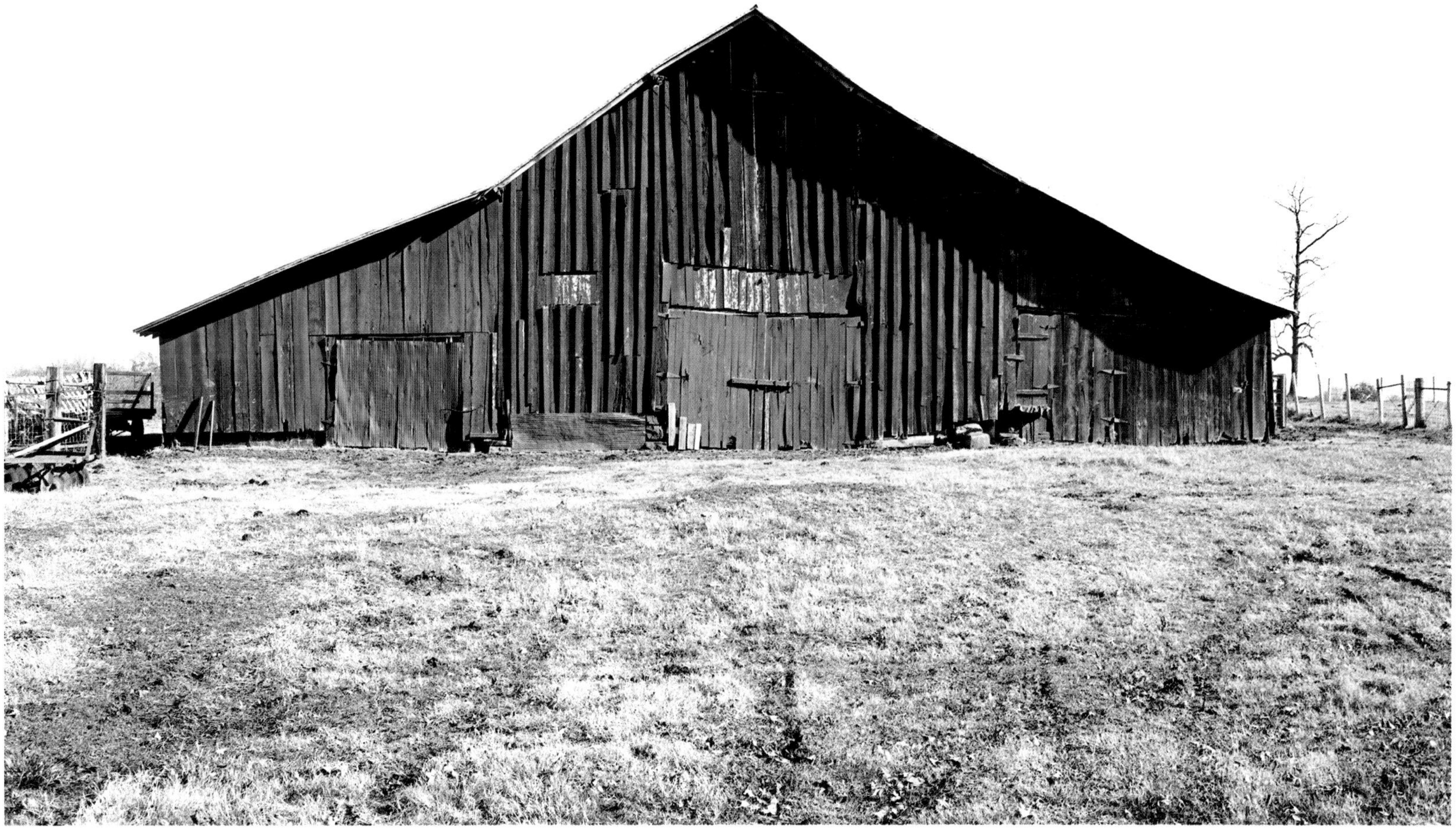

Wood frame box and batten barn with much-altered doorway
Scott County, Arkansas

When I was a boy, growing up in Forester, I was always looking for a way to go out into the log woods to watch the men and the mules at work. My mother didn't want me out there in the woods where they were bringing down those giant trees. She thought it was dangerous. But there was a guy, his name was Roy Nichols. He was a logger, and he had a son my age. He drove a big logging truck, and he would pick us up in town and sneak us out into the woods to watch those logging teams at work.

That was something I will never forget, seeing those giant trees come crashing down. The squirrels and coons and possums would all come flying out as those trees came down, and it was just fascinating to watch the men and the mules at work, hitching up to those logs and loading them onto the trucks.

I don't know who was tougher, those men or the mules. I guarantee you they were *all* tough, but I was always fascinated most of all with the mules. Years later, they had mechanical skidders, but at that time the mules would skid the logs up to the trucks, then those mules would come right around to the other side of the truck. The men would throw the chains over, hook up those huge logs again, and the mules would just pull them up, one at a time, onto the truck. When they had the log on the truck, the men would pop the lines, and those mules would go right back and start skidding another log.

After they got the town built and the mill was up and running, they had my dad working as foreman of the rough shed. My mom had come to join him by then, and they had both thought that they would be teaching in the new school there. But Rosborough told my dad, "I can pay you twice as much to stay on as foreman of the rough shed," so he did. He was the foreman from 1930 or 1931 until 1952, when they cut the mill out. The whole town moved away after that, so all you have there now is a county park that marks the spot where Forester once stood.

Billy R. Wilson
Little Rock, Arkansas

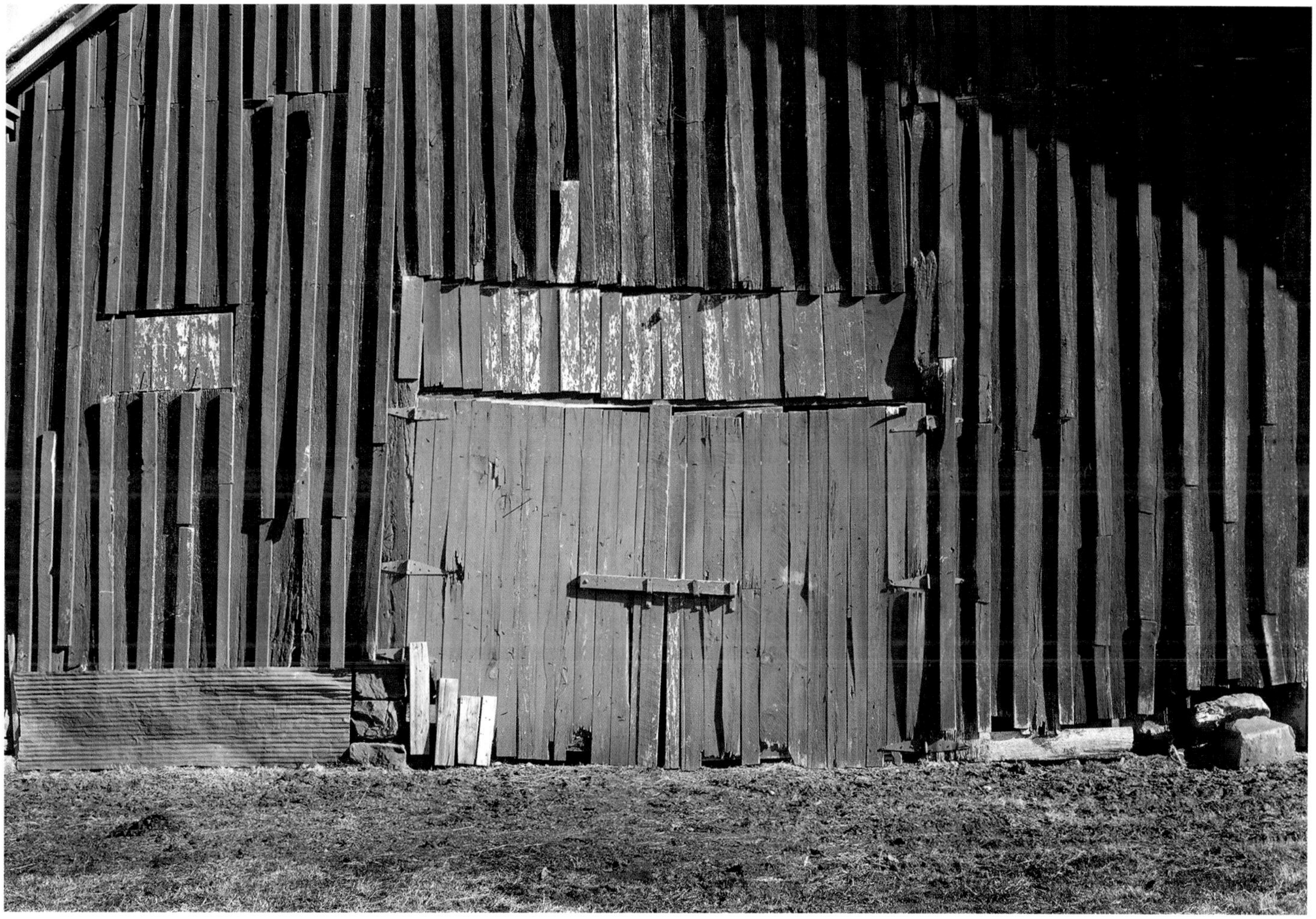

Wood frame box and batten barn with much-altered doorway
Scott County, Arkansas

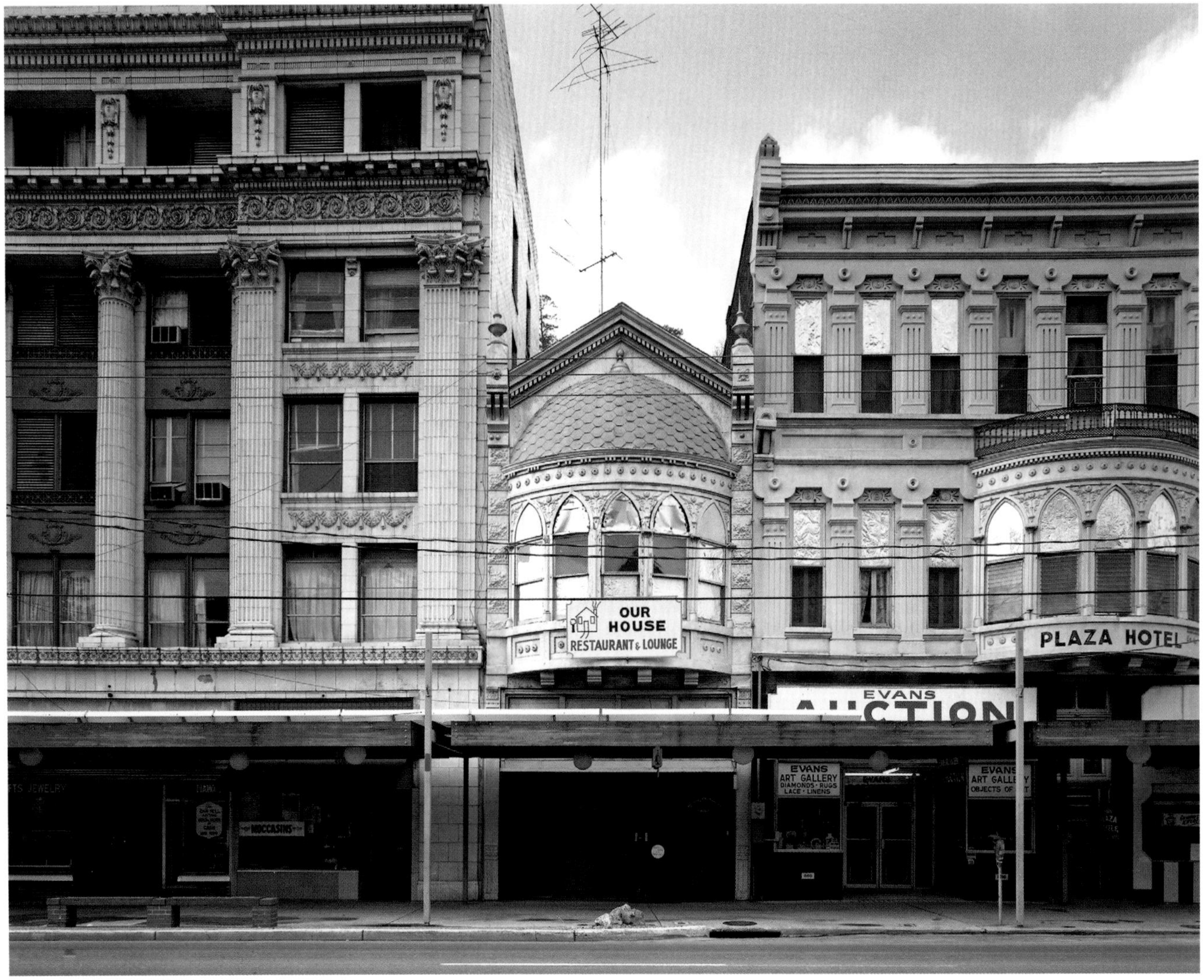

Exotic domed in-fill between commercial buildings
East Grand Avenue
Hot Springs (Garland County), Arkansas

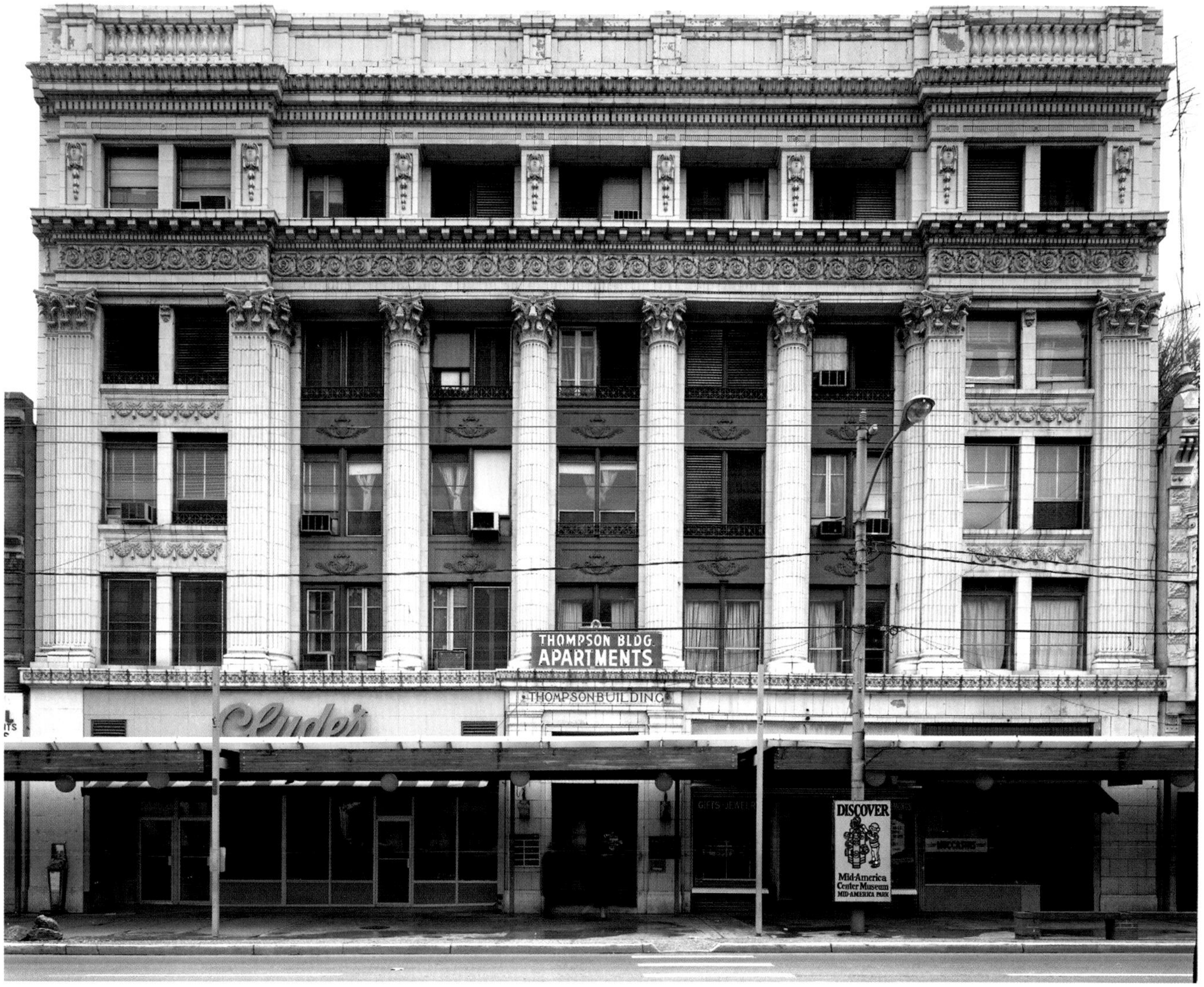

Beaux-Arts commercial building with Corinthian colonnade
East Grand Avenue
Hot Springs (Garland County), Arkansas

Before they invented Las Vegas, even before they invented Florida, *Hot Springs* was the place. At one time or another, everybody who was anybody came to Hot Springs. Don't take my word for it, just read the history. Al Capone and all his gangsters, they put down their guns and came to Hot Springs whenever they needed to take a break. Sam Houston came to Hot Springs before he got around to going to Texas. Jesse and Frank Jones—the Jones boys—came here to rob stagecoaches. Hell, even Bat Masterson came here from Dodge City.

By the 1920s, Hot Springs was at its peak and everybody that was famous came through here. You could see Babe Ruth walking the streets or hanging out at the track, betting on horses. Dizzy Dean was a regular. All the major league baseball teams came to Hot Springs for spring training, drinking the mineral water to get strong and sharpen the reflexes. Famous opera singers came here, poets and politicians. But they didn't just come for the water and the baths. They came because this was *the place* to come, to celebrate, and to have a good time.

The clubs and floor shows here were famous all around the world. People *lived* just to get back to Hot Springs and the Southern Club, the Belvedere, the Palm Club, the Tower Club, and the Vapors. Hot Springs, back then, was what we called an *open* city. Gambling was everywhere. You could gamble on any street corner. Prostitution was open. You could snap your finger and have a woman. Miss Daisy's Piggly Rooms was the most famous house of prostitution in town, and it was here from the turn of the century until they tore it down in '66. It had a saloon on the first floor and rooms on the second floor. Hell, everybody had a story about going to the Piggly Rooms. ▶

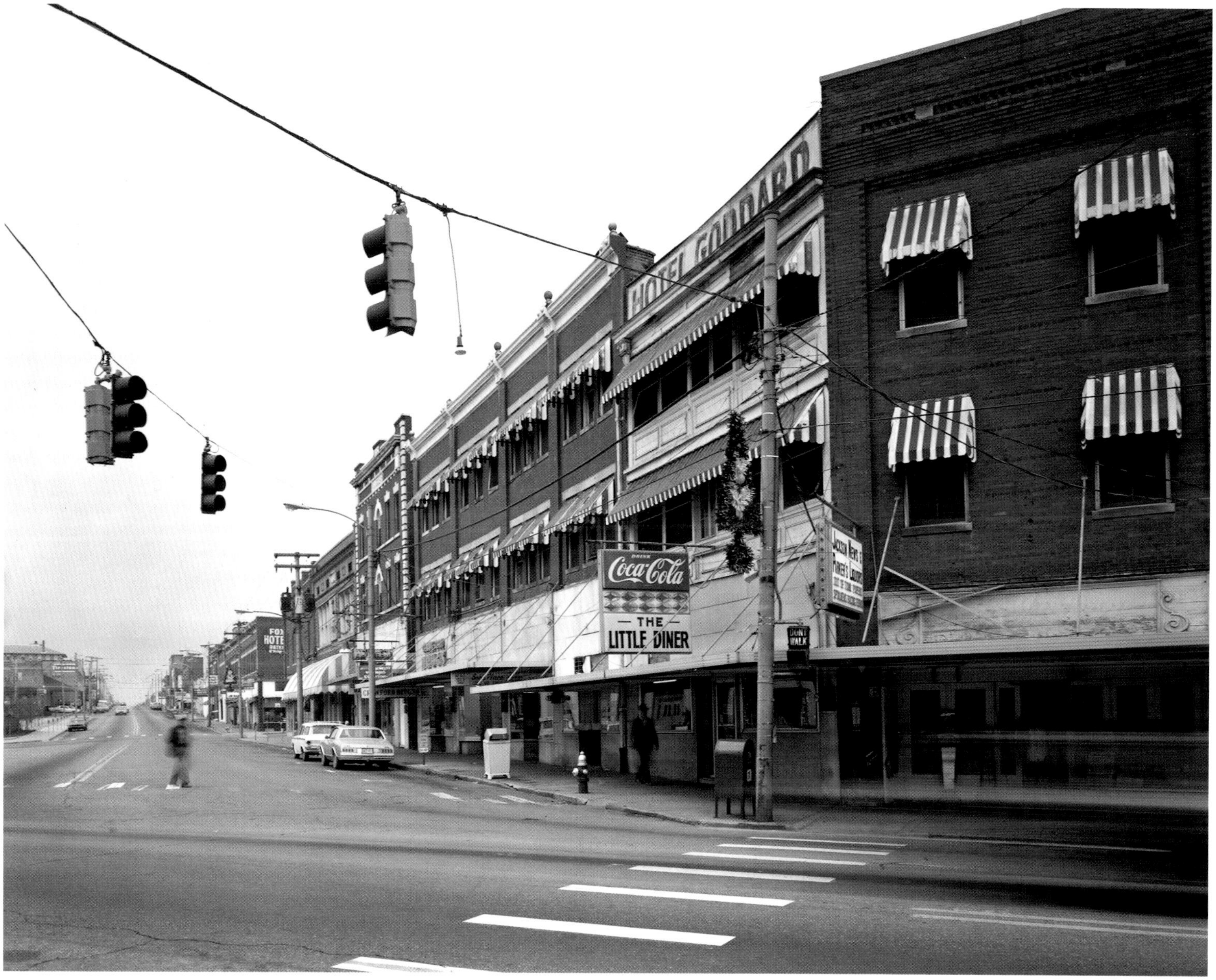

Intersection of Central and Ouchita Avenues
Hot Springs (Garland County), Arkansas

Yes sir, Hot Springs was River City, as they say, there was plenty of *trouble* right here in River City. The politicians was always fighting about who was in charge, and those were bloody fights. There were fires that burned most of the city to the ground, and flash floods that nearly washed it away. But Hot Springs always came back. What finally took Hot Springs down for good was politics. Politics and the church people. Governor Faubus finally had to pull the plug. He closed down illegal gambling in Hot Springs, and that was the beginning of the end. That was in '64, and Hot Springs—the great place that everybody came for fun—was a goner from that day on.

Now look what we got. We got an amusement park, just like every place else has, and we got a bunch of art galleries. It's all legal, and I guess that's good.

But what have we lost? They turned the old Belvedere into a golf course and country club. What used to be the Southern Club is a wax museum—I wonder how much fun they were having in the wax museum last night?—and the Vapors Club was converted to a *church* building.

What we have lost is *Hot Springs, Arkansas*, because Hot Springs is gone.

David Garner
John's Shoe Repair
Hot Springs, Arkansas

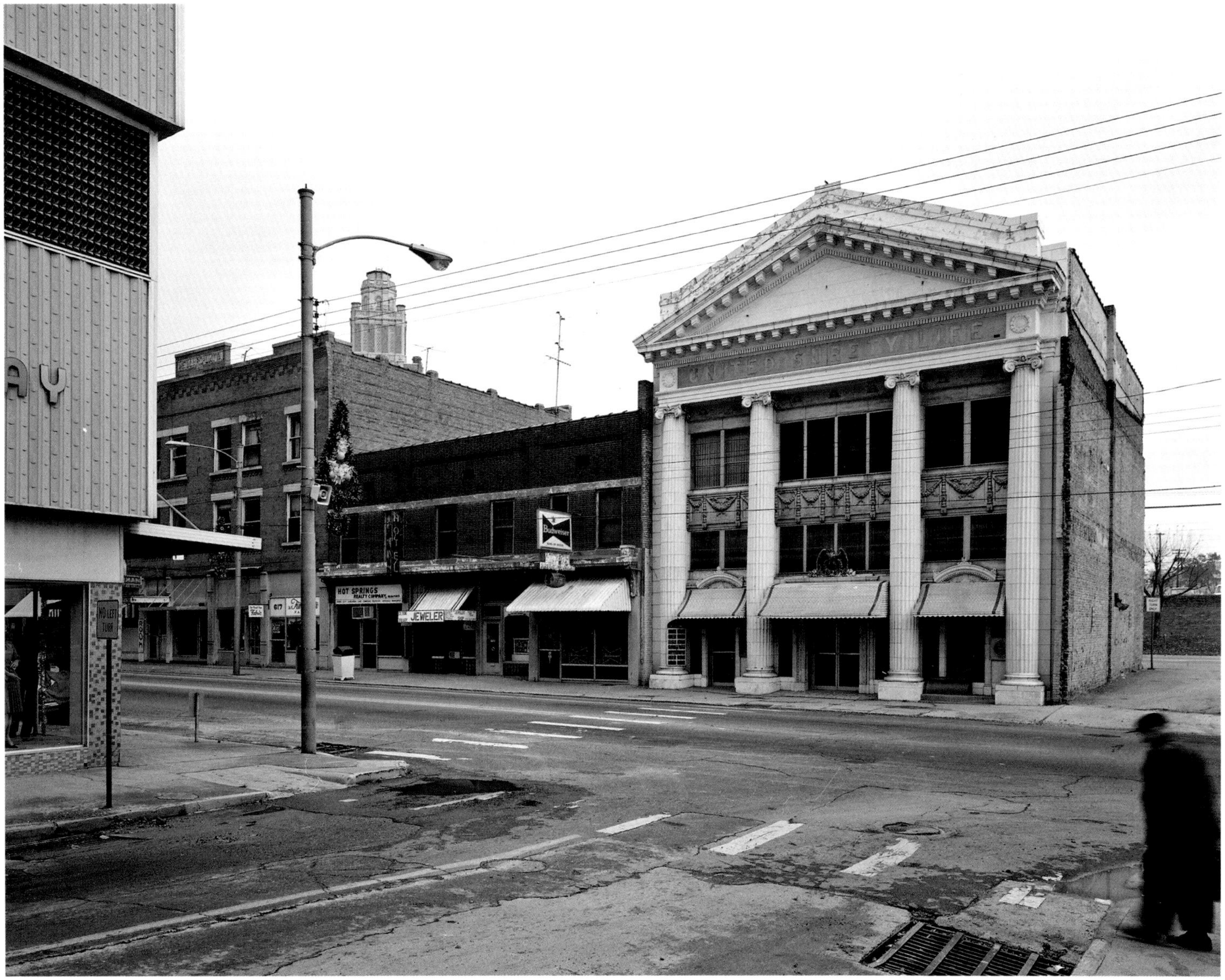

Beaux-Arts commercial building with attached Ionic portico
Central Avenue and West Maurice Street
Hot Springs (Garland County), Arkansas
(demolished)

WHAT YOU DON'T KNOW UNTIL YOU GET OLD is that a place can disappear. You wake up one morning and a place that has been there all your life is just *gone*. I worked in that building right there, the old Goddard Hotel, every day for all those years. My barbershop was right there, on the ground floor, on the west end of the ground floor. They had a café in there, too, and a jewelry store—Holiday Jewelry was the name—and of course they had the old newsstand, Jackson's News, that carried newspapers from all around the world. You could go in there and buy a newspaper from any city in the world. Over there on the other side of the newstand, just outside of the picture, that was where they had the entrance to the sleeping porch. If you couldn't afford a room, you could pay a dollar to sleep overnight on the open sleeping porch.

You know, that looks a lot like old man Britt there. He was one of two brothers who came here from Illinois, bought the hotel, and ran it for many years. That sure looks like old man Britt.

Over time, the old hotel just wore down. It got old and it wore down. When the roof started leaking in the shop, I told myself I better get out of there before the whole place comes down on my ears. So I moved on out of there. By the time I moved my shop out, the newsstand and the jewelry store had already gone. I was the last one to leave.

The old hotel just sat there, the roof falling in and getting to be a safety hazard. Then a woman—I think she was from Chicago—she come in and made an offer to buy it. She was planning to put a lot of money in it and fix it up. She was connected with a church group, the Nazarenes, as I recall, but the word was that she had been a call lady herself. I never figured that one out. Anyway, she put some money down on the old hotel, talked about what she was going to do with it, fix it up and all, and then she didn't make another payment. So they took it back and finally, in '08, they tore it down. That's the story of how that place disappeared.

William Bennett
Hot Springs, Arkansas

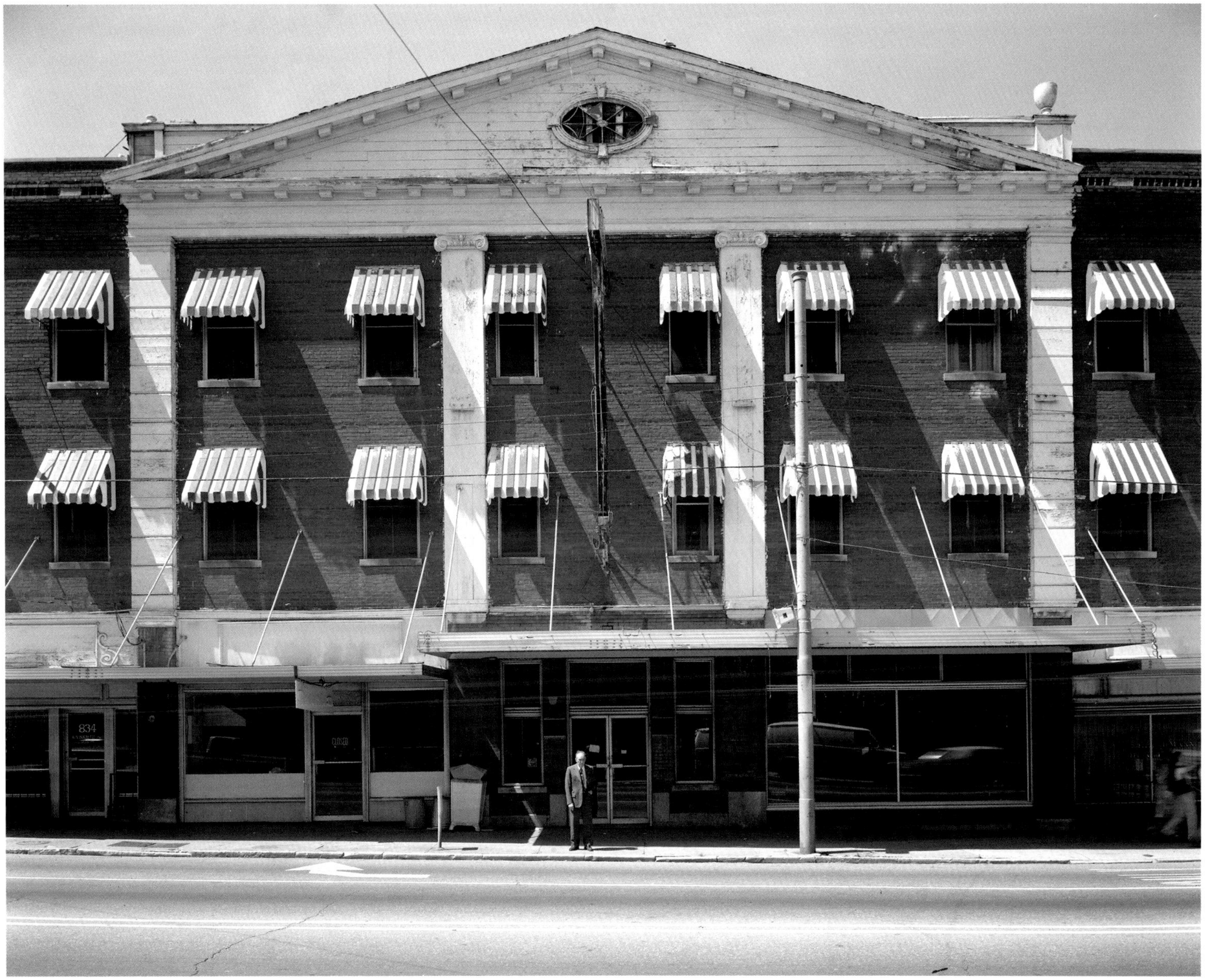

Colonial Revival hotel of brick with attached colonade in antis
Goddard Hotel
Grand Avenue
Hot Springs (Garland County), Arkansas
(demolished)

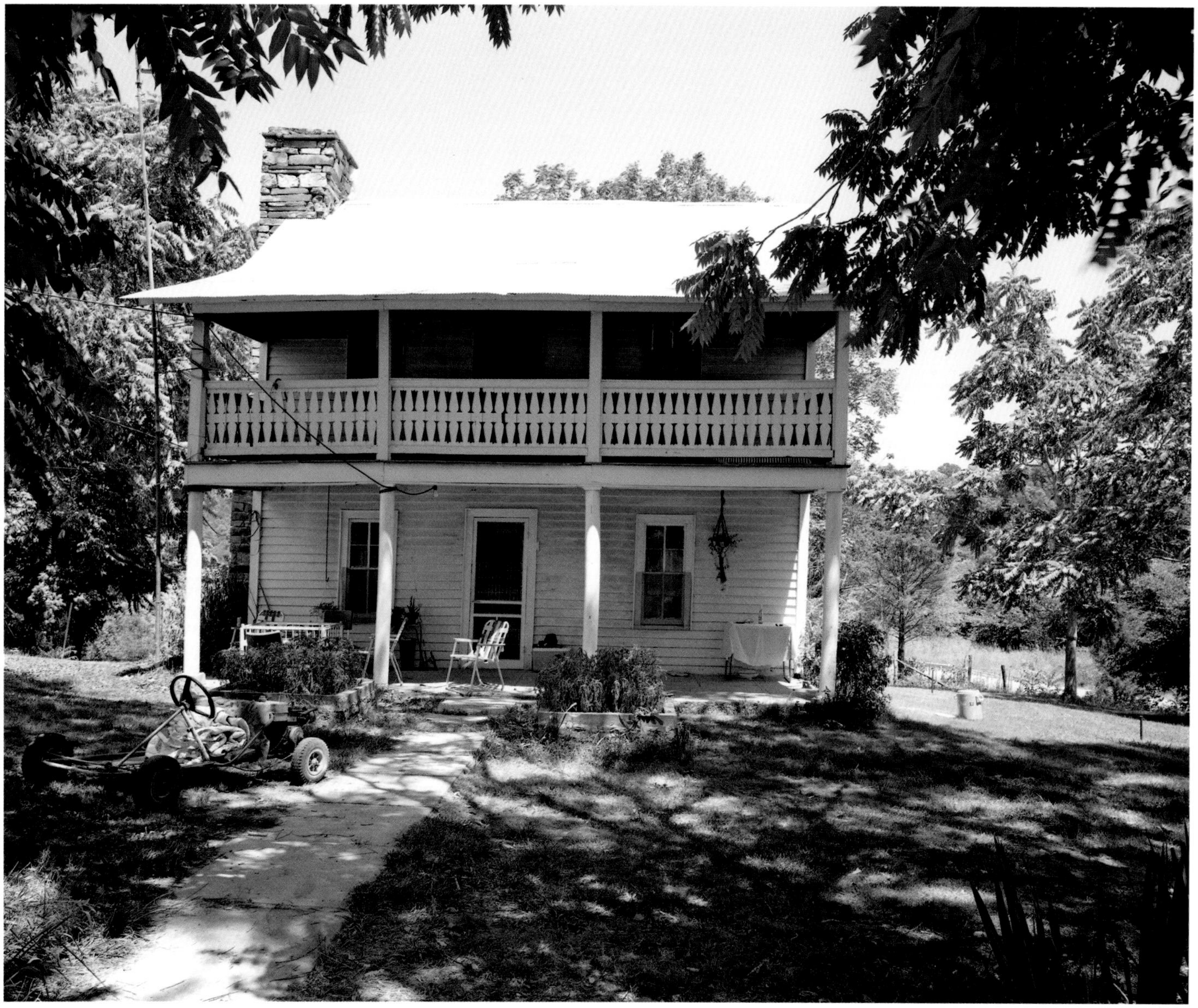

Mountain house with profile gallery railing
Wesley (Madison County), Arkansas

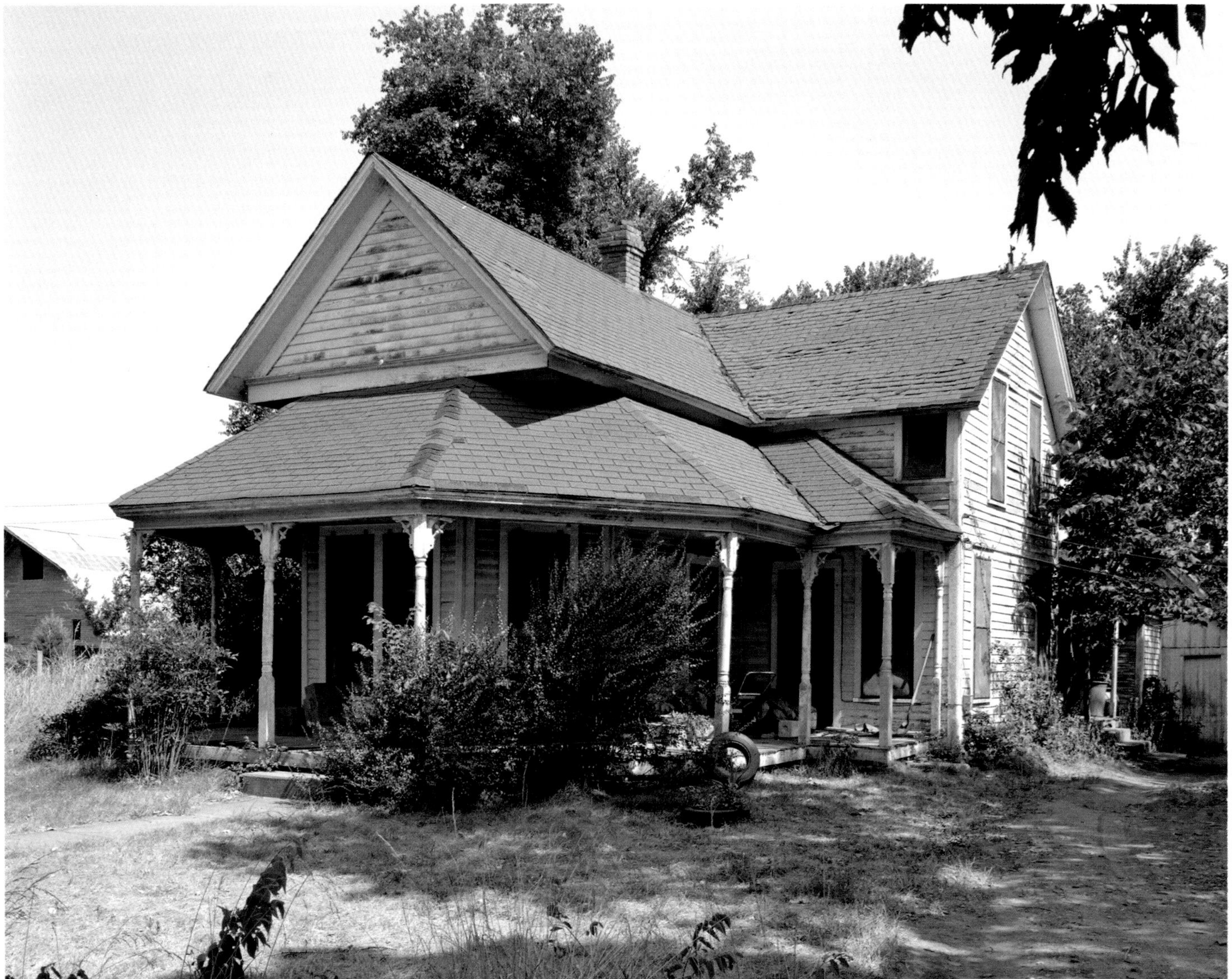

Sophisticated wood frame Queen Anne cottage
Mountainberg (Crawford County), Arkansas

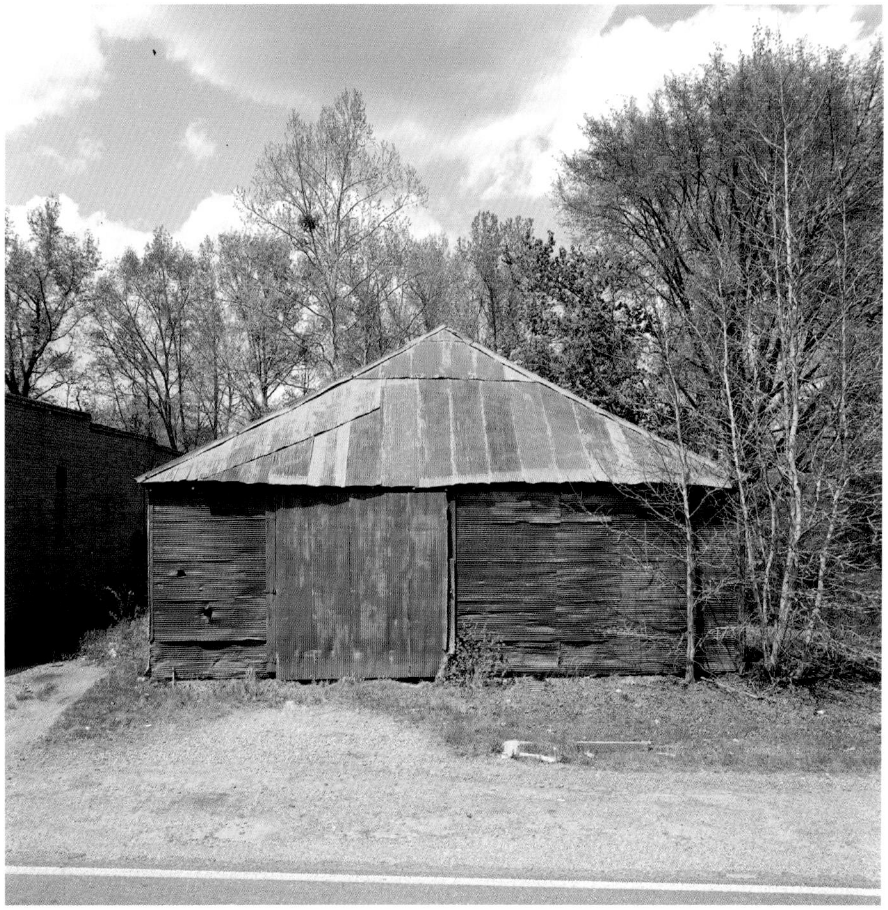

Roadside commercial building with corrugated metal siding
Havana (Yell County), Arkansas

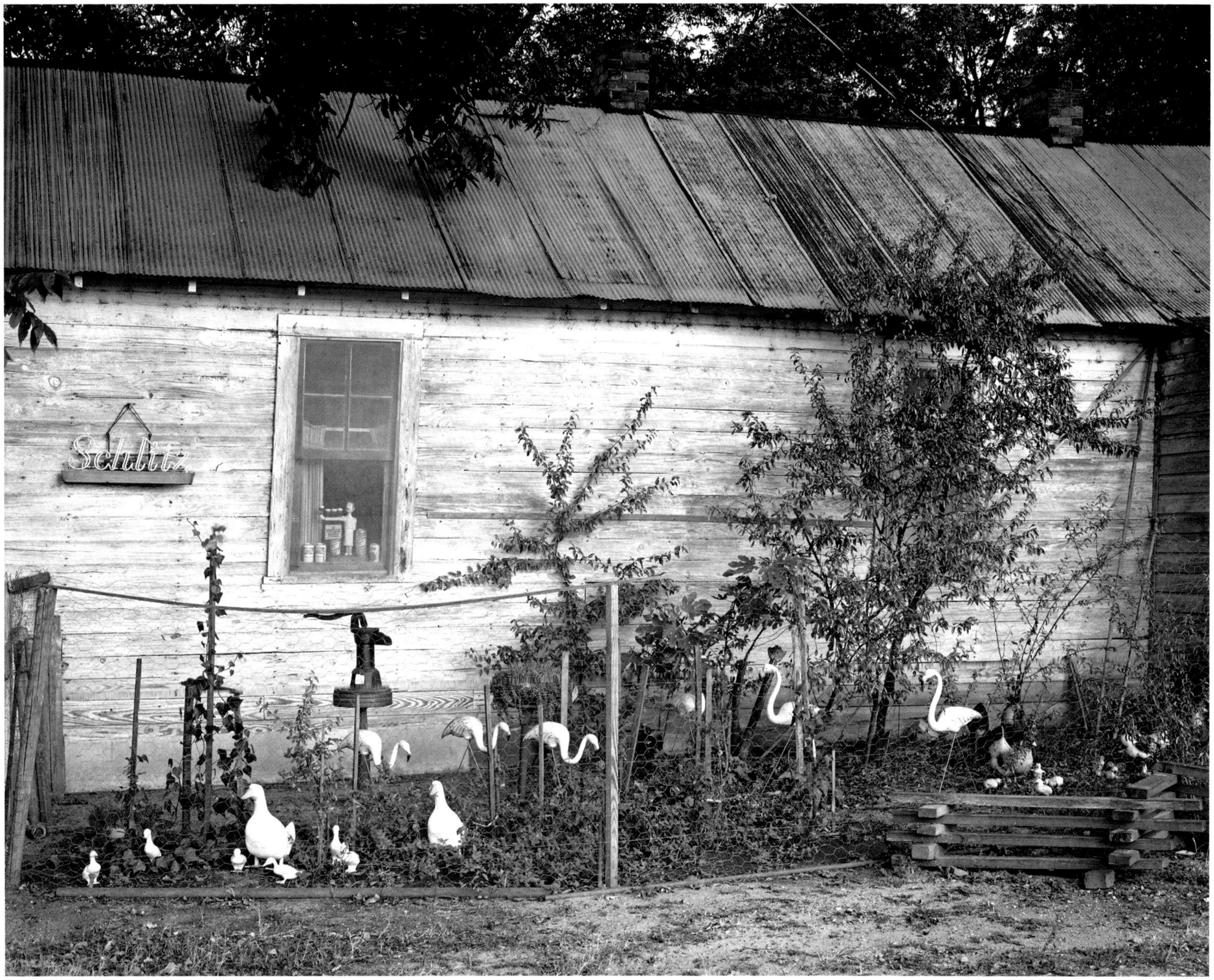

Wood frame shotgun house with ornamental yard figures
Arkadelphia (Clark County), Arkansas
(no longer standing)

THAT WAS THE COUNTZ BUILDING. It was a beautiful building, and why they tore it down, I'll never know. It had a grocery store, liquor store, butcher shop, feed store, pool hall, barbershop, post office, and a mo-tel on the top floor. I feel like Ola died when they took that building down. Now the town is just a ghost of its self, and it's a sad thing to see.

The original name of the place was Red Lick. That's what I been told, but I don't know where they got the name. Then the town took the name Petit John, after the river just north of here. You'd say it like in French, "*petty-john.*" That was before the railroad come in, right about nineteen hundred, the Choctaw Railroad, coming out of Dardanelle. Up to then, there was nothing but a dirt road and oxcarts to take all the cotton from here up to the riverboats at Dardanelle. After the railroad come in, they built a power plant, then a bottle works, a flour mill, and a cotton gin. Ola was a booming town.

It's hard to say what killed it all, but the tornado that come through in 1930 did its share. That was a hell of a storm and it just about leveled the town. Lots of people picked up and left after that. Just moved on. My momma, I remember, the rest of her life whenever she saw a dark cloud coming, she would run for the storm shelter. She would stay in that shelter all night, scared to come out, remembering that tornado.

The Countz Building was one of the few buildings that survived the tornado. Bully Countz run his grocery store on the ground floor, and my family used to buy groceries from him. I remember that deal he had where you could buy from him on credit. He'd write it out, write it on a ticket, and then he'd put that ticket there with your name on it in a little file box. When you was ready to pay your bill, Bully would pull out all your tickets, add 'em up, and you would pay. Used to have five, six grocery stores in Ola. Now we hadn't got *one* grocery store in town. Not *one*. We got to drive all the way to Russellville or Dardanelle just to buy our groceries.

Jackie Harrison
Ola, Arkansas

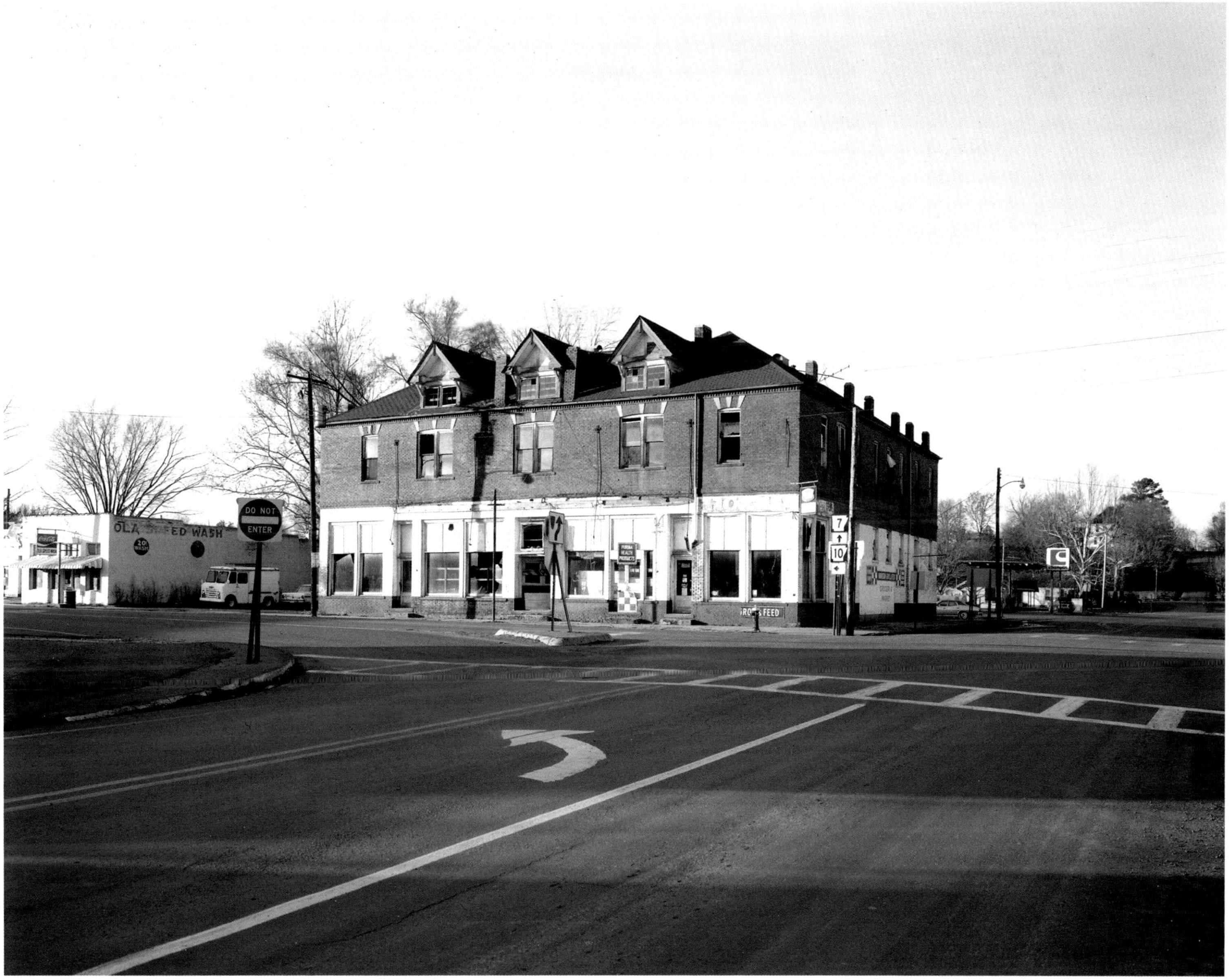

Brick commercial building of combined purposes
Countz Building
Ola (Yell County), Arkansas
(demolished)

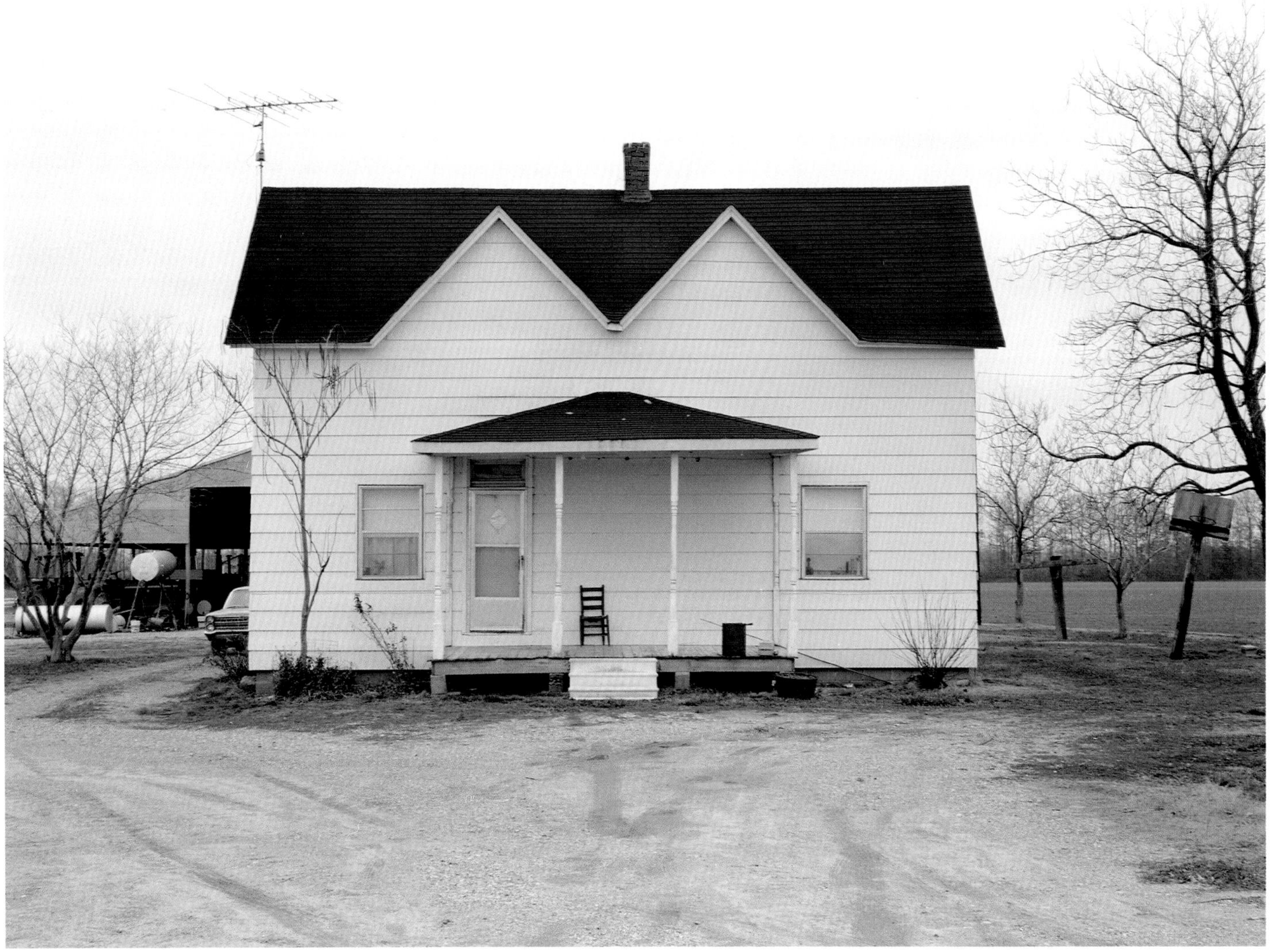

Wood frame double house articulated by gable, metal siding
Mist (Ashley County), Arkansas

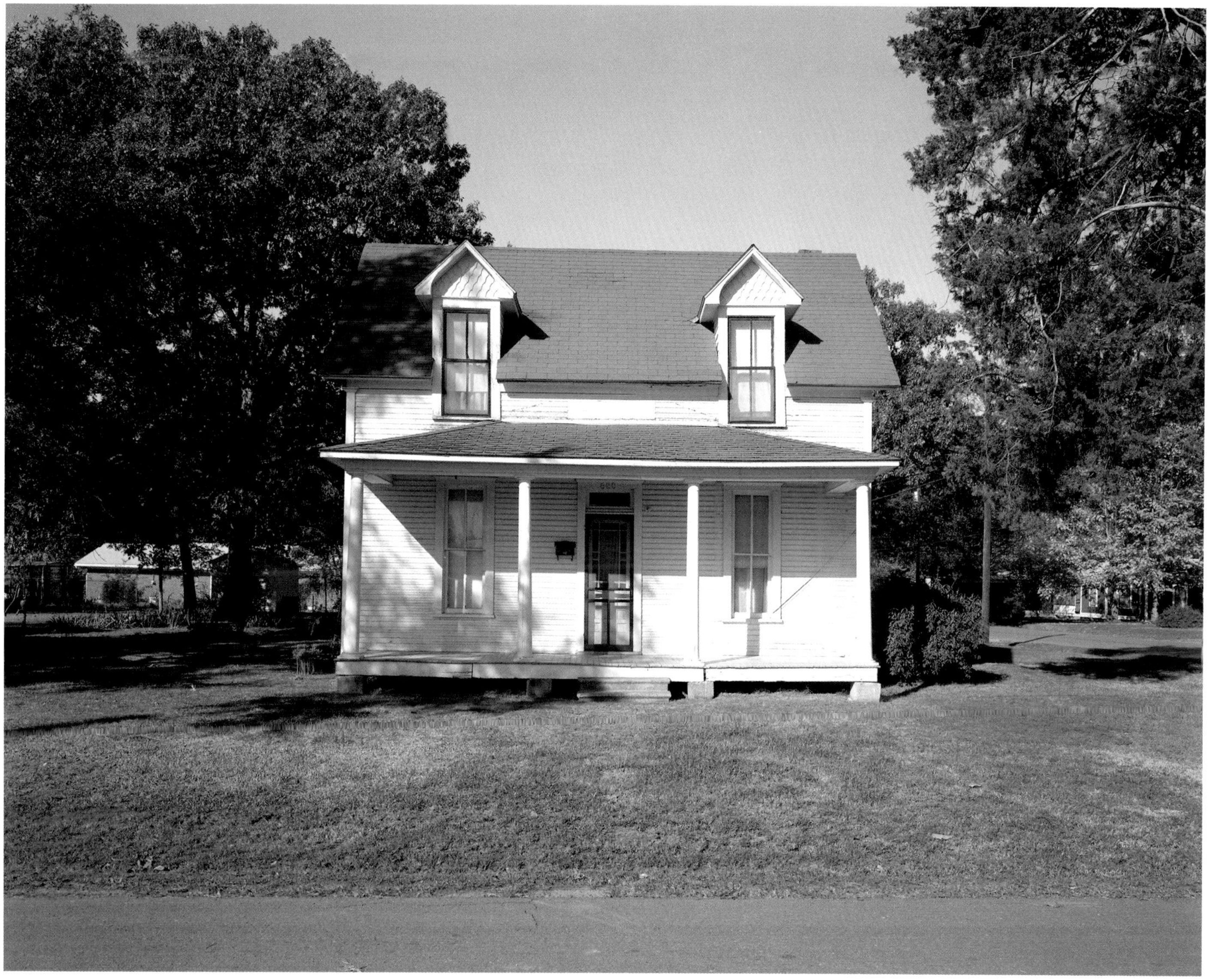

One-story wood frame cottage with inset dormers
Roe (Monroe County), Arkansas

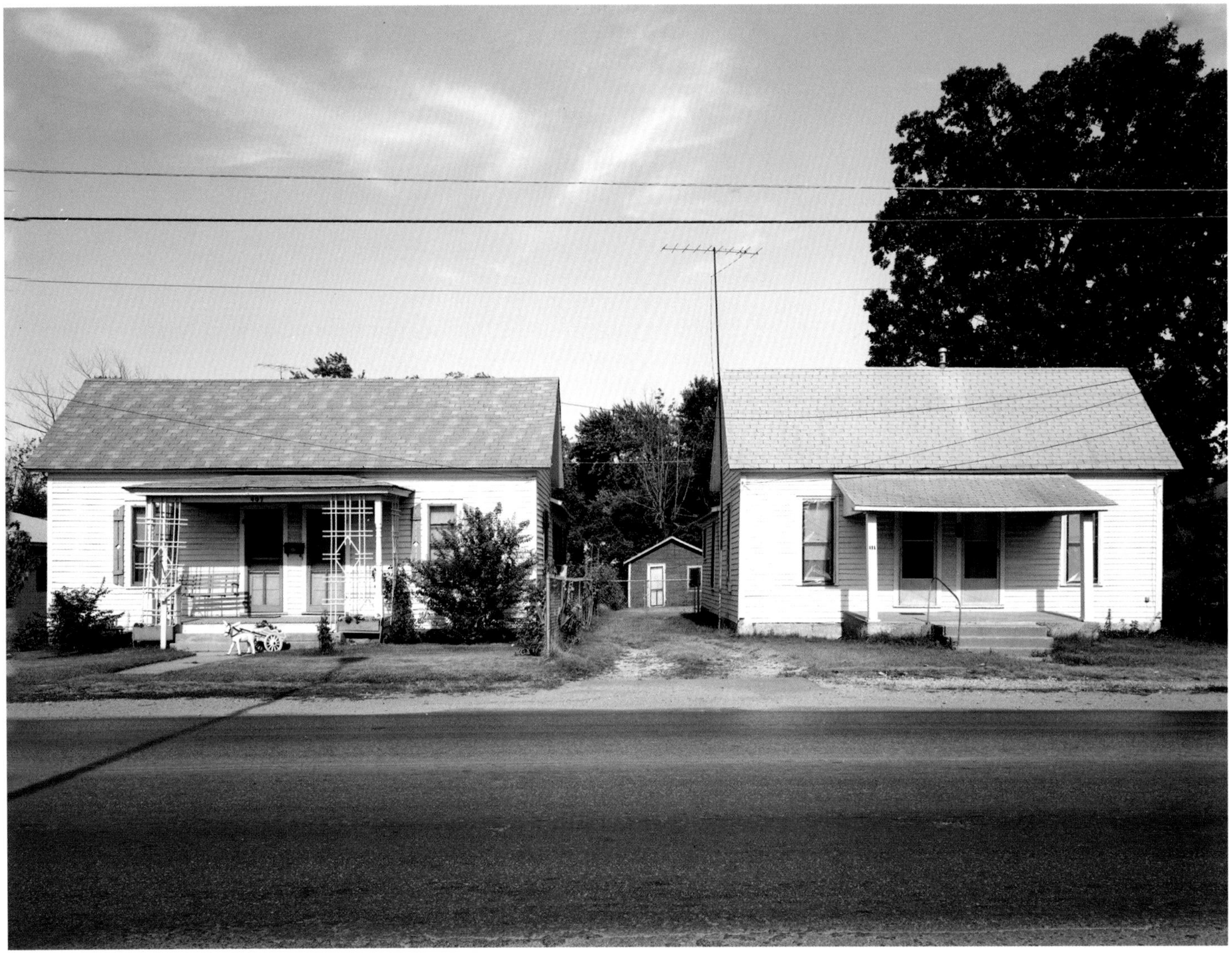

Two wood frame double cottages
Ozark (Franklin County), Arkansas

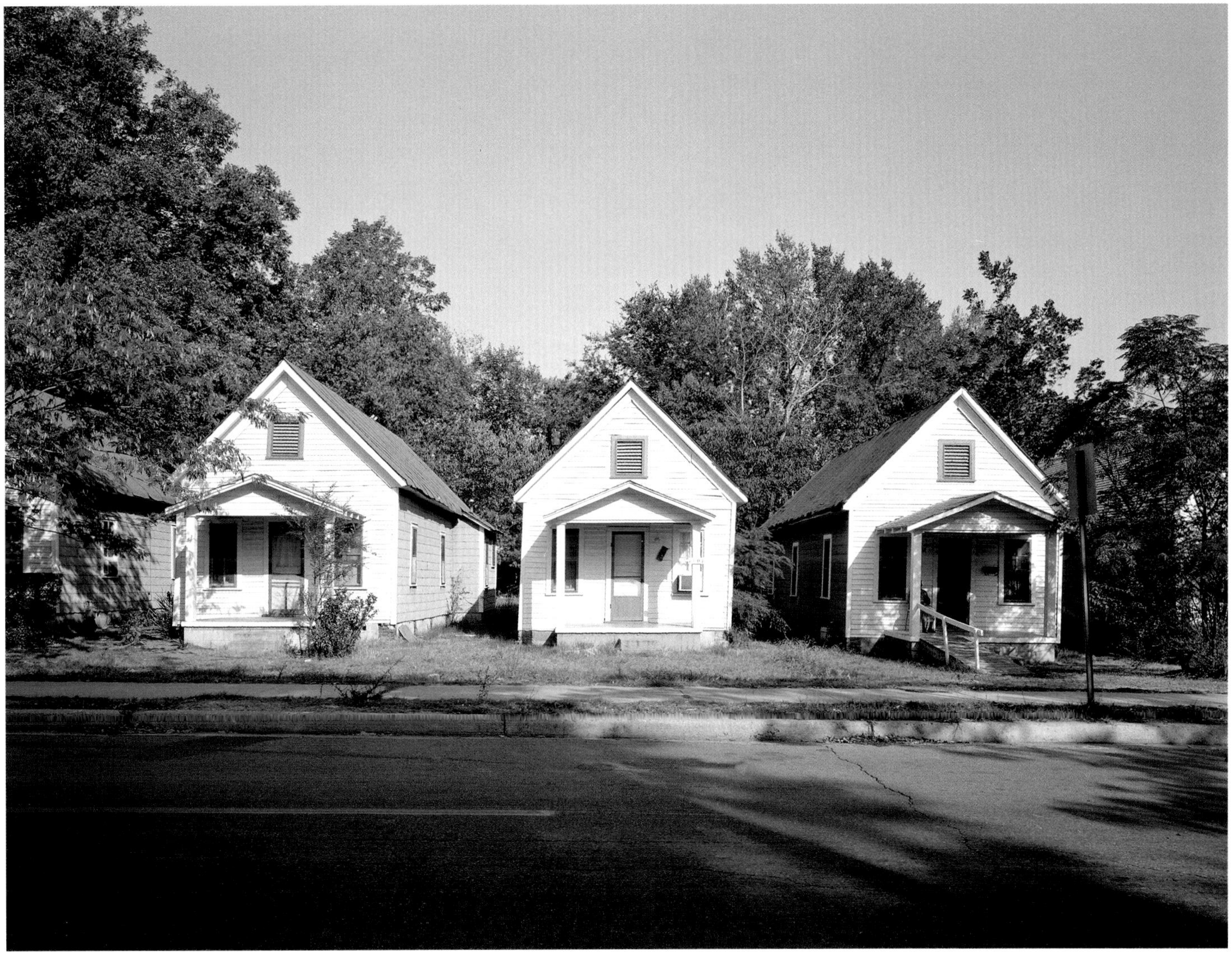

Three identical wood frame shotgun houses
Little Rock (Pulaski County), Arkansas
(demolished)

THIS USED TO BE A SLEEPY LITTLE TOWN SQUARE, a lot like every other town square you would see all over the state. It used to be that when you came to town you had to drive *around* the square to get through town. The road through town took you *around* the square, past all the stores and cafés and whatnot. You had to do that to get through town, and that was good for all the businesses on the square. Of course the courthouse was right there on the square, too, and so many people came into town from the country just to go to the courthouse. They came to the courthouse to get married or pay their taxes or go to court or whatever.

Then, back about 1972, there was a big fight about this, but when it was all over they just cut the highway right through the middle of the square. They took out the little park and the bandstand and just let the highway run straight through the town. I know they had their reasons for doing that, but I don't even like to walk over to the café anymore. I just hate crossing that busy highway.

What else has changed is the Hispanic population, and that's plain to see. All you got to do is look at all the Mexican restaurants and you know. We got two of them on the highway coming into town and two more going out. Two Mexican restaurants on each side of town. They're popping up all through the Ozarks, while most of the other restaurants are fizzling out. The Mexicans have been coming and settling here in bigger numbers for I would say the last fifteen years. Some of them are here legally, and I assume that some are not. But you don't hear much mouthing about that because they're good people, family people. They obey the law, they work hard, and they don't ask for any handouts. We have a chicken processing plant outside of town here that employs a lot of workers. A lot of the Mexican people work there, and the truth is that there are not many locals—and by that I mean *white* people—who will work all day pulling the guts out of chickens. It's too easy to draw welfare, or disability, or sell drugs. That's just the way it is. You can make what you want of it.

I went to school in Greenforest, the next town over. I like to say we have a dialect here and I call it hillbilly. That's all we ever heard growing up. Hillbilly. That's all we heard and so that's all we knew. Now you hear people in the street talking to each other in Spanish. You go into the stores and you see signs in Spanish. Even on the loudspeakers in the schools, they make the announcements in English and in Spanish.

Berryville has become a two-language town.

Vineta Wingate
Berryville, Arkansas

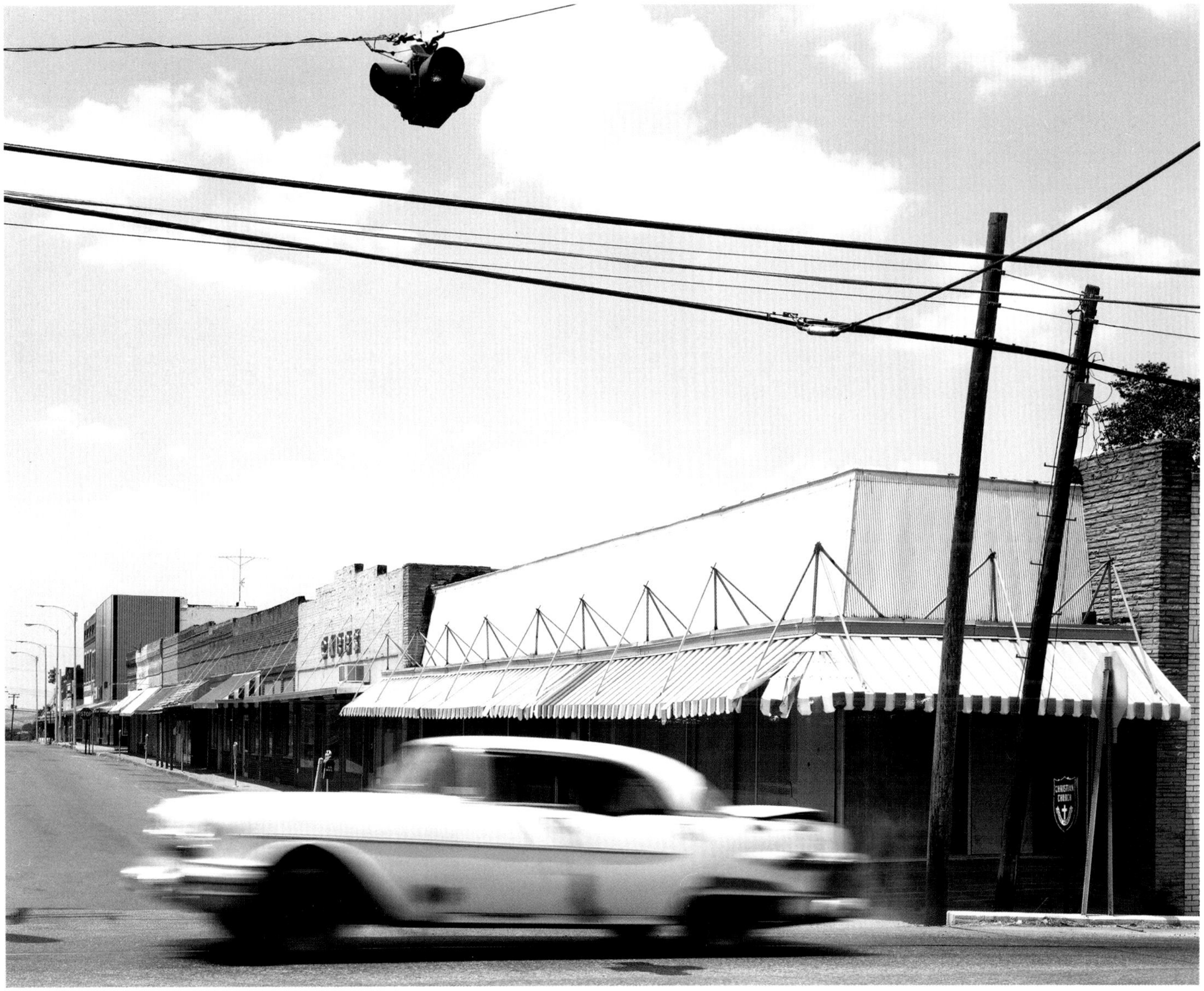

Town Square
Berryville (Carroll County), Arkansas

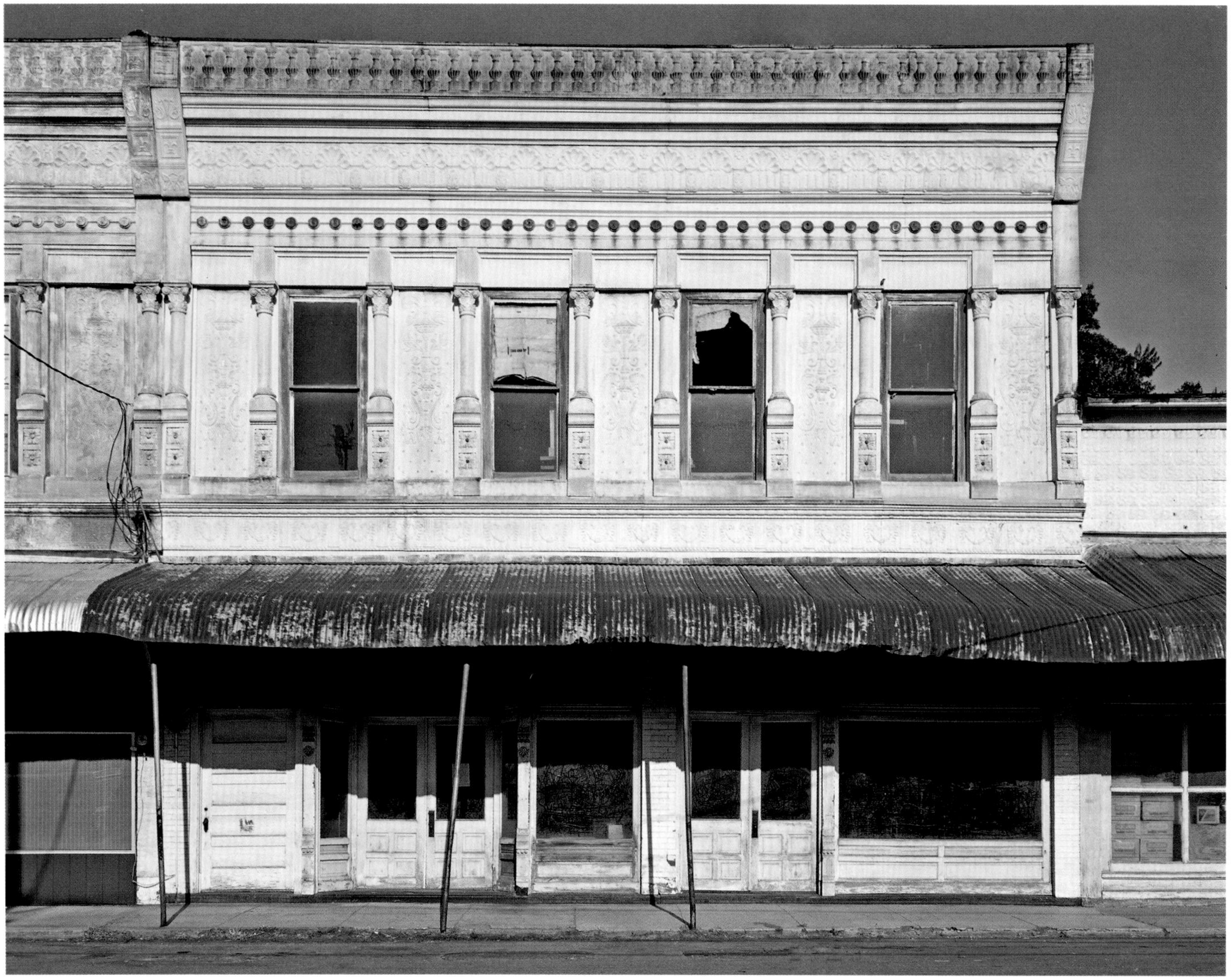

Tin front commercial building with residential quarters above
Prairie Grove (Washington County), Arkansas

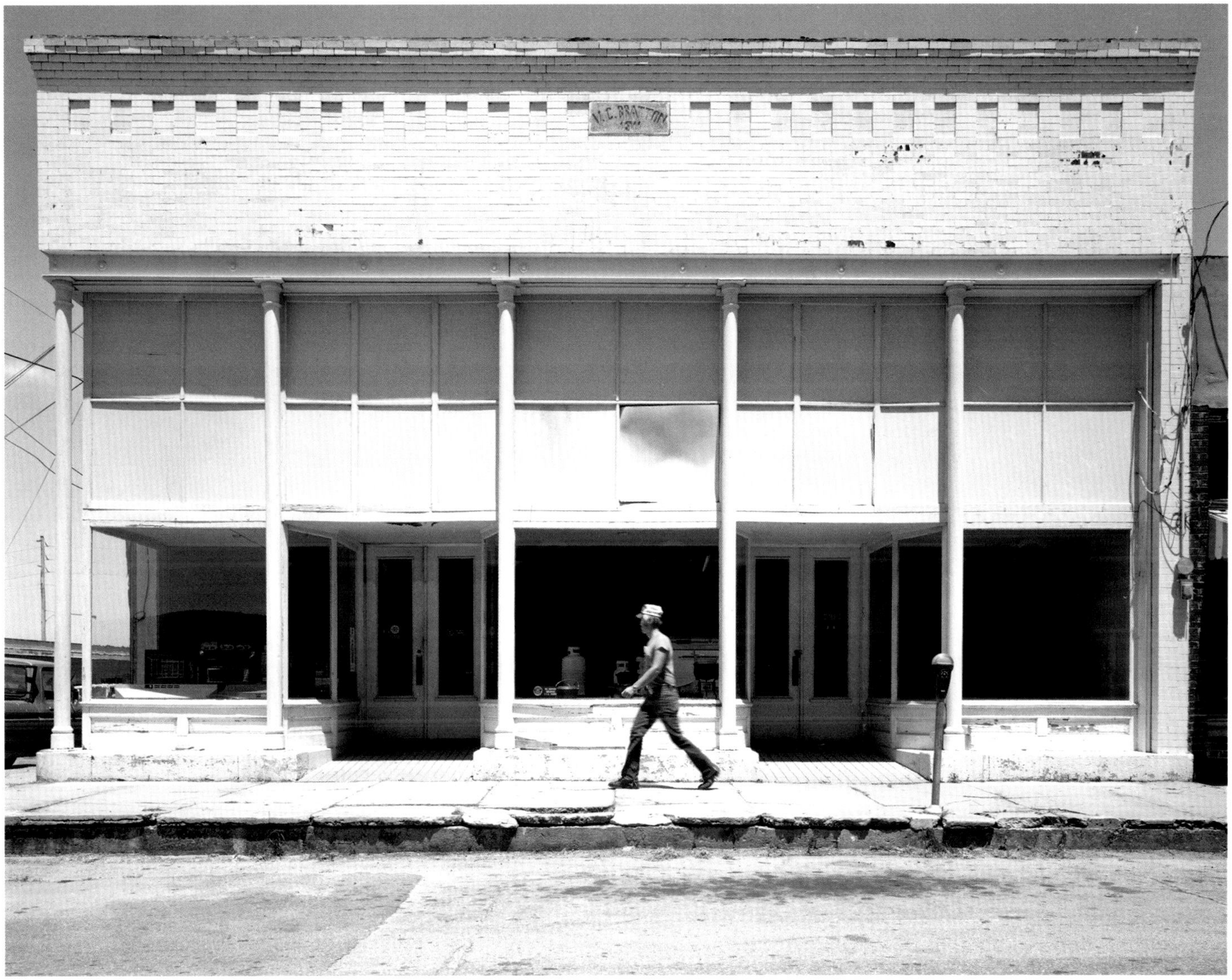

Brick commercial building with cast iron colonnade
V. C. Bratton Building
Marshall (Searcy County), Arkansas

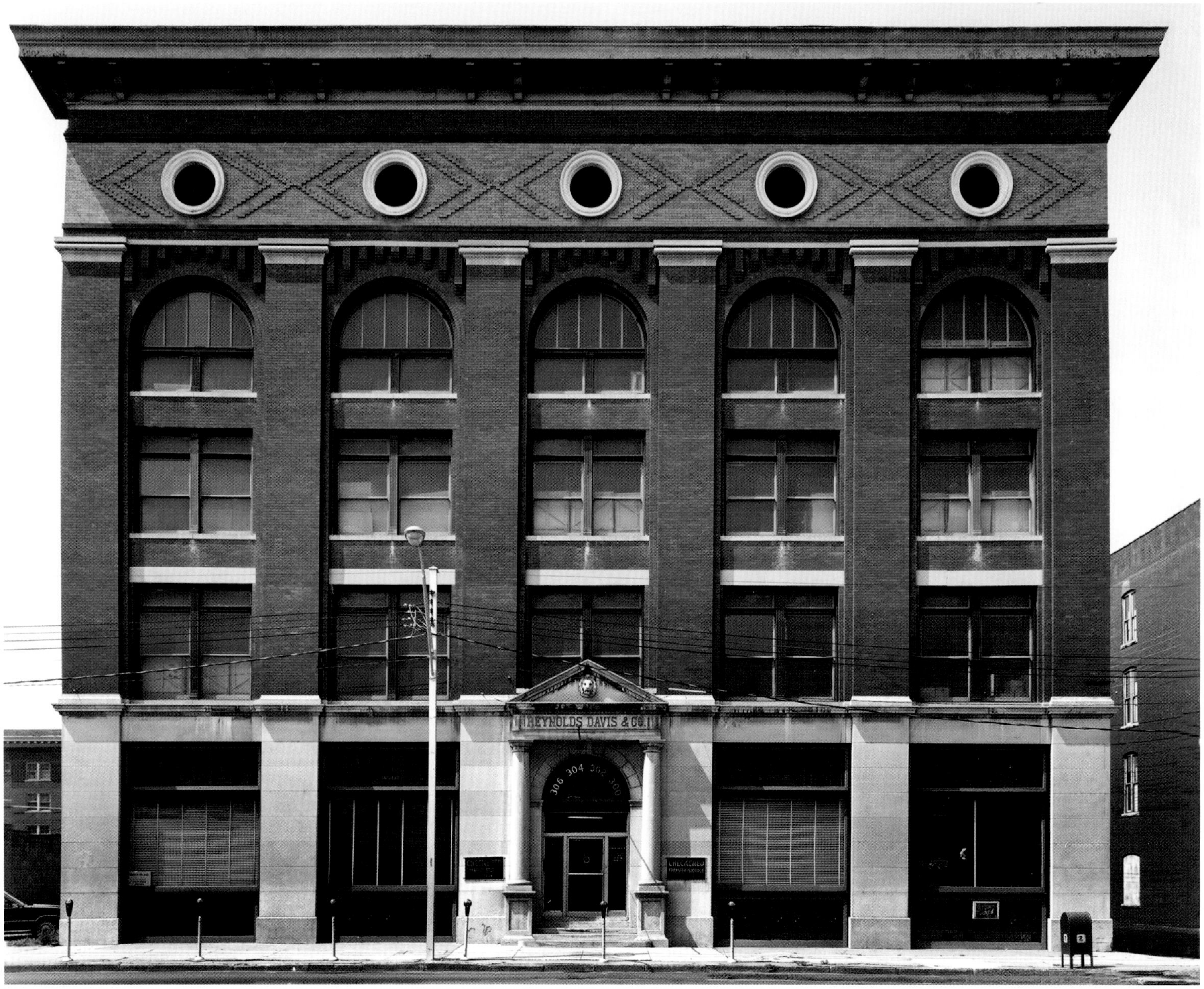

Brick and terra cotta office building with store fronts on ground level
Fort Smith (Sebastian County), Arkansas

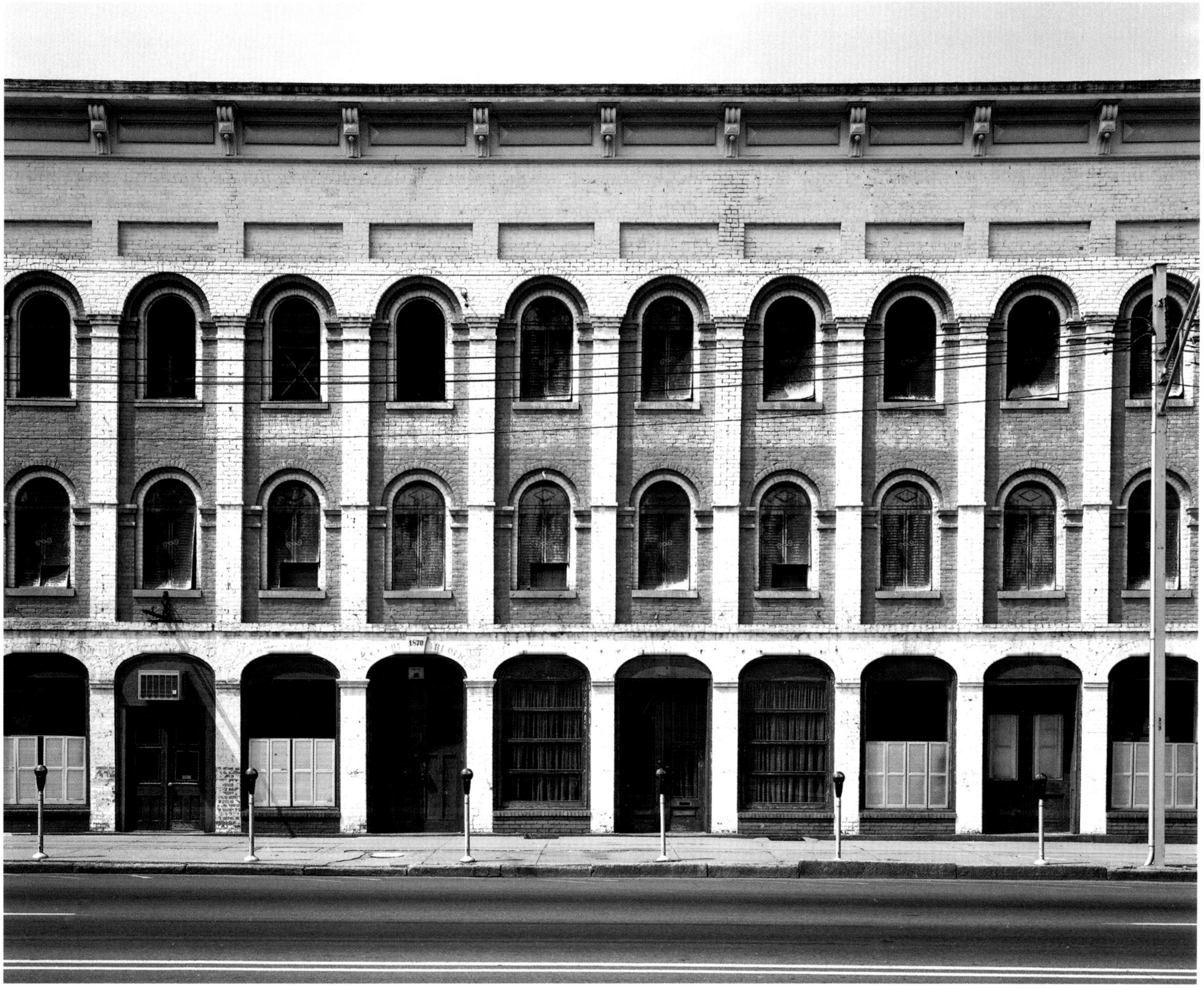

Arcaded brick and iron office building
Fort Smith (Sebastian County), Arkansas

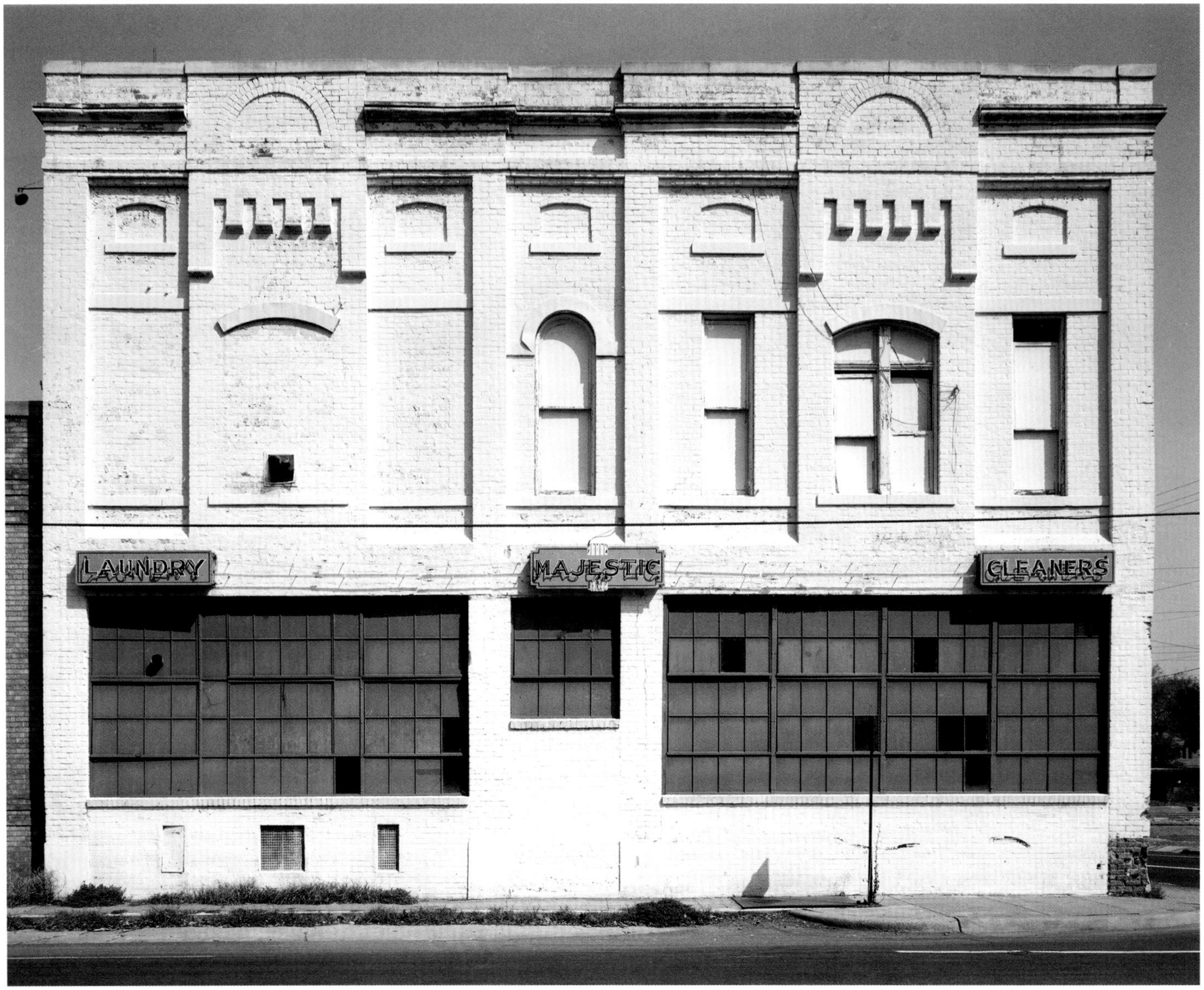

Brick commercial building with Romanesque details
Little Rock (Pulaski County), Arkansas

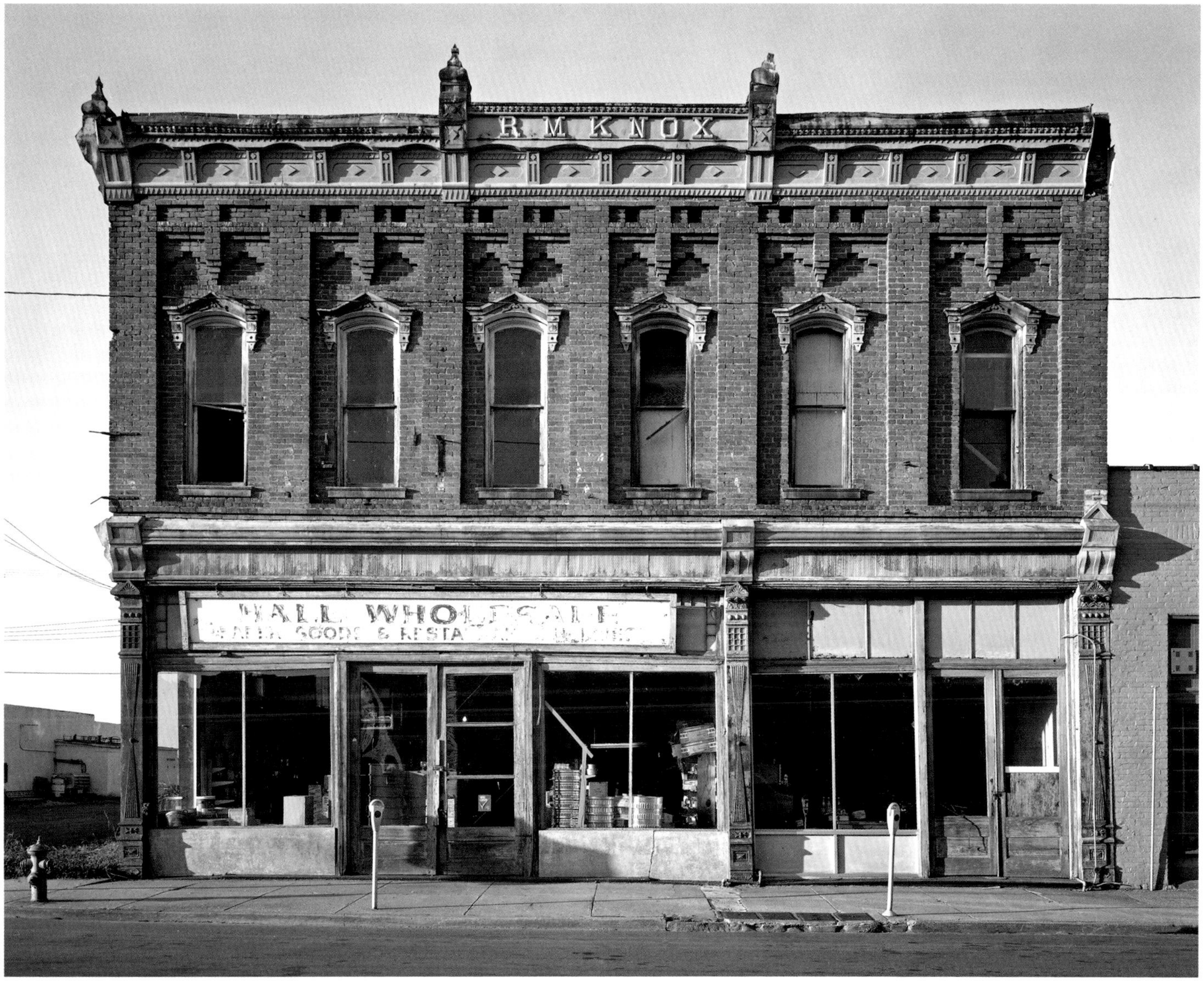

Brick commercial building with Renaissance Revival details
R. M. Knox Building
Pine Bluff (Jefferson County), Arkansas

THIS WAS OLD MAN WOLFF'S STORE. Rufus Wolff was his name, and I used to ride my bike down to his store every afternoon. Back then I could buy a drink and a candy bar for twenty-four cents. I'd be sitting right there on the porch, eating my Milky Way and drinking my Coke, and Mr. Wolff, he'd come out there and sit with me and talk.

Old Rufus Wolff, he catered to everybody. He sold whatever the farmers around here needed. He had a dock on the back of the store where he sold feed. He sold groceries. He sold clothes. He even carried these high-laced, pointy-toed shoes that was real popular with the ladies back then. Powell White, he lived down the street, and he liked buttermilk. So Mr. Wolff, he kept buttermilk in the store icebox, just for Mr. White. And of course the Bingen Post Office was right there in the store, with a personal mail slot for everybody in town. When they finally come to take the store down—that was sometime in the '80s—there was still mail in some of those mail slots, even though the post office had closed down for over twenty years.

The day they took the store down, I set up there on the side of the road, set there on a log where they had cut down one of the trees that had grown up right by the store, and I almost . . . well, let me say it was just a very sad thing to see something like that, them taking that store down. I don't know why, but I expected them to find a treasure chest or something under the store when they got it all down. So I asked one of the workers that day, when they was hauling that store away, I asked him, "Did you find anything under that store?" He said, "Yes sir, we did. We found about a million bottle caps."

Where am I *from*? I come here from the end of electricity, out of Yellow Creek Farm, out south of Saratoga, between Saratoga and McNabb. We had a farm down there, my family did. We had 480 acres. We homesteaded down there, come from up east and abroad, you know, back when everybody migrated west, right after the Indians and the tea parties and all that. We homesteaded there, in the blackland bottoms, what we called it.

Then I met this young lady who lived here in Bingen. Her parents homesteaded this property, but they got up in age and moved to town. There was a little what you call *camp house* out here. It wasn't much, but the roof didn't leak and the wind didn't blow in. So that's where we lived after we got married, and I started fixing it up. Of course, Mr. Wolff's store was right down the road, and he must of seen that I could drive a nail and saw a board. Seen I was handy. Course he didn't know how many screwdrivers I burnt trying to wire that place.

When people ask me what I do for enjoyment, I tell them I watch the grass grow. To me, this is a little piece of paradise, what with the quiet and the grass growing all around and the creek moving through. You know, God intended this life to be a paradise. He meant for us to sit on the creek bank and enjoy life, have a one-on-one conversation with Him, not this rat-race, stick-it-to-you world we got today. He gave us a paradise to start with, then Adam and Eve went and messed it up for the rest of us, and we been paying for it ever since. ►

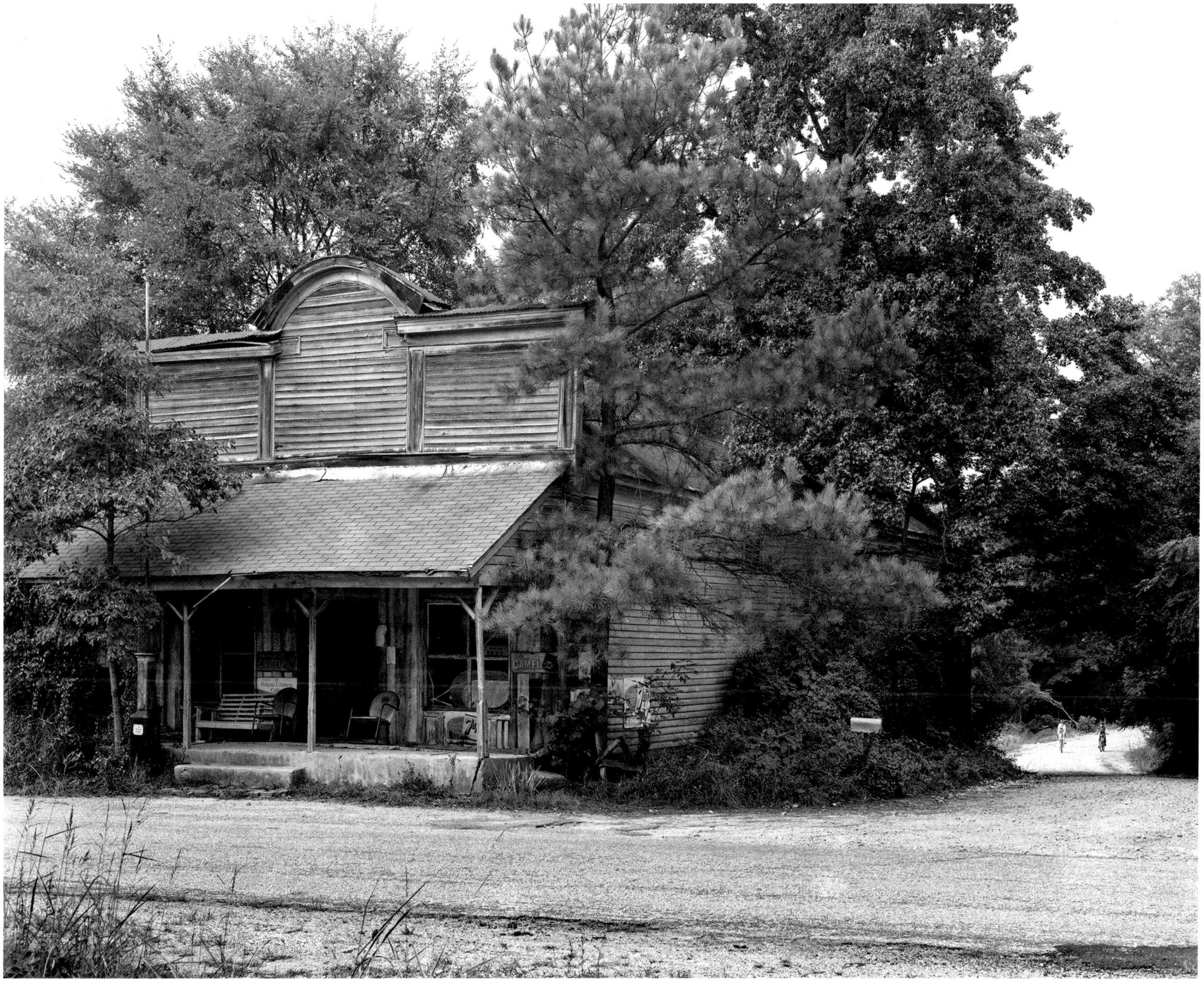

Wood frame commercial structure with false front
Wolff Store
Bingen (Hempstead County), Arkansas
(relocated)

You know, I seen lots of the world since I been driving that truck. I delivered Sheetrock all over this country, north all the way to Chicago, west all the way to San Antonio and south to Florida. I seen it all. I go to Houston a lot, and I've learned my way around all the highways down there. I can take you straight to the skyscrapers, without so much as one wrong turn, but there's no way I'd live down around there. No way at all.

Last week I was I was down there in the skyscrapers, down by that Minute Maid stadium, what they call it, and I saw a place where they were feeding people who been living in the streets. Homeless people. They was sitting at picnic tables behind a eight-foot chain-link fence. They was feeding those people behind that fence, right there next to that multi-billion-dollar stadium, and I stopped my truck so I could look. But I couldn't understand that. *I just couldn't understand it.* What can you say? Life goes on.

I remember one day, way back then, old man Wolff told me that the university—the Muleriders, what they call them, from over at Magnolia—they was wanting to buy some of his land and move that school over here. But he wasn't going to sell his land to them. These people, the Wolff family, they just didn't sell their property. You had to be part of the family or you wasn't going to get any of their land for any price. That's just the way they was. So that's why nothing much happened here in Bingen. The Wolffs, they owned all the land, and they shut everybody out. Finally, they all died, and everything they built just started falling down.

Long after old man Wolff died, and the store had just been sitting here all those years, some guy from Little Rock, I think his name was Anthony, he bought the old store. I heard that he bought it partly because his daughter was in the antique business. So she came down and took everything in the store. Those old high-top, pointy-toed shoes, still in the box, I was told she got two hundred dollars a pair for them. She took everything out of that store but what was nailed down. That was in the '80s. Then the store just set there like an empty shell for years. Some people thought it was haunted, and for sure it was a sad thing to see. People was coming and pulling planks off the wall, taking them away to to make picture frames.

I still take care of the property, up there where the store used to stand. I keep it mowed and I weedeat it. It's just a sort of a good neighbor thing that I do, keeping the property clear. Seems like the least I can do. After I finish mowing it, sometimes I just sit there for an hour or so and I try to understand how it can be . . . how that can be that that store is *gone.*

Clay Hester
Bingen, Arkansas

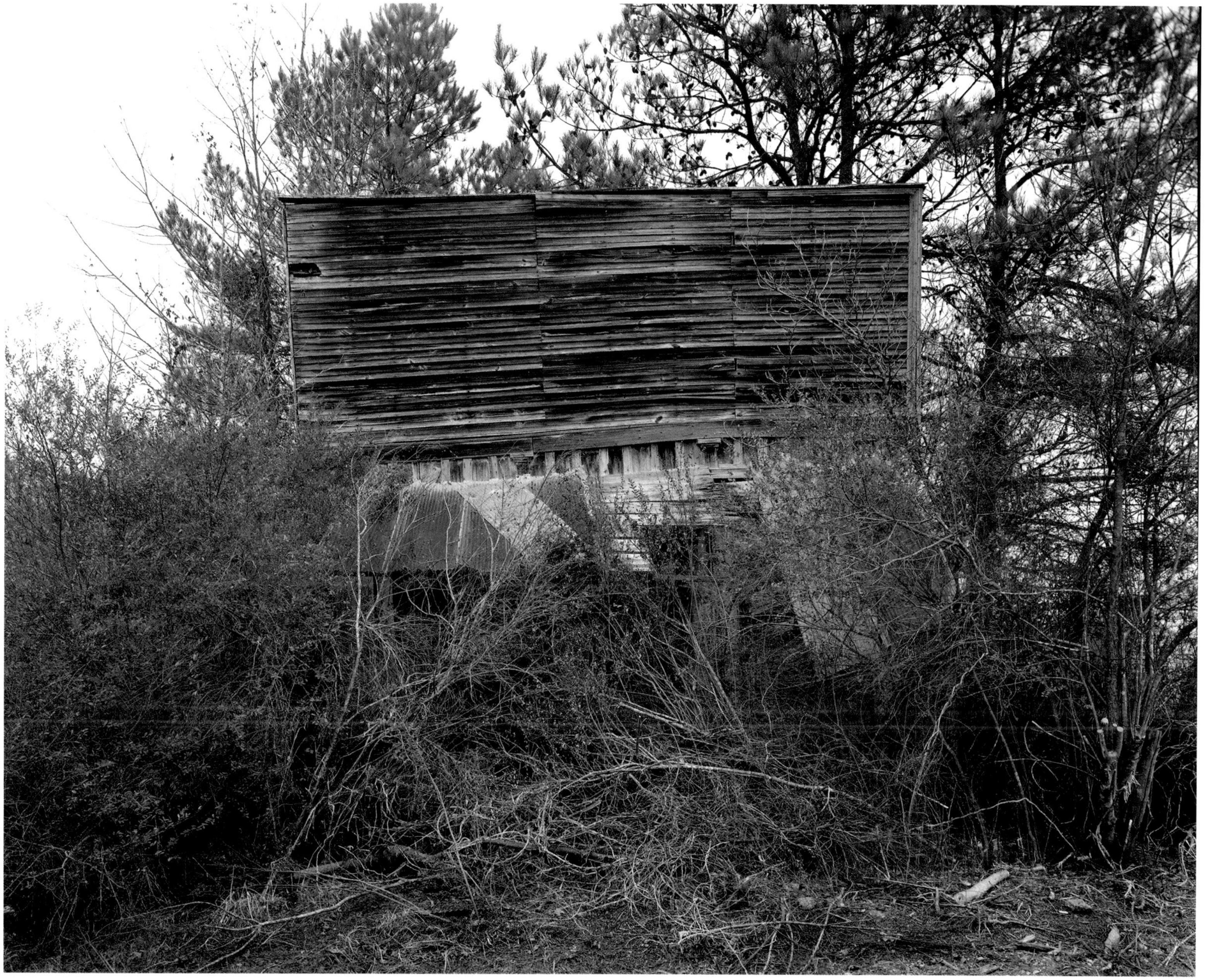

Abandoned wood frame commercial structure
Bingen (Hempstead County), Arkansas

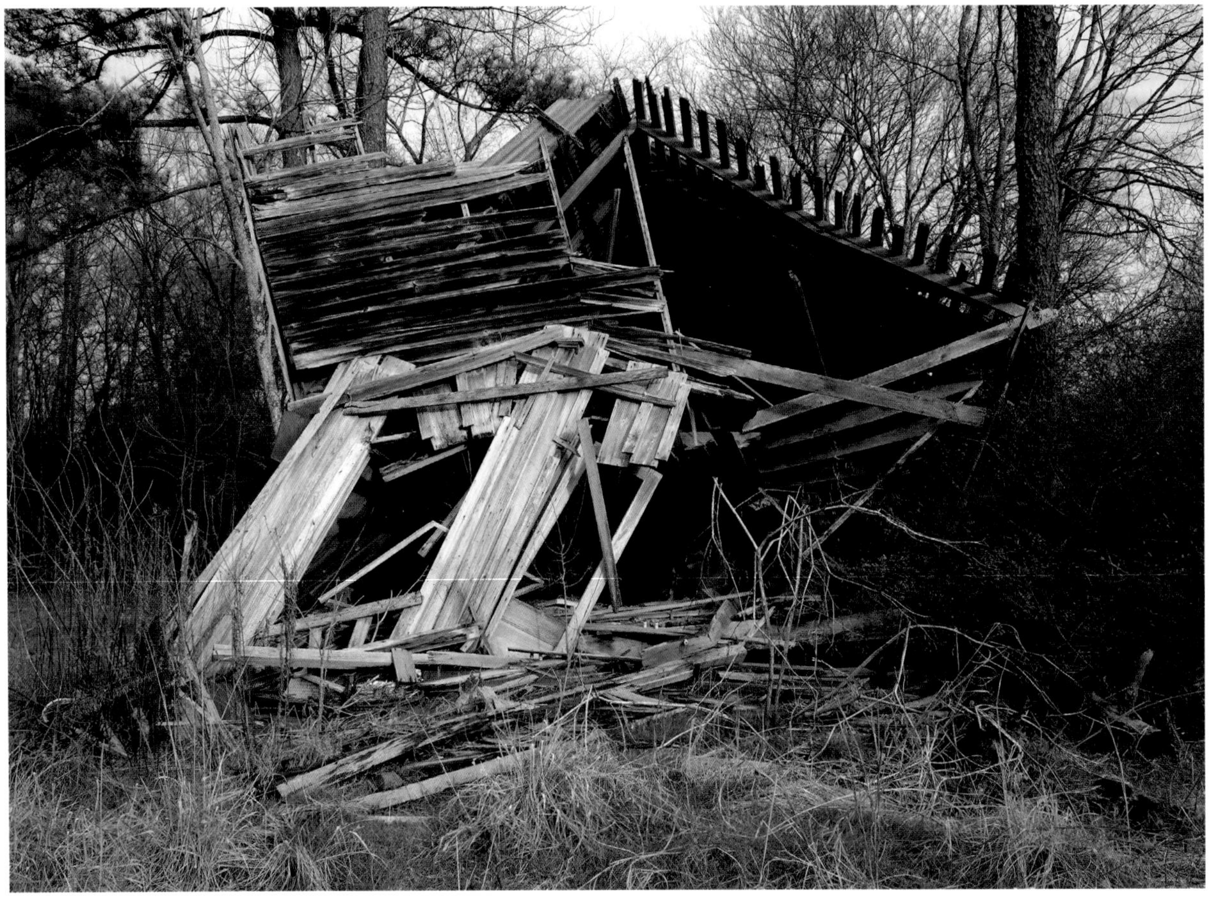

Collapsed wood frame store
Bingen (Hempstead County), Arkansas

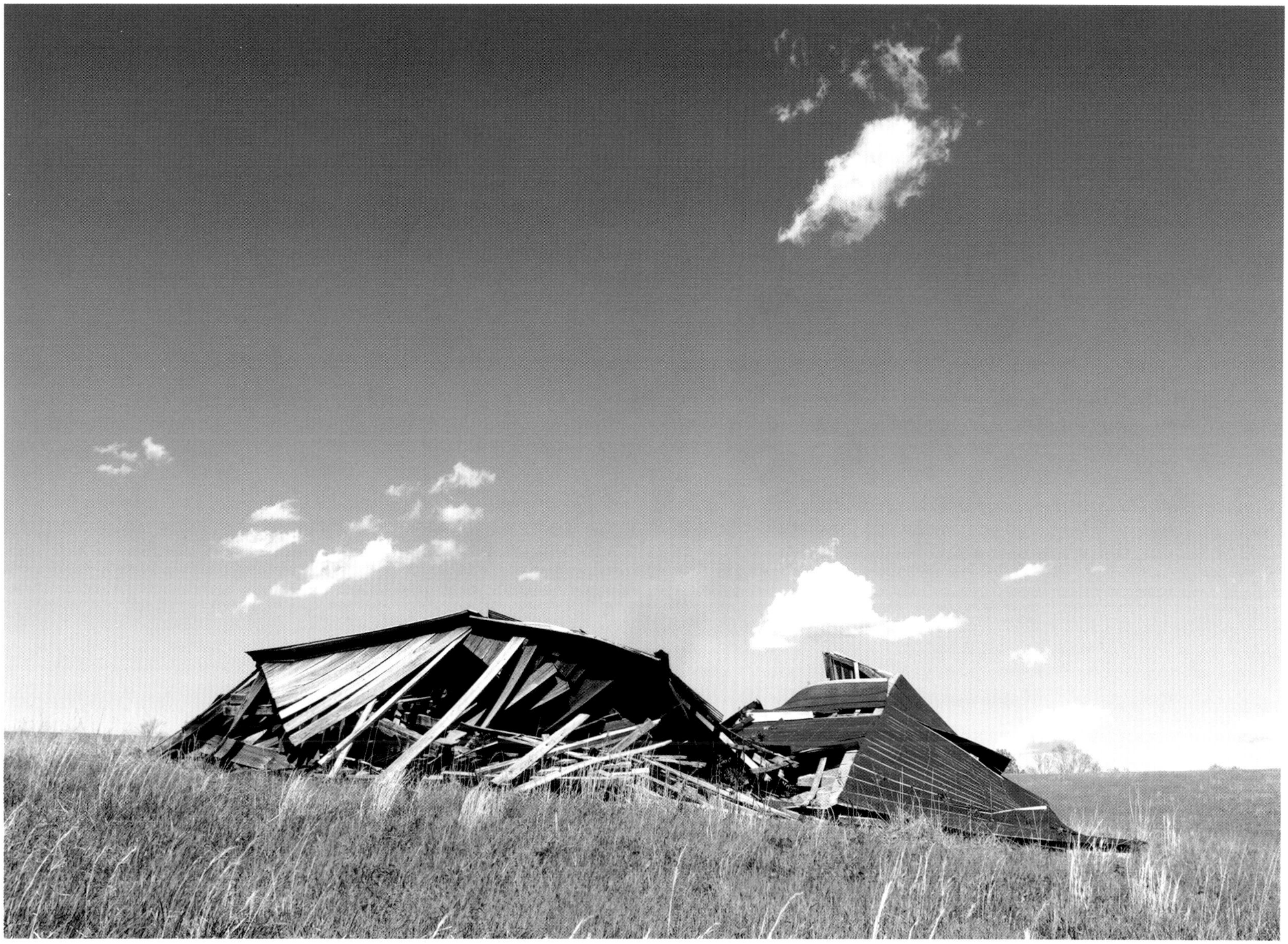

Collapsed wood frame barn
Franklin County, Arkansas

I WAS BORN HERE IN MARIANNA IN 1921. I grew up here. Marianna was a booming river town back then. Riverboats would come up the Mississippi and then up the St. Francis River to Marianna. The paddleboats would come and dock at what we called Miller Landing, and they would bring "drummers," as we called them. Those were the salesmen who came from all over, bringing their goods, their samples and whatnot, in suitcases that were shaped like drums. I guess that's why we called them drummers. So here they came, off those riverboats. They would just *pour* into town. The people from the Hotel Marianna would go down there with carts and bring all their suitcases to the Hotel Marianna, which I could just cry about because somebody bought that beautiful old hotel and just *tore it down*.

Anyway, the boats would come in and bring all the drummers and they would have their samples to show. All the retailers in town would come and look and place their orders. Years later, the drummers came in on the Missouri Pacific Railroad. They'd come in to the old depot down there on Mississippi Street. There was a Magnolia Inn and a Travelers Hotel and the Hotel Marianna, and all of them had their—we called them "redcaps"—but at that time they were all blacks and they all had pull carts. They would take all the drummers back to where they wanted to stay, get them all registered, and show them where everything was.

Marianna was such a booming town back then and such a wonderful place to live. It was an entirely different town than what you see now. We had three old-fashioned drug stores with marble countertops and fancy stools. You could go there and get a milk shake or a chocolate soda. Those drug stores were the real thing, you know, with soda fountains and ornate mirrors on the wall. They're all gone now, of course, and I could cry over that, too. ►

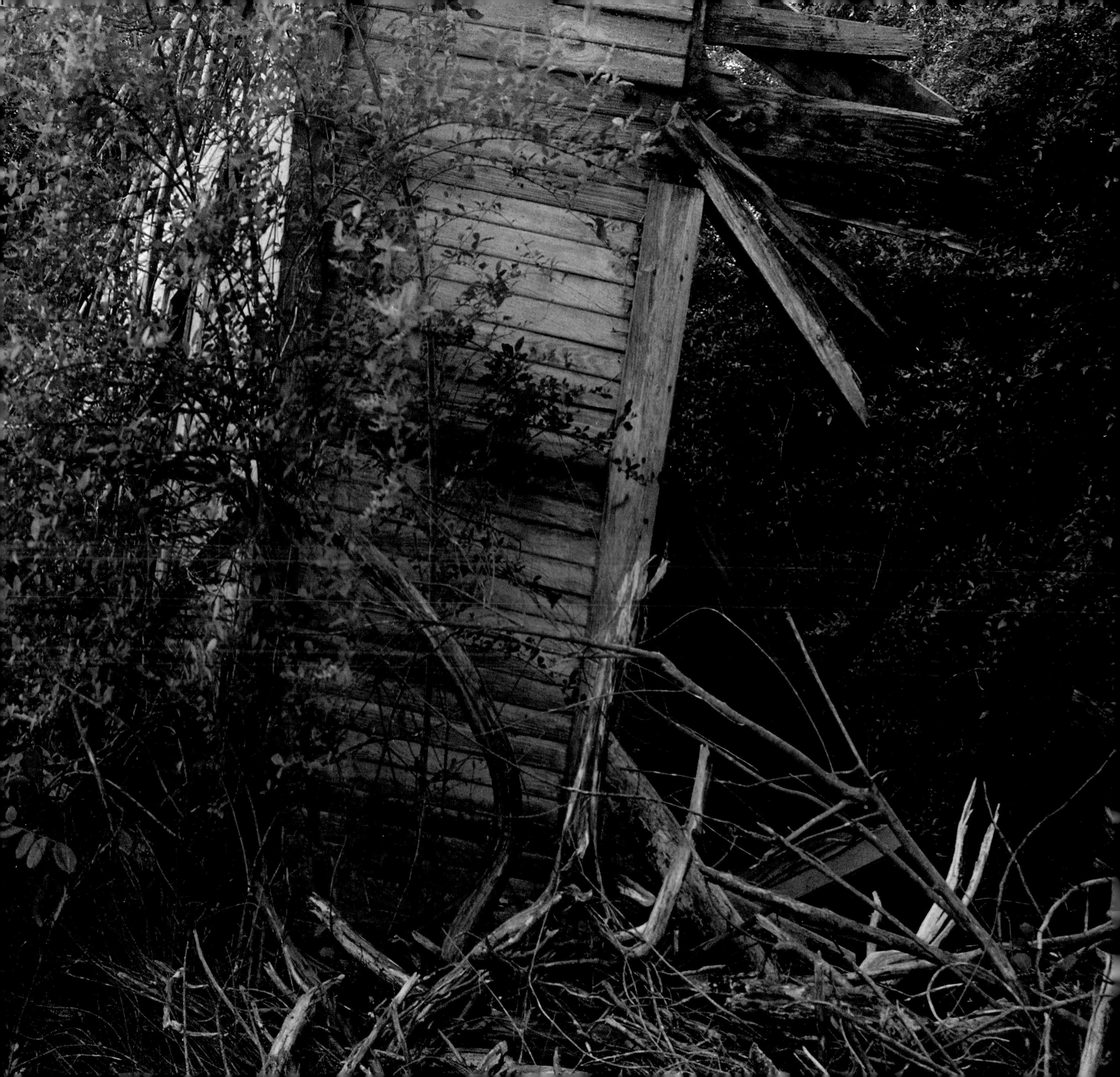

Boxley Valley
Newton County, Arkansas

Acknowledgments

In March of 1980, I met with the late H. Charles Johnson, then president of First Federal Savings and Loan of Arkansas, in his office in Little Rock. It was there that Johnson laid out the original idea that led to this project and this book. First Federal was nearing completion of a new, modern office building, and Johnson had a vision for the art he wanted to hang on the walls of the new offices. He told me that he was looking for "a good photographer with a big black and white camera," who would travel all across the state of Arkansas and photograph the best barns, stores, churches, houses, and other everyday buildings. The commission I was awarded from First Federal to do that photography provided the foundation for this project, which comes to fruition with the publication of this book, thirty-four years later.

The late Cyrus Sutherland, professor at the Fay Jones School of Architecture at the University of Arkansas, was my primary collaborator and partner during the early years of the project. Parker Westbrook was my guide and advisor on other occasions in the early years of the project, particularly in the region around Nashville, Arkansas, where his family had settled generations ago. In more recent years, as I worked to identify many of the structures that I had photographed three decades earlier, Parker gave me his untiring assistance.

I wish to thank Professor Terrence Doody, my colleague at Rice University, who helped me shape the book from its initial concept, and William Seale, who generously contributed his time and architectural expertise in helping me compose the captions for the photographs. I also received valuable suggestions from several people who studied early versions of the book, including Jimmie Killingsworth, Elisa Holquist, Joshua Chuang, and Jon Evans.

I thank the Arkansas Humanities Council for the grants that enabled me to complete the research for the book and that supported its publication, as well as Tom Dillard, former head of Special Collections at the University of Arkansas Libraries, and Ethel Goodstein-Murphree, professor at the Fay Jones School of Architecture at the University of Arkansas, who served as humanities scholars for the grants.

Finally, I express my deepest appreciation to Jeff Shannon, professor and former dean of the Fay Jones School of Architecture, whose enthusiastic support made possible the completion of the manuscript and the publication of this book.

G. W.

INDEX TO THE PHOTOGRAPHS BY LOCATION

INDEX TO THE STORIES

This publication made possible by grants from:

Arkansas Humanities Council
School of Humanities, Rice University

First Edition

ISBN-10: 1-55728-659-0
ISBN-13: 978-1-55728-659-8
17 16 15 14 13 5 4 3 2 1

Manufactured in China by Everbest Printing Company
through Four Colour Print Group

Designer: David Timmons
Map by Mapping Specialists, Inc.

∞ The paper used in this publication meets the minimum requirements of the American National Standard for Permanence of Paper for Printed Library Materials Z39.48-1984.

Library of Congress Control Number: 2013948314